MW01092731

HORYO

MEMOIRS OF AN AMERICAN POW

Richard M. Gordon
Major, U.S. Army, Ret.
Bataan, P.I., 1941–42
(1921 —

With the assistance of
Benjamin S. Llamzon, Ph.D.

PARAGON HOUSE
St. Paul, Minnesota

First Edition, 1999

Published in the United States by
Paragon House
2700 University Avenue West
St. Paul, MN 55114

Manufactured in the United States of America.

Library of Congress Cataloging-in-Publishing data

Gordon, Richard M., 1921-
    Horyo : memoirs of an American POW / Richard M. Gordon; with the assistance of Benjamin S. Llamzon. — 1st ed.
        p.   cm.
    Includes bibliographical refefences.
    ISBN 1-55778-781-6 (cloth)
        1. Gordon, Richard M., 1921- 2. Bataan (Philippines: Province), Battle of, 1942. 3. World War, 1939-1945 — Prisoners and prisons, Japanese. 4. World War, 1939-1945 — Personal narratives, American. 5. Prisoners of war — United States Biography. 6. Prisoners of war — Philippines Biography. 7. Prisoners of war — Japan Biography. 8. United States. Army Biography. I. Llamzon, Benjamin S. II. Title.
    D767.4G68   1999
    940.54'25 — dc21   99-27861
                                                                              CIP

10 9 8 7 6 5 4 3 2 1

For current information about all releases from Paragon House,
visit the web site at http://www.paragonhouse.com

DEFEAT AND VICTORY ARE ONE

Defeat has been my capture, victory my survival.

2nd Lt. Thomas Austin Marshall, Texas
Bataan, Philippines 1942

To Jean, my first wife of forty-seven years, and to Lyn, my present wife, both of whom gave me loyal and affectionate support in writing this book. Without them at my side this project could not have been completed.

I dedicate this book to my son, Richard, and my loving children, Kathleen, Michael, Suzanne and Judith, who had to bear with the raw scars and nerves that marked their father's life during their childhood. To them I give my profound apologies and assurance of my affection which never wavered, no matter how it may often have appeared otherwise.

Above all other fellow prisoners of war, I owe my life to one Cecil Fernandez of the Royal Air Force, Special Training Corps, captured in Singapore and held with me in Mitsushima, Japan. His help and friendship aided my survival.

For we do not want you to be ignorant,
brethren, of the affliction we experienced in Asia,
for we were so utterly, unbearably crushed,
that we despaired of life itself.

II Corinthians 1:8

I see no gleam of victory alluring
No chance of splendid booty or gain
If I endure—I must go on enduring
And my reward for bearing pain—is pain
Yet, though the thrill, the zest, the hope
Are gone
Something within me keeps me fighting on.

Lt. Henry G. Lee
HQ Co., Philippine Division
Bataan
R. Gordon's platoon leader and friend

CONTENTS

PREFACE

In the Japanese prisoner of war camps of World War II, many POWs were "so utterly, unbearably crushed that [they] despaired of life." Many of these prisoners 'despaired' to such an extent that they resorted to any means to survive, at the expense of their fellow prisoners. As unbelievable as it may sound, many became quite wealthy in these camps. They made exorbitant profits selling simple foodstuffs and medications. These individuals were the "predators." It was the "free enterprise," "what the market will bear" instinct in its most depraved form, and it existed in every prison camp which held American prisoners of war.

Nor were Americans alone in such behavior. British, Australian, and Dutch prisoners were also guilty of such conduct, but to a much lesser degree. Their countries had been at war for some time, thus deprivations were not unknown to these men. Another element enters into the definition of predator, namely a lack of military discipline. This vital part of a soldier's life was missing from the American soldier captured in the Philippines. In contrast, the discipline of the British soldier generally was to be admired. Added to the absence of military discipline on the part of the American soldier was the poor quality of leadership offered by company and field grade officers to their enlisted men inside the prison camps. Once the colonels and generals were separated from their troops by the Japanese (such officers were sent to Formosa and Manchuria), discipline became a much greater problem. Junior officers were primarily interested in their own survival. Many of these young officers were relatively new to the American military in the Philippines, having been recently called into active duty as reserve officers or National Guard officers with little or no military experience. This lack of discipline and leadership enabled the predator to ply his trade.

In the fall of 1942, conditions in the main American prisoner of war camp, Cabanatuan, where most American POWs were held, improved noticeably. Food, Red Cross supplies, and medication came into the camp for the first time since opening in early June 1942. As a result, the death rate among the prisoners fell dramatically. During the first early months of the camp's existence almost 3,000 prisoners died in Cabanatuan, and 90 percent of those deaths were survivors of Camp O'Donnell who had been moved to Cabanatuan on 6 June 1942. The hellhole called O'Donnell had witnessed 1,600 American deaths in forty days and over 25,000 Filipino deaths in three months. That death rate so alarmed even the Japanese that they began paroling Filipino POWs who promised not to bear arms against the Japanese.

Shipped by train and truck on 6 June, 1942 (with 500 men left behind as undertakers and caretakers) from O'Donnell to Cabanatuan, dying of disease, starving and without medical care, these men soon filled the graves at Cabanatuan, their second camp. Their fellow American prisoners of war, captured not in Bataan but a month later on the island fortress of Corregidor in Manila Bay, were luckier. Taken immediately and directly to Cabanatuan, they were appalled at the condition of their fellow Americans. Corregidor's captives to this point had had a relatively easier time. In much better physical condition and with much better food rations, with little or no disease, the American POWs from Corregidor entered prison life better able to withstand the conditions at Cabanatuan.

With the improvement in food and medical supplies to Cabanatuan, homosexuality began to appear. While the military had its share of homosexuals before the war, they were of the "closet" variety. The upswing in the men's condition did much to encourage and create homosexuality.

The predators meanwhile, recognizing the improvement and not wanting to leave this environment for the cold, unknown rigors of Japan and Manchuria, were determined to remain in Cabanatuan at any cost. Most did so until late 1944 when the Japanese, in dire need of laborers, finally decided to move POWs from the Philippines. In addition, with the Allies moving closer to the Philippines, the Japanese wanted to make sure that the fewest number of prisoners were rescued by the advancing Americans.

Fate played a cruel joke on many predators. Because of the ever tightening blockade of the Philippines by the Allies, more and more Japanese vessels, many carrying prisoners of war, were sent to the bottom of the Pacific by American submarines and aircraft. Almost 5,000 American prisoners of war aboard these ships, including predators, went to their deaths in late 1944 and early 1945 (probably the greatest number of Americans ever lost to "friendly fire").

The means predators used to remain in the Philippines until finally forced to leave in those hell ships is a story in itself. Many did so by bribing American officers in charge of preparing shipments of workers to Japan. Others decided to have "dysentery" by buying stools from dysentery patients in the hospital at Cabanatuan. If and when these men were marked for shipment outside the Philippines, they would enter the camp hospital by presenting the purchased stool samples as their own, knowing that the Japanese did not want dysentery patients as workers. The Japanese were deathly afraid of such a disease entering Japan. This "fear" became ironic when one considers how many prisoners of war held in Japan in fact had dysentery. Dysentery wards were just as prevalent in prison camps in Japan as they were in Philippine camps.

A ridiculous, almost comical scene could be observed when prisoners disembarked in Japan. Each prisoner was made to strip naked and was then sprayed for body lice before being allowed on Japanese soil. For if ever there was a common problem among prisoners of war in Japan, it was body lice.

The contemptible behavior of too many American prisoners of war in the Philippines, as I just mentioned, will be a recurrent theme of this book. Many, far too many, American POWs died as a result of predators' actions. But as will become clear, the actions of our own government, too, brought about the deaths of thousands of Filipinos and Americans fighting in defense of the Philippines. It can truly be said that American military personnel in the Philippines were victims of their fellow Americans both before and after their capture.

For a number of years preceding World War II, the American military establishment firmly believed that it was impossible to adequately defend the Philippines against any attack by Japan. General Dwight Eisenhower, then serving as an aide and chief-of-staff to General MacArthur in prewar Manila, was one of the first to admit to the impossibility of such a defense. Most military authorities at that time calculated that they would need at least two years to successfully reinforce the Philippines if attacked by Japan. That projection could not, of course, include the destruction of Pearl Harbor. As a result, World War I weapons originally sent to the Philippines during Teddy Roosevelt's administration were to be used in World War II against a far superior Japanese attack force.

With such gloomy predictions, Washington was reluctant to send anything in the nature of war materiel to the Philippines, especially after the outbreak of war in Europe. In the minds of many, sending supplies and equipment to the Philippines would be a waste. It was not until July 1941 that General Douglas MacArthur, retired army chief of staff, and field marshal of the Philippine Army, was given complete command of all forces in the Philippines. It was he who convinced General George C. Marshall, army chief of staff, and President Roosevelt that the Philippines could be defended for a period of six months. MacArthur firmly believed that the Philippines could hold out for that time if given adequate men, supplies, and planes. Personally, I find it hard to believe that MacArthur was unaware of the general belief that the Philippines were a "lost cause," "doomed from the start." Yet none of this, I think, would have deterred MacArthur from having the Philippine Army under him heroically defend the islands. His ego and reputation would not allow any other alternative. That, however, is a story already taken over by historians. Suffice it to say that troops in the Philippines were considered expendable in the event of war.

When war finally did come, Secretary of War Henry L. Stimson (governor general of the Philippines in the late 1920s) summed up the position of the Philippine defenders with this remark to newspaper reporters: "There are times when men must die." He said this in early December 1941, before the Japanese landed in the Philippines.

Those then who did survive were truly "victorious" while those who died "suffered their defeat." They had been denied "victory" not only by the Japanese but by their fellow Americans. It is up to the reader of this book to judge whether that is true.

FOREWORD

The reader will want to know how I came to know Richard Gordon, Major, U.S. Army (Retired); and why I took a busman's holiday in my retirement from the groves of academe to work on his manuscript.

When World War II broke out on December 8, 1941, I was a gangly twelve years old, in first year high school in Manila. I would walk every day to school in Intramuros, the Walled City. On the way I passed Sternberg, the U.S. Army hospital by the Botanical Garden, and continued on along the sunken gardens before the fortress walls—places that Gordon mentions in the early chapters of the book. At that time, Manila was every bit the lovely city that he fondly recalls. How was I to know that among those American infantrymen then training and drilling on those grounds before my eyes was a sergeant I would one day, more than fifty years later, work with on this book! How was I to know that the souls and bodies of those American soldiers who looked so impressive to us Filipinos, as they went through their drills and exercises, would soon be laid bare and found woefully wanting in the harsh light of captivity under the Japanese.

In the next three years and a half, 1942–45, I was to catch fleeting glimpses of these bedraggled American men, many of them walking skeletons, as they were herded to work by their haughty captors who brandished fixed bayonets and encircling machine guns mounted on military trucks. It was impossible ever to come near them then, nor after their liberation. In the intervening fifty years since, I never managed to meet any of them. Hence in May 11–18, 1992, when the roughly 1,000 survivors of this group—all who were still alive then, and in their seventies and eighties—con-

vened for a full week in the Marriott in San Francisco for the fifti-
eth anniversary of the fall of Bataan and Corregidor, I hastened
from my home in Evanston, Illinois, and flew out to join them. I
had my tape recorder with me, and for the first three days I did
nothing but circulate among them and record as much as I could
of their grim reminiscences. By the fourth day I began to notice
one individual who stayed on the outer fringe of all the socializing
camaraderie. It was Dick Gordon, and he preempted my intention as I approached to interview him.

"All those tapes—how will you sort out the truth?" Dick asked.
The question suddenly conjured up in my mind the phrase "devil's
advocate." Then I looked back to the milling throng of ex-POWs
from Bataan and Corregidor in the lobby. It was the start of a sinking feeling that only took deeper hold as I worked on this manuscript. That sinking feeling is what this book is all about.

Several motives impelled me to this project. Of those, three are
worth mentioning. The first is subjective and may prove to be elu-
sive. Yet its practical impact on my life is palpably real, and it may
serve the common good to spell it out here. The other two are
directly and empirically recognizable in their implications for our
national life in America today, as the foremost example of a self-
renewing democracy.

In the book Gordon talks about the bewildering emotions that
welled up in him on his departure from home, at the site of his
enslavement in Mitsushima after liberation, and at meeting his
family again during the Thanksgiving season back in America. So
too, bewilderingly, I have never quite understood my voracious
impulse to read every book I can lay my hands on about the atrocities of Japanese soldiers during World War II, all the time that
such reading repulses and pains me. Working on this book has, I
believe, helped to organize these psychic crosscurrents inside me
into some degree of clarity.

I now thoroughly adhere to what may be called, "Pascal's Bet
Revisited." This book points up the fact that some of the few who
never forsook the basic human values of decent behavior, order,
and discipline, even in the seemingly bottomless depths of a living
hell, survived equally, as did the predators, to the day of liberation.

So too, in the lottery of life, whether in the mere ordinariness of everyday living or in the worst of circumstances, to me this book of horrors is really saying that it makes sense to put your money (i.e. action and behavior) where your mouth should be, namely, on the side of decency.... Why not? After all, the odds remain the same for everybody, those who do not make it and those who do.

My other motive revolves on the conviction that our democratic freedoms, so dearly paid for in war by the blood of fellow Americans, cannot be preserved in the ensuing epochs of peace and prosperity unless they are locked onto a passion for truth on a nationwide scale. All the turbulent crosscurrents sweeping our land in domestic crises under President Clinton bear testimony to the fact that truth must pervade the large picture of our three branches of government or our nation will unravel in disarray. But truth-telling in that large picture is impossible unless the overwhelming majority of the citizenry itself is imbued with the virtue. Unfortunately, what we see taking over today in alarming proportions is what Allan Bloom has called "the closing of the American mind," the full-scale relativism so characteristic of the *me, myself, and I* generation. This is alarming since the truism still holds that a people gets the kind of government it deserves.

People devoid of truth are what T. S. Eliot called "hollow men," incapable of the self-imposed order and discipline which are the indispensable foundations of democratic freedom. Physical beatings such as those Gordon describes being given by Watanabe, "The Bird," maim and kill. But the collapse of order and discipline among the POWs recounted here ensued when these men gave up on all notions of right and wrong, leaving only the fragile shred of individual survival at any cost as the ultimate belief. This book enables us to peer into the kind of life that is sure to ensue when basic moral values and decency are abandoned—the life that ensued when that happened in Japanese prison camps. The ruthlessness of captivity under the Japanese was then redoubled as the prisoners themselves turned on one another as mutually ruthless predators. Note how, ironically, the only order and discipline possible came from the iron fists of their captors. It is a terrible

picture we cannot afford to forget. Where only falsehood and all
the other vices it spawns rule, the situation will always invite a
mailed fist from the outside to intervene. Order of any sort, after
all, is better than its complete evaporation among hollow men.
Thus on a deeper level, this book is about the inseparability of
truth and freedom.

Lastly, I would like to underline Gordon's lament about the
woefully inadequate training American soldiers in the Philippines
had before the war. Because he was a professional soldier who had
undergone training in the Philippine jungles before the war—
unlike the raw recruits from the National Guard units who arrived
just before war broke out—his training paid off, especially during
the Death March. His military experience helped him again in
the death camps, the hell ships, the slave years in Japan, and indeed even in the heady days after liberation.

Before the cataclysmic engagements in World War II, notably
D-Day in Europe, and on the eve of the greatest naval battle in
history off Leyte Gulf, General Eisenhower and Admiral William
Halsey broadcast the assurance to their men that they had received
the best training for battle that it was in the power of their country
to give. The time had now arrived, the supreme commanders announced, when the men, in turn, must put that training to valiant
use to bring about their country's deliverance, honor, and glory. It
was a rousing battlecry that neither Generals MacArthur nor Wainwright could broadcast in truth to their troops on Bataan and Corregidor on the eve of the Japanese assault in early 1942.

In closing, I would like to emphasize that my work on this book
extended only to editing, vetting, and all the work that preparing a
manuscript for publication generally require. At no time and in no
place did I ever intrude into its contents. Gordon, not I, was horyo.
So, on these matters any blame must be laid at my door.

My affectionate thanks go to my wife, Georgia, and our two
children, Lily and Clark-Belmonte, who cheerfully tutored me in
the wonders of computer technology. The decisive job of putting
the manuscript into final format was done by Sharon D. Connor,
another computer wizard, an eagle-eyed professional and a nice
and easy friend. I thank Elizabeth Frangedakis, of Rethymnon in

Crete, Greece, and Oman, the manager of Hotel Splendid in Buyukada, in the Sea of Marmora, off Istanbul. The facilities they provided me made my work a pleasure.

Ben Llamzon
Evanston, Illinois, Easter, 1998

PROLOGUE

This book is the memoirs of a "Horyo," a soldier captured by the
Japanese on Bataan. It is written plainly just as I saw things happen over five years of military service before, during, and after World
War II. I hope that the reader, and my children, will better understand and have a more in-depth appreciation of what the phrase
"hell on earth" really means after going through this book.

The Allied calamity that was Bataan in April 1942 began with
the surrender of Major General Edward P. King Jr., commanding
general of the Fil-American forces on Bataan, of the largest number of American military personnel ever turned over to an enemy
force in the history of the United States. General King, very mind-
ful of the significance of the date 9 April, when Confederate soldiers under General Robert E. Lee surrendered to General Grant
at Appomattox, Virginia, thus ending the Civil War, decided that
any further resistance on Bataan was useless and would only result
in more bloodshed. Knowing that his immediate superior, General Jonathan Wainwright on Corregidor, had expressly forbidden
any surrender, he accepted full responsibility for his actions. He
was to spend the remainder of the war in a Japanese prison camp
wondering what sanction awaited him for this capitulation.

To some, especially the Japanese military of that era, surrender
was, to say the least, a disgrace. To this day some former prisoners
of war who were captured in the Philippines still feel disgraced by
being taken prisoner. It may be, however, that these men feel more
guilty about surviving than surrendering. It is true that these men
did not give in of their own volition. Rather, they were given orders by their commanding general to lay down their weapons. In-

deed, most U.S. troops were unaware of the surrender until Japanese forces were almost upon them. In some instances the Japanese massacred those who, because of poor communications, continued to fight until the command reached them belatedly.

Colonel T. S. Drake, U.S. Army, offered the following consolation to many prisoners of war. "Let no man believe that there is a stigma attached to having been honorably taken captive in battle. Only the fighting man ever gets close enough to the enemy for that to happen. That he is not listed among the slain is due to the infinite care of Providence. Be proud that you carried yourselves as men in battle and adversity. You will be enriched thereby."

Surrender was hardly on the mind of General Douglas MacArthur, overall commander of Fil-American forces in the Philippines, when he left Corregidor on 11 March 1942 for Australia in accordance with President Roosevelt's orders. Upon leaving he gave explicit orders to his replacement, General Wainwright, to "hold on" until he returned. Wainwright assured MacArthur that he would or would die trying. Future events were to make that promise impossible when he too was compelled to surrender Corregidor a month after Bataan fell.

To disobey a lawful order in the military was, and is, a court-martial offense. (Like General King, all through his captivity General Wainwright too agonized over his surrender). When MacArthur left the Philippines he sincerely believed that he would be able to mount a rescue effort to save his men there. Once in Australia, he soon learned that no Allied force was available to him and that he could not keep his promise to Wainwright. Yet, upon learning of both King and Wainwright's surrender he became furious with both men. He was even more incensed when he learned that Allied soldiers in the southern Philippines, under General William F. Sharp Jr., commanding general of the Visayan-Mindanao forces, had also been surrendered by Wainwright. MacArthur of course was completely unaware of the nightmarish conditions on Bataan or the impossible situation facing Wainwright on Corregidor.

The fall of Bataan, especially, deeply affected MacArthur for the remainder of the war and for years after. The very mention of

Bataan during the war often prompted tears in his eyes. He had visited Bataan but once during the fighting there, and many of his men were openly critical of him. They called him "Dugout Doug," a term that deeply hurt him as it was a challenge to his courage, never before questioned by anyone. As late as the Korean War in the early fifties, MacArthur flew around in his plane called "Bataan."

Wainwright, confronted not only with defeat but annihilation on Corregidor, did attempt to keep the southern forces fighting in the Philippines while contemplating surrender. He sent the following message dated 6 May 1942 to General Sharp. "All forces in the Philippines except those on the fortified islands at the entrance to Manila Bay are released to your command. Inform all concerned report at once to MacArthur for orders. I believe you will understand the motive behind this order. Wainwright."

The motive was not only obvious to General Sharp, it was also very obvious to Lieutenant General Masaharu Homma, commanding general of all Japanese forces in the Philippines. Homma had already taken too long to complete the taking of the Philippines and was in disfavor in Tokyo. Meaning to bring the fighting to an abrupt halt, he refused Wainwright's surrender unless it included all the forces under Wainwright's command, including Sharp's forces in the south. Faced with this dilemma, Wainwright then sent Sharp a second message explaining that Homma refused his surrender of the fortified islands of Manila Bay (Corregidor and surrounding islands) unless it included Sharp's forces. His message to Sharp read "...you will therefore, be guided accordingly and will repeat will surrender all troops under your command." Sharp, after being informed of the entire situation on Corregidor by Colonel Jesse Tawick Jr., Wainwright's emissary, then ordered his troops to surrender. Sharp directed all of his forces to cease operations against the Japanese and "to raise the white flag." In his message to his command, Sharp reiterated what Wainwright had stated via Tawick "this is imperative and must be carried out to save further bloodshed." Here however, Sharp's commands were questioned by some of his subordinates inasmuch as their units had been unhurt by the Japanese. One, Colonel J. Christie, commanding in Panay, took the position that he needed "MacArthur's okay or surrender may be treason." In his response to Sharp, Christie further stated, "I do not even see a small reason why this unit should be surrendered because some other unit has gone to hell or some Corregidor shell-shocked terms are issued." Sharp replied that he had orders and expected his subordinate (Christie) to follow those orders. Realizing that he had no alternative but to obey, Christie surrendered his group. All units in the Philippines faced the same decision as Sharp and Christie, and every man was expected to obey.

At stake was the survival of every man, woman, and child on Corregidor. At least such was the belief of General Wainwright after being threatened with extinction by General Homma.

What really did happen when Corregidor was given Homma's ultimatum? The true story did not become known until years after the end of World War II. It is possible that Corregidor's fall might have taken a different turn if all the facts had been known to Wainwright.

Homma, subsequently executed for his role in the Bataan Death March, had over 14,000 men for his invasion of Corregidor but an insufficient number of assault barges for the task. With the limited number of 2500 men, he initiated the invasion rather than incur Tokyo's wrath over his delay in taking the Philippines.

Unknown to Homma, the tides along the Manila shore shifted eastward near "the Rock," as Corregidor was known. His landing craft began drifting apart, with most of them heading for the wrong part of the island. Floating directly under the guns of Corregidor, they were caught broadside and blown out of the water. Only about 800 Japanese soldiers survived to reach a landing site on the island.

Homma, upon learning of the destruction of his landing craft, assumed that all was lost and was prepared for his defeat in the attempted landing. To his surprise, word came to him that about 800 men had managed to secure a beachhead. A Colonel Sato took charge of this contingent and informed Homma of their situation. In addition, three tanks managed to get ashore and Sato's force soon made its way to Malinta Tunnel, headquarters for General Wainwright on Corregidor and refuge to all Allied personnel who managed to gain shelter there. The day after the initial Japanese landing a force of approximately 300 stood before the tunnel's entrance. This small force brought about the capitulation of Corregidor.

It is a fact that while Corregidor had over 12,000 men on the island, most were inside the main and lateral tunnels. Shelled for thirty consecutive days from Bataan after that peninsula fell, and after four months of almost daily bombing attacks, most of Corregidor's defenders were shell-shocked and incapable of mounting a strong defense. A relatively few defenders met and attempted to repel the Japanese on the beaches. This group fought bravely, but received no support from those within the tunnel and were themselves forced to fall back to Malinta Tunnel. The three Japanese tanks were soon at the mouth of the tunnel. Believing that a much stronger Japanese force threatened his troops, Wainwright opted for surrender.

Many American historians are really unaware of what happened on both Bataan and Corregidor. A number of myths have emerged from this lack of knowledge, many perpetrated by the survivors themselves. Some historians of today, writing on the fall of the Philippines, have also provided erroneous information. It certainly is a good example of the adage, "when history becomes legend, print the legend."

A case on this point can be found in William Manchester's book *American Caesar*. Manchester writes that the prisoners on Corregidor were taken to Bataan and underwent the infamous Bataan Death March. Bataan fell on 9 April 1942, and the last group of marchers entered their first prison camp, O'Donnell, on 24 April 1942. Corregidor did not fall until 6 May 1942, and the men defending it did not leave the island until 20 May 1942. To insure the surrender of the southern forces under Wainwright's command, Americans were held on "the Rock" as hostages, pending that surrender.

For any Corregidor captive to take part in the march out of Bataan, he would have had to leave Corregidor while the Japanese were shelling the island. Then, he either would have had to swim or obtain a boat to make it across the two-and-a-half miles of shark-infested water to the shore of Bataan, with the absurd objective of joining the Death March! His only alternative would be to walk on water and only one man has ever done that. Yet today, a number of Corregidor survivors claim to have made the Bataan March.

Another myth from the Bataan-Corregidor campaigns, that still exists even in the halls of the United States Congress, is the belief that all Marines in that campaign defended Bataan, then Corregidor, and then made the Bataan Death March. Less than three years ago, congressional legislation was proposed to award the Bronze Star medal to those Marines "who defended Bataan and survived the Death March." Eventually a number of Bataan survivors convinced Congress that their information was erroneous. The medal was then awarded, rightly so, "to the Marines for their defense of the Philippines."

In December 1941 the vast majority of Marines captured in the Philippines had arrived in those islands from China. These were the Fourth Marines, a unit primarily in garrison duty in China to protect American interests there. Almost immediately these Marines were posted to Corregidor and assigned beach defense duties. A small detachment of Marines, along with a small group of naval personnel eventually did fight on Bataan and were captured there. About forty-three Marines and a handful of sailors arrived at Camp O'Donnell, the first prison camp for Bataan defenders. This small detachment of Marines and Navy personnel fought with distinction and brought great credit upon themselves and their organizations.

In early 1992 the secretary of the navy acknowledged that Congress was armed with good intentions but a poor knowledge of history. The secretary was quick to point out that the Bronze Star award to all naval personnel was not for having participated in the Bataan Death March but for their defense of the Philippines, a recognition they truly deserved. The original myth, if left unchallenged, could have again distorted the history of Bataan and Corregidor. Bataan survivors prevented this by contacting their congressional representatives and asking that the erroneous information be expunged from the records.

As part of the 50th anniversary remembrance of the end of World War II, the official committee appointed to commemorate the event issued paintings of Marines in action. Among them was one painting showing the Marines' participation in the Bataan Death March. Obviously the myths continue even at the Department of Defense level.

It is the belief of this writer that the American people and our military need to recognize to what level an American prisoner of war, poorly led and poorly disciplined, can sink while holding onto some vestige of civilization. While some truly deserved the name "hero," they were few in number. They are the ones who died in battle, prison camps, or aboard prison ships headed for camps outside the Philippines. These are the men I enshrine with this book.

CHAPTER 1

THE ADOLESCENT YEARS

B orn in New York City's Bellevue Hospital in 1921 and raised in that city's notorious "Hell's Kitchen," I can say without fear of contradiction that my "ghetto" upbringing prepared me well for what life had in store. I knew nothing of my father. He deserted his family of five when I was eight. One day he simply walked away and was never seen or heard from again. I always wanted to believe that he despaired to such a point over his inability to provide for his family that he simply gave up as did so many men of that day. Such men however still showed some signs of love for their children. Events later proved such was not the case with my father. His desertion has never been forgiven. He took the coward's way out. His own family said so.

Thus abandoned, the two oldest children were given the responsibility of supporting the others. My older brother, age ten, and I, found ourselves doing any available work. With little chance for real work, we would find ourselves shining shoes after school and selling newspapers at night before going to bed. Shining shoes on a windswept corner of New York's garment center at five cents a shine was hardly productive, especially with the "city's finest" constantly chasing us away from our place of business. Badgered by the shop owners the police had no choice. It soon became a game of finding a street corner and setting up shop again where the police had already checked and were unlikely to appear, at least for a while.

Summers however were pleasant for us. My mother was always able to enroll her sons in the *New York Herald-Tribune* Fresh Air

Fund which offered the "underprivileged" two weeks in a camp or private home. In our neighborhood the Hudson Guild Settlement House was the conduit for these summer programs.

On several such summers we found ourselves with our hair cut to the skin in order to prevent head lice. We "baldies" paid a dear price for that haircut in the way of a very bad sunburn atop the head. (I remembered those sunburns years later when the Japanese gave their prisoners a taste of the sun on a daily basis during the march out of Bataan).

It was during one of these summer experiences that I entered puberty, and the woman of the house that had taken me in had an interest in me that I found disturbing. The lady apparently had several extramarital affairs and I found myself caught in the middle. On one occasion this very attractive farmer's wife had a liaison with a young fellow in the family canoe. The husband, upon returning home, stumbled upon "the scene of the crime" and became violently drunk. He quickly found his .45 caliber pistol and chased his wife into the cornfields, firing at her as she ran. Unfortunately I was running with her and heard the bullets whizzing by. I felt it was not safe for me to remain in that house, for I too was now a suspect. Upon returning to New York, I told my mother of the incident. That was the end of my three annual visits to that farm.

Yet working on a farm picking "taters," though hard work, was a memory I always recalled fondly. When not picking potatoes we would drag our feet in moccasins along a shallow waterway, clamming. After selling the clams for seventy-five cents a bushel, we would spend our money at a very small country store, drinking Doctor Pepper and discussing the local maidens. This one night a week, Saturday night, was a much sought-after pleasure as we sat on the store's front porch. To get to "town" where the store was meant putting our shoes on after a week of going barefooted. Boy, did our feet hurt! It was here that I had my first crush, a young lady in her first year of college. I was obviously too young for her, so the romance went nowhere.

After shining shoes during the afternoon and a quick dinner, my older brother and I would walk up to the Grand Central Terminal, where we newsboys would buy the next day's newspapers, armed with the profits of our afternoon shoe shining. New York had a number of newspapers in those days, but we would purchase the best-selling papers, the *New York Daily News* and the *New York Daily Mirror*. Both papers had a tremendous following. Paying two cents for each copy, the "going price," we bought as many as our shoe shining efforts that afternoon would allow. With newspapers under each arm we set out for our home on the west side of town, stopping in every bar along the way. The bars were numerous. We banked on the bar patrons to show us compassion by way of generous tips, and soon our business was flourishing. Only rarely did we receive less than a nickel for a paper. Result, over 100 percent profit. Many bar customers were very kind, and also inebriated. We often received as much as a dime and even—on holidays such as Christmas—a quarter! With the exception of keeping money for our school lunch, probably the only balanced meal we had, all earnings were given to our mother. Shining shoes on Saturday and Sunday helped swell our income, but I found shining shoes on Sunday very demeaning. The best place to "set up shop," which consisted of a homemade box containing a footrest and our equipment, was on an avenue near a church. Unfortunately, this meant that friends, male and female, not as bad off as we, walked by going to church. I remember on several occasions ducking into the entrance of a store so as not to be seen when a friend walked by. With the boyfriends it wasn't too bad, but the girls were a different situation. We couldn't bear being seen by them in our lowly trade.

My mother, of stout Irish stock, was an extremely proud woman and very proud of her heritage. To accept charity was difficult for her to say the least. But often we would be compelled to join soup lines for food, or at Thanksgiving to line up at one of New York's Child's restaurants, which annually served a full course turkey dinner with all the trimmings. Of all the meals during those days, I remember Child's the best, and we looked forward each year to Thanksgiving. There were many in line for this dinner, but it was certainly worth the wait. Accepting charity however, in light of my mother's pride, was humiliating to us all.

Rather than seek out her family's help, Mother attempted to raise her children on her own. She soon realized the impossibility of the situation and turned to her parents for shelter when she was unable to pay the rent on our flat. While my mother was a Catholic, my father was not. This interfaith marriage caused a schism in our family, which culminated in two children being placed in New York City's borough of Queens Shelter while she and the other two children lived with her parents. The two non-Catholic children, myself and one other, were left at the shelter.

A strange arrangement had developed between my parents while they were together regarding the religion of the children. The first-born was baptized a Catholic. The second child, myself, was given over to the Protestant belief. The third son also was a Protestant and the fourth a Catholic. While never discussing how this all came about with my mother, I can assume that each parent had a choice at certain births. Nevertheless, the two non-Catholics ended up in the shelter, and I am convinced that arrangement was brought about by my Catholic grandparents, who had little room themselves.

In a few months my mother came and took us from the shelter to her parent's house. Apparently she had convinced them that she wanted to be with all four children. While my grandmother, a very strict Irish woman from the old country, did show her grandchildren some consideration, my grandfather was another case. A stevedore who worked extremely hard unloading the ships of England's Cunard Line in New York City, he accepted us with obvious reluctance. He made no bones about it, we were to work to earn our room and board.

While living with our grandparents we two oldest brothers were expected to earn as much money as we could. On days when shining shoes was impossible, we helped about the house. I vividly recall being sent to the local pub by my grandfather for a "scuttle" of beer, with the instruction "don't spill a drop." There was no cover for the canister so this was difficult, considering I had to walk up three flights of the tenement house.

My grandfather had a temper, which is a gross understatement. We lived in fear of him. Drinking, which he did regularly, made him even more ill-tempered. Being cuffed about the ears by him on a number of occasions is an unforgettable childhood memory. On one particular weekend, Grandpa came home in his usual Saturday shape. Saturday was payday and all the "boys" would gather at the local pub, just like in the old country. This one Saturday he looked for his dinner and finding a ham on the table, asked my grandmother what it was. Objecting to ham as the entree, he proceeded to throw it through the kitchen window. The window wasn't fully open and we hastily retrieved the ham-thru-window from the backyard three floors below. Even though the ham had some glass in, it served as supper once Grandpa went to bed. Yes, Grandpa was unpredictable. When one of his sons brought home a prospective bride and introduced her to him, Grandpa inquired, "Where did you dig that up"? He was notorious for such biting one-liners.

Finally, my mother could no longer stand it at her parents' house, and after saving some money she moved us to another apartment. We moved so many times from the time I entered elementary school until graduation, that my school records consisted of two 3x6 inch cards with addresses on both sides. Without a doubt we must have broken a school record for moves in our eight years. Strangely enough, we graduated from the same grammar school that we first entered (Public School 11). My mother loved to move (actually on most occasions she was forced to when unable to pay the rent). I recall moving into one flat on Roosevelt Avenue in Queens, New York, one evening and moving out the next morning. Moving was relatively easy in those days. Not much furniture or belongings, and the use of child labor, the kids, was there to ease the move. Never was a thought given to hiring movers who had to be paid.

Attending school under such conditions became more difficult with each move. Working after school and at night allowed no time for homework. Saturdays found me working from seven in the morning to one o'clock the next morning in a butcher shop. For this I was paid two dollars and fifty cents for the entire time, plus tips I earned from delivering groceries up the many tenement stairs. I could bring home as much as five dollars a day. In between making deliveries I was also required to clean the butcher's block, sweep the sawdust on the floor, periodically clean the showcase windows after closing, and be available for any other chores thought up by the two butchers.

On one particular Saturday an incident gave me my first guilt complex. I became a "thief" at the age of nine, or so I thought at the time. While freshening up the floor's sawdust I discovered a ten dollar bill. With visions of what I could do with such a large amount of money I hastily put it in my overcoat pocket hanging in the rear of the shop. Upon returning from a delivery I was told that a customer had reported losing a ten dollar bill, and I was asked if I knew anything about it. Not wanting to part with my newly found wealth, I denied any knowledge of the money. The butchers then questioned me for the rest of the evening and assured me that I would not be allowed to go home unless I produced the money. In retrospect it was wrong for me to have kept that money, but I also knew that if I had returned it to the butchers the customer would never have seen the money either.

At about 1:30 A.M. I was shocked when they told me I could leave. Walking up the avenue I felt exhilarated that I was free. But when I reached into my coat pocket I found the reason why the butchers had allowed me to go free. The ten dollar bill was gone, and to add insult to injury they had refused to pay me my wages for the day. At no time did they mention that I was fired. I never had a doubt as to who finally received that money: my friendly butchers! At any rate, my embarrassment kept me from ever returning to that store. What hurt the most that night was having to give all my tips to the house to make up for the loss of my wages.

It can be said unequivocally that neither son ever held back a nickel from our earnings. As a reward for our weekly work, we each received from Mom fifty cents, which paid for a Sunday movie, a hot dog, and a cold root beer. The theater manager of the Arena Theater on Eighth Avenue and Fortieth Street in Manhattan gave out free root beer to encourage the kids to leave the theater after one performance.

In addition to the treat of a weekly movie, we could look forward to the somewhat dubious joy of listening to "Two Hours In Ireland" on radio station W-A-R-D from Brooklyn. The kids—out of earshot of our mother—called it two hours of agony. The title should be self-explanatory, but let me add that it was two solid hours of Irish jigs and folk music. My mother insisted that we listen each week as part of her culture program for us. A further "treat" awaited us periodically when we would be taken at no cost to an Irish vaudeville show held locally. Mother was indeed proud of her heritage and wanted to instill the same pride in her children.

While life was extremely difficult for most during the Great Depression, many endured as best they could while hanging together as a family. In our case, the problem of being without a father was soon compounded by alcohol. My mother, unable to make ends meet with the limited help provided by "home relief," or welfare as it is known today, soon despaired and took to drinking away the money earned by her sons. Her alcoholism became progressively worse. Soon her drinking periods would last four to six weeks, depending on the money. These drinking bouts we called "benders" or "binges," and both names became household words.

During these "benders" life became even more unbearable. When sober, my mother was an extremely clean woman and our house was as clean as could be. Half awake during a drinking period, she would come into where we boys were sleeping and awaken one of the two "non-Catholics," usually with a broom handle. (Rarely did she ever awaken the oldest or the youngest in such a fashion or for such a purpose.) The two "shelter graduates" would then be told to clean the entire flat. While the place certainly needed cleaning, 3 A.M. was not the time to do it. But it was her time to be awake. She held inspections of our work which an Army drill sergeant would find difficult to match. We tried sleeping under the bed in a false belief that we were safe there. The danger under the bed was greater as the broom handle hit vital parts.

One night during such a binge I was awakened by the broom handle and told to clean the house. On this very cold night in February, I attempted to escape both the broom handle and the chore by running through the flat. Unable to escape my mother's pursuit, I climbed out onto the tenement's fire escape, outside the kitchen window in my shorts and undershirt. Not to be outdone, my mother proceeded to lock the window, ensuring I could not get back in the house. Climbing to the roof, I found the hallway door also locked. That night I spent about three hours standing barefoot on the metal grill of the fire escape. Soon, my feet began to stick to the grill as a result of the subfreezing temperatures. After numerous attempts at calling for help, I gave up and waited until my older brother entered the kitchen at about 7 A.M.

Early in my childhood my mother became a full-blown alcoholic, and during the Depression very few people gave much concern to treating the disease. I recall an ambulance coming to our apartment one night in answer to a neighbor's call for my mother. The person I assumed to be a doctor lectured my mother for what she was doing to her children as a result of her drinking, hardly the correct treatment. Eventually things worsened, more ambulances were called to the house, and on several occasions my mother was taken to St. Vincent's Hospital in Greenwich Village. When we visited her there we were told by relatives that "she had stomach problems." Upon release from the hospital she seemed to be a new person. Alas, she quickly fell back to her old ways as soon as the money came into her hands. Eventually stomach problems did result and those problems took her life at age forty-two.

In those days my grandparents achieved some recognition from neighbors living in New York City's Greenwich Village: My mother's second cousin, Gene Tunney, had emerged onto the boxing scene and was fighting for the world's heavyweight championship with Jack Dempsey. My grandmother, a very proud Tunney, was to die from diabetes soon after Gene won the title. It was her proudest moment as an Irish woman that one of her "clan" had been accepted. The Irish-American of that era knew discrimination as much as any nationality in America. Being discriminated against did not stop them from discriminating against others, however. They discriminated against my father because he was not a Catholic and against my mother because of her "mixed" marriage.

Thankfully my childhood passed and at age sixteen, after considerable prompting to quit school and get a job, I joined my older brother in the full-time work arena. He had found employment at sixteen as a messenger for the Postal Telegraph Company, one of two major national firms that delivered telegrams, flowers, and packages. I, in turn, joined the competing firm, Western Union. All messengers were given complete uniforms when hired. My brother's uniform was blue. He later wore the same color in the United States Marines, while I wore a color similar to that of the United States Army uniform (an interesting coincidence). My uniform gave me a sense of pride, as I felt much better wearing it than my skimpy "civilian" garb.

Having long since decided on becoming a soldier, my Western Union uniform gave me the feeling of "being on my way" to that goal, and I felt very much at ease wearing it. I must acknowledge a great debt of gratitude I feel for that organization. They — in accordance with the law — provided a continuing education in their schoolrooms to those who left high school at age sixteen. My former high school days were a disaster. Forced to work almost immediately after coming home from school and with absolutely no time for study, my grades suffered tremendously. Each day was an experience to fear if called upon by a teacher. School social life, experienced by most youngsters, did not exist either for me or my older brother. One of my high school hopes was to play football and possibly earn a scholarship. This was now out of the question — my football days were confined to a sandlot after church on Sundays. Western Union changed my life and gave it the structure it was missing.

One day a week, each employee my age had to attend classes in their main building at 60 Hudson Street. Going to "continuation school" provided me with a chance to play basketball for Western Union's school. When employees reached age seventeen, the company offered a chance for advancement to those they deemed deserving. Called upon by numerous companies in the New York City area for recommended individuals, I was offered a position at a fixed salary, as compared to the percentage salary paid by Western Union. The job would pay me fifteen dollars weekly (a good wage for a seventeen year old) at the firm Wood, Nathan & Virkus of 112 Charlton Street. Jumping at the chance of a fixed income, I found myself the new shipping clerk.

A year went by and the war in Europe was now almost one year old. My immediate superior was a German-American, really more

German than American. I always believed he was a member of the Bund so prevalent in New York City at that time. Mr. Schneider, the boss, decided I was a little too outspoken in my criticism of Adolf Hitler and I was fired.

Things at home had gotten so bad that I decided to move out while I was still working, but once fired I found myself without a place to call home. As a result I slept at night on a billiard table in a one-room clubhouse that some childhood friends had found for me. This group of friends, to whom I owed so much, seemed to be the only people interested in what happened to me. Later, when given the opportunity to make a radio broadcast from Japan during my captivity, it was to the New York Cubs Athletic Club that I sent my best regards. With no rent to pay for my billiard table bed I could afford to eat at supper time, while breakfast was non-existent. Lunch consisted of a sandwich and a glass of water. I finally turned eighteen, the legal age for joining the army with a parent's consent. Due to my strained relations with my mother, and by now a stepfather whom I detested, I obtained my mother's written consent. She hesitated, for whatever reasons. My promise to send a portion of my monthly salary finally won the day and I headed for the army recruiting office anxious to get away from home.

My mother remarried several years before I enlisted and her second marriage was as disastrous as the first. Her second husband was also an alcoholic who enjoyed beating his stepchildren. (Five years after I joined the army he also disappeared from our lives after ducking out on my mother's funeral bill.) At the age of seventeen I had the wonderful experience of paying him back for his cruelty. After coming home from football practice one day, I became the object of his anger. A fight broke out between us and I had the pleasure of reminding him that I had grown up. Unfortunately my mother stepped between us and I caught a sneak punch from him flush on the mouth (the scar is still on the inside of my mouth). The biggest casualty of the day: one broken couch when this "stepfather" landed on it after taking a punch from me.

Chapter 2

ARMY RECRUIT DAYS

On 5 August 1940, I entered the army. This was for me the fulfillment of a boyhood ambition. My love affair with military life began at West Point. After seeing the school during numerous trips up the Hudson River aboard New York City's River Lines, I fell in love with the United States Military Academy and wished for such a life. Unfortunately, family economics precluded even the slightest chance of my attending. Even with an outstanding high school education, something I never had, the chances of an appointment were slim to impossible. With that knowledge, and with the war in Europe heating up, I felt that the time had come to join. Besides, I knew that once in the army, I would never go hungry again (so I thought).

Approaching the recruiting office at 39 Whitehall Street in downtown Manhattan, I noticed the familiar "Uncle Sam wants you" sign with Uncle's finger pointing right at me. On the reverse side of the sign was a poster extolling the virtues of joining the 15th Infantry in Tientsin, China. The offer satisfied two of my purposes in life: To become a soldier, and get as far away from New York City as I could.

Upon completing the necessary paperwork and taking the oath of allegiance, I soon discovered that the 15th Infantry was no longer in China and had not been for years. Nevertheless, the army was not going to waste a good poster on a small detail like that! The recruiting sergeant explained, after the oath, that only Marines were stationed in China.

Crestfallen over this unexpected turn of events, my spirits were soon lifted when the good sergeant promised me the 31st Infantry Regiment located in the Philippines. I remember asking him where the Philippines were. His response was that they were near China. Immediately taken by the friendliness of the recruiter (all recruiters of that time were very friendly, initially) I readily agreed, though I wasn't exactly sure where the Philippines were. Handed a slip of paper to cover the cost of the five cent subway ride, I was soon on my way to Fort Slocum, an island off New Rochelle, New York.

Looking back now on my life prior to joining the army, I get a great deal of satisfaction in focusing on the "positives" of my pre-army life. It is my firm conviction that the miseries, discomforts, and deprivations of that period aided me immeasurably in withstanding what was to come. Even then, I felt as I do now, that nothing could bother me after such an upbringing. I am equally positive that my "training" for Bataan and what followed began on the streets of New York City. Surviving Bataan and prison camp was not much different from surviving my childhood.

As a result, I have a love-hate relationship with New York City. While it will always be a reminder of a very unpleasant part of my life, it was also my home for better or worse. I still have fond regards for the city of my birth. As the saying goes, you can take the boy out of the city but you can't take the city out of the boy. Unfortunately the New York City of today bears little resemblance to the city I knew. Yet to quote the song Frank Sinatra made famous, "if you can make it there you can make it anywhere."

Fort Slocum was an army post primarily for recruits assigned to overseas areas, i.e., Panama, Puerto Rico, Hawaii, and the Philippines. On an island a short ferryboat ride from New Rochelle, it was an ideal place for raw, homesick recruits about to leave the country. Passes were limited as recruits were not expected to remain there very long.

One of my first objectives on reaching Fort Slocum was to discover exactly where I was going to start my new life. From an old *National Geographic* magazine I soon learned that the recruiting sergeant knew his geography. The Philippines were indeed as close to China as an American soldier could get. I now knew where my

home for my anticipated two-year tour of duty of overseas would
be, at least on a map. I might add that ignorance of our destination
was shared by twelve other recruits reporting for duty in the Philippines that particular day in August 1940. *Most were like me.* They
all wanted to be soldiers, and where they went to soldier was sec-
ondary as long as it was far away. Hawaii would have been great. It
had a good athletic reputation, but as we all found out on enlist-
ing, Hawaii was "closed." Too many "jocks" signed up to go there.

Issued ill-fitting uniforms late that afternoon, we fell out for retreat formation on the parade grounds for our very first time as
soldiers. A field artillery piece belched out the smoke of a blank
round of ammunition and we stood at some degree of attention
while the flag of the United States was lowered. That marked the
end of the soldier's day. The post band began to play our national
anthem, and while I have heard that song many times in my military and civilian career, it never sounded more beautiful than that
first time in the army. My back stiffened with each note.

Up to this time the army had consisted of approximately 175,000
men. All enlisted serial numbers began with the number six. Our
group however came into the army with all of the first numbers
beginning with one. The second number designated the army area
from whence you came. In my case, number two designated the
Second Army which encompassed New York.

Numbers were important to us. We knew that any serial number beginning with "six" indicated an "old soldier," that "two" indicated National Guard troops, and "three" spoke out loudly for
draftees. In a fireside chat President Roosevelt promised that no
draftees would be sent abroad. But the draftees sitting in their
dayrooms listening to the speech knew he really didn't mean it.

At bedtime that first night, still so excited that sleep would not
come easily, I heard the bugler play "taps" for the first time. I still
vividly hear the mournful sounds of that call closing out my first
day as a soldier. It provoked chills along my spine then as it still
does today. I vowed that night that the army was to be my life. Had
I been offered the opportunity to reenlist the next day I would
have jumped at it. I made this vow and I kept it. I have never—
regardless of what came my way—regretted my vow. The Army

truly was now my life, and I was home at last.

The following morning I was introduced to army food. Food, such as French toast, that I had never seen before. Where had this delicacy been all my life? It was merely a question of time until I was eating dishes totally unfamiliar to me. Creamed beef on toast, all the pancakes I could eat, roasts of every kind, bacon and sausage with eggs, served in any manner you desired. What food for a kid from Hell's Kitchen! Hot dinner rolls for lunch and dinner; ice cream, all you could eat. This truly was Nirvana! It was always a source of amazement to me to hear soldiers complain about army chow. I knew for a fact that very few of them had ever eaten as well. We were all coming out of a Depression!

The image of white, clean, starched bed sheets on my bunk that first night still lingers in my memory. Yes, this was truly home, and I fully intended to stay home! Fort Slocum was a beautiful assignment, albeit a brief one. The five weeks spent at that old army post were five of the most pleasant weeks of my life. In addition to three fabulous meals a day, the likes of which I had never seen, I found a camaraderie among my fellow recruits that I had never experienced before. The warm summer days of August slipped by all too quickly, and on weekends we would be given a two-day pass. For me, living in New York City, it was a simple matter to ride the subway to Manhattan. Wearing uniforms for the first time in a civilian world, we stood tall and proud. Unfortunately the civil populace of that era did not see us in the same light. Prewar soldiers were unpopular to put it mildly. It was not uncommon to see signs in bar windows saying "No dogs or soldiers allowed." The reasons were simple. We did not have much money! We usually left the area very quickly, and we cut into the locals' relationships with the females. There was also the owner's constant worry of a bar fight involving servicemen and the subsequent damage to the establishment. After the war's end I spent considerable time in bars in Tacoma, Washington. The treatment accorded us then made me feel we were in a totally different country than the one we left.

While at Fort Slocum, I would spend my days taking instruction on what the field manual called, "Military Courtesy and Drills." We learned to salute everything that moved and to paint everything else. In addition we became very proficient at "policing the area," another term for picking up cigarette butts on the parade grounds and streets. On those warm summer nights I would perch myself on the seawall surrounding the post and listen to Glenn Miller, at no cost. Miller was playing at the Glen Island Casino near New Rochelle, and the sounds of his music would float across the water. A devoted fan of Glenn Miller then and now, I found a great deal of happiness just sitting and listening, and it was free.

Happiness comes in many forms. For example, Uncle Robert visited me while I was at Fort Slocum. Now a visit by a relative to a young army recruit was no big deal in those days, but this was a special visit. Uncle had joined the army in 1937 for want of a job. Assigned to the 16th Infantry Regiment stationed at Fort Jay on Governors Island adjacent to lower Manhattan, Bob had reenlisted about the time I joined up. With his reenlistment came the glorious rank of corporal. He now was one of the "elite" in my eyes. He came to Fort Slocum with the largest corporal chevrons available, and the extra-wide cross-stitching on those stripes made them look a little bit like sergeant stripes. Now that was an important man! I immediately became somewhat of a celebrity among my fellow recruits. After all, I had a noncommissioned officer as a relative. That just might help me go far in this man's army. I remember Bob, all of four years older than I, acting with the true dignity of a noncom of that era.

While the army kept us busy in the five weeks at that post, we did not attempt any formal basic training such as became mandatory for all servicemen later on. Instead, our basic training was to be given by our parent unit, the 31st U.S. Infantry Regiment in my case. No one foresaw it, but this method of basic training was to backfire on the military in the Philippines.

Shortly after the Fil-American forces took up predesignated positions on Bataan, it became necessary to convert Army Air Corps personnel (who had no planes and who had never learned anything but handling a monkey wrench) into infantrymen. Without even very basic infantry training, these men were ill-prepared to fight as infantrymen. In general, because of their lack of training they were placed in line positions where Japanese attacks were not anticipated. The quality of the Allied effort on Bataan could have definitely been aided with universal basic infantry training.

It was not uncommon for Air Corps units placed along a defensive line as infantry to seek out infantry units supporting them and ask assistance in accomplishing the simple task of cleaning a jammed or dirty "gun." Nothing is more abrasive to an infantryman than hearing a rifle referred to as a "gun." The lack of proper training undoubtedly cost Filipino and American lives.

Five weeks after arriving at Fort Slocum, recruits assigned to Panama, Hawaii and the Philippines boarded a ferryboat for a trip down the Hudson River en route to the Brooklyn army base, in New York City. Friendships made during our stay at Slocum were to continue throughout the days ahead. As always, soldiers place great reliance upon others to ease the pangs of homesickness and the need for protection that lay in having a buddy to support you in a hostile environment. Thirteen soldiers entered Fort Slocum on 5 August 1940 en route to the Philippines. I find myself at this writing to be the sole survivor of that group. We were very close, but we were reduced to two survivors by the war's end.

Our stay at the Brooklyn army base was intentionally brief. Arriving on a Monday afternoon, we were told we would be "shipping out" on Saturday morning. With absolutely nothing to do but play table tennis (I managed to win the base's championship during that week) we were allowed out every evening. Brooklyn was no different than New Rochelle, however. Before being allowed to leave we were warned to be sure to walk near the curb of the street on our way to the subway. Walking near the houses of the street could prove hazardous as flower pots landing on soldiers' heads were not uncommon occurrences. (Just think: we were going off to defend our country, even though its people did not think they needed any defense.)

While the out-of-towners headed for the bright lights of New York City and its excitement, I headed home knowing I would soon be leaving for several years. Each night of that week was spent visiting friends and family. On Thursday I visited my mother with full intent not to visit her the following evening. Parting from one's family is always difficult, and while I did not expect such feelings I found myself in some emotional distress over leaving my mother. Knowing that my ship was leaving on Saturday, my mother felt certain that I would not return the next night as I promised. She read me well.

As I walked up the street from our apartment house, I looked back and saw her watching me from the roof. Her intuition proved correct, as I could not bring myself to return. This prompted a sense of guilt which was quickly erased when the army announced on Friday that no one would be allowed to leave that night. We were confined to the base. A decision, I am sure based on much experience in losing recruits due to be shipped out.

CHAPTER 3

EN ROUTE TO THE PHILIPPINES

On Saturday morning 14 September 1940, I along with several hundred other enlisted men and a small group of officers, boarded the U.S.A.T. *Grant* for duty overseas. As we walked up the gangplank on that very bright and beautiful morning, a representative of the Mennen shaving products handed out a small bag containing samples of their wares. While the gift was of little monetary value, the act of giving a gift to those leaving their country in a peacetime atmosphere was sincerely appreciated by many others and me. I am sure that Mennen gained a considerable number of lifetime users of their products with that very small and insignificant gift. Each recruit felt just a little bit more special after receiving it.

The ship we were to travel on had been in service as a troop transport for a number of years, and it was originally built in Stettin, Germany for the Hamburg-American line before the Great War for tropical service on the run between Hamburg and Buenos Aires. While in this commercial service under the German flag she was known as the *Köenig Wilhelm II*.

At the outbreak of World War I the ship was interned at Hoboken, New Jersey. When the United States entered the conflict, the ship was used by the Army Transport Service for eighteen months, thereby earning the right to wear the three gold chevrons adorning her funnel the day we boarded her.

When troop movements after the cessation of hostilities had been completed, the ship was returned to the control of the United States Shipping Board. A year later she was again assigned to the War

Department for permanent use as a transport and renamed the
U.S.A.T. *Grant*. With a crew of two hundred and nineteen officers and men, the ship never exceeded thirteen knots. In normal
times the *Grant* made two annual trips from New York to Manila
(stopping at San Francisco for west coast recruits) and a total of
four trips from San Francisco to Manila. The ship played a major
role in the defense of the Philippines as it transported most of the
American defenders to those islands.

As the ship pulled away from the pier I noticed a one-star pennant flying from the ship's mast. "Old soldiers" explained that it
meant there was a brigadier general on board. We soon learned
through the ship's daily mimeographed newspaper that our general was Jonathan M. Wainwright, headed for his place in American military history. In addition to Wainwright, several senior ranking colonels, whose names are now part of the defense of Bataan,
were aboard. Colonel Albert Jones, who was to be my regimental
commander in the 31st Infantry Regiment in Manila and later a
corps commander as a major general; and Major General Edward
P. King Jr., who, defying orders and expecting a court-martial for
doing so, surrendered more men than any American general before him when he surrendered Bataan on the seventy-seventh anniversary of Appomattox.

New York City's skyline slowly disappeared from view as we
steamed out of the harbor. I watched it fade on the horizon with
mixed emotions. My initial feeling of sadness was mixed with the
excitement of an adventure about to begin. Shortly, a new feeling
came over me, seasickness. As darkness fell the troops assembled
on the ship's fantail to watch a very recently released movie, "Boom
Town," with Spencer Tracy and Clark Gable. As we watched a
very small portable screen, I noticed the screen moving up and
down with the rolling of the ship. This began a nightmare of being
seasick that was to last the entire journey to the Philippines.

I had been seasick from my first half hour aboard ship, and soon
found out that I could not go below decks, as I was unable to stand
the stench of the ship's innards. Fearing that I would feel even
worse if I could not breathe fresh air, I remained on the main deck
for the entire voyage. I slept each night, in fair weather and foul,

under one of the lifeboats using a blanket as my mattress. While the deck was hard and often very wet from waves washing over the ship, I preferred those sleeping quarters to any below.

Shortly after the end of the movie we had our first negative experience in the army. To cut the wind sweeping around the officers' deck while the movie was in progress, a roll of canvas was lowered to the railing on their section of the deck. When the movie ended, a detail of crewmen and recruits climbed the railing to raise the canvas. One young soldier, wearing his recently issued heavy army overcoat for protection from the surprisingly cold wind, lost his footing and fell overboard.

The ship sounded its alarms and came to as rapid a stop as possible. Small boats were lowered into the dark water while searchlights plied the sea. For over an hour the men in these small boats combed the area. Their efforts in vain, they were recalled to the ship by the captain. We got under way once again but the men grew strangely quiet. We had lost our first comrade.

All aboard were fully convinced that the young soldier, falling so close to the ship's stern, was chopped up by the propellers, or that his fall had rendered him unconscious and the weight of his overcoat had drowned him. We preferred to think the latter.

The ship was soon moving through the darkness toward its first port of call, Charleston, South Carolina, where it docked the next morning to discharge cargo. The time had come, I thought, to get off the ship and away from this terrible seasickness. Harboring thoughts of going AWOL (absent without leave), I started for the gangplank only to see two huge M.P.'s, one at the top of the gangplank and the other at the bottom. In those days, M.P.'s selected for such duty had to be as big as possible. Their size usually resolved small incidents. The mere sight of them erased all thoughts of escape from my mind.

After leaving Charleston we headed toward Panama, following close to the coastline of the United States. We soon entered Gatun Lake leading to the locks of the canal, and a great commotion came over the ship. We discovered that we were in a freshwater lake and that we could have a fresh water shower. Bathing in salt water had proved very unpopular, yet that was our only choice during the entire trip to the Philippines, excluding Gatun Lake. The ship's fresh water supply, extremely limited and always guarded by an M.P., was reserved for cooking and drinking. All aboard, excluding the officers, were compelled to shower and wash their clothes in saltwater. A common sight aboard the *Grant* was army fatigues (blue) washed in salt water (with a white appearance from the salt) flapping against the side of the ship to dry. The sight of such "slapping" laundry became an everyday sight in the Philippines. There, Filipino laundrywomen would wash the clothing in a nearby freshwater stream, pounding the clothing against large rocks at the water's edge.

After bathing and laundry chores, we entered the famous Panama Canal. To kids from the farms and cities of America it was a most fascinating sight to see the procedures that allowed a ship to pass from the Atlantic to the Pacific. Upon docking in Panama City we were all authorized twelve-hour passes. Warned to avoid certain areas, we rushed to go ashore. I would have gone anywhere in order to put my feet on solid ground. Many times I have thanked God that I did not decide on a naval career. What a wonderful feeling to be on terra firma! Some of those off the ship decided to ignore the warnings concerning prohibited areas. The American M.P.'s, outstandingly dressed in their formfitting army suntans, which fit them more like gloves, with pegged britches fitted into tall black boots (all their leather was black including the weapon holster and Sam Browne belt) and pith helmets, immediately recognized the recruits for what they were in the "off limits" areas. A wave of a black nightstick in the direction of the errant recruits sufficed. A half hour before the expiration of our passes, these same M.P.'s began rounding up all of those off the *Grant* and steering us back to our pier. Before rejoining the main body however, we managed to find a few of the local bars and quench our thirst. Panama was hot! No one was missing from roll call taken immediately after going aboard. The M.P.'s had done their duty remarkably well.

In Panama City I first became fast friends with Alban Harvey, a farm boy from Chester, Pennsylvania. While we had joined the army on the same date, our friendship began in Panama when he protected my back and I his while in one of the local establishments mainly frequented by the navy. Forming a two-man protective association, we saw the sights of Panama City, and in those days that was one city that required a friend. He and I became close friends and we remained so until Bataan, when we were separated due to my new assignment. After that separation I never saw him again. Returning to the Philippines in 1986, I discovered Harvey's name engraved on the wall of the Cabanatuan Memorial. Harvey was one of the three thousand young American boys who died in that camp. Ninety-nine percent of those fatalities died in the first six months of the camp's existence. The overwhelming majority were men of Bataan who survived Camp O'Donnell only to die in their second prison camp.

Harvey and I were inseparable. Assigned to the same infantry company of the 31st Infantry, Company F, one of us could not be found without the other being nearby. Upon discovering Harvey's name on the memorial, I said a silent prayer. A flood of memories of our friendship rushed through my mind. How could such a fine young man as he have died in such a place? Al Harvey was not only a fine soldier but a gentleman in a group and time of very few gentlemen. He has been sorely missed by me these past fifty years.

With our departure from Panama we set sail for the west coast. On 1 October 1940 our one-star pennant atop the ship was lowered and a two-star flag was hoisted in its place. It was now Major General Wainwright aboard the *Grant.* A considerable amount has been written concerning Jonathan Wainwright, both pro and con, but no one ever questioned the loyalty that this man could inspire among his troops. This "old soldier" belonged in the days of cavalry charges (he ordered the last cavalry charge in U.S. Army history when he sent the 26th Cavalry [Philippine Scouts] against the Japanese on Bataan). He became a victim of circumstances. Sent to the Philippines in 1940, Wainwright felt he was being "put out to pasture" while younger officers were destined for the coming battle with the Germans. It was my pleasure and honor to know General Wainwright at Fort McKinley in the Philippines prior to World War II.

The general had three personal mounts brought with him aboard the *Grant* and he exercised those horses every day possible in the Philippines. The early months of his tour were relatively quiet, and on any day the general could be seen riding one of his horses around Fort McKinley's parade ground outside Manila. His other two horses would trail behind him, with one usually ridden by one of his two aides and the third by an enlisted man. On several occasions, because of my assignment at Fort McKinley, I would be that third rider, having learned to ride at McKinley's stables.

That Wainwright was a heavy drinker was well-known, but so were most regular army officers of that era. At no time however did his drinking interfere with his soldiering. The army in sending Wainwright to the Philippines may have felt that they were putting an old soldier out to pasture, but if that was their reasoning, and from all research it was, then they did a disservice to the troops in the Philippines who eventually needed a leader after MacArthur was pulled out of the Philippines in March 1942. Wainwright—in the estimate of many—was ill-prepared to assume the role placed in his hands. He was a great second-in-command, but not the type to be the decision maker.

Shortly after our arrival in San Francisco we were taken to Fort McDowell, located on what is known as Angel Island in San Francisco Bay. On our ferryboat ride to the island we passed the infamous Alcatraz for the first time. It seemed appropriate that the prison was also known as Devil's Island, in view of its close proximity to Angel's Island.

In fairness to Fort McDowell, it must be pointed out that it was a fine military post with a busy history during World War II. It was a stopover for troops en route to the Philippines. Due to the large number of troops awaiting shipment to the Pacific at that time, nine meals a day had to be served to accommodate all the troops on the relatively small base. Three breakfasts, three lunches, and three dinners were served, all "family style."

While we had to line up and eat from trays at Fort Slocum and aboard the *Grant*, the army did it differently at McDowell. Each table contained a certain number of men assigned to it, and K.P.'s (kitchen police) served food on heated platters. To feed such a large number of men, and three meals at each sitting, required a large number of K.P.'s on duty in the kitchen. This meant constant work from 4 A.M. until 1 A.M. the following day. I was unfortunate to be among those chosen for such duty and I don't recall ever working as hard as I did at that time, and I include my labor for the Japanese as a POW!

Gaining a weekend pass, my buddy Al Harvey and I found ourselves touring San Francisco, known to me only from books and movies. The beauty of San Francisco in 1940 was unmatched by any other city I had seen. Looking for lodging for two nights, we soon settled for the YMCA on Embarcadero Street. Looking out the windows of our immaculately clean and reasonably priced room, we could see a very tall tower containing a huge clock near the piers of the city. For young soldiers away from home for the first time, both Harvey and I were deeply impressed by our good fortune in obtaining such a place to stay. Later on, many times we reminisced over our days in San Francisco.

Harvey wanted to tour the city on Saturday, our first day. I wanted to see my first college football game. With almost two months pay in my pocket, I could not pass up the opportunity to see the University of California play St. Mary's University. Harvey went his way and I went to Berkeley. Long after the game and the band's rendition of both schools' hymns, I lingered in the stadium. The sun setting over that arena awoke a feeling of homesickness I had never experienced until then.

I was finally forced to leave and had to rush to meet Harvey for dinner and share the experience of our last night in the United States for a while, we thought. For Harvey, it was the last night in his country.

The next day, Sunday, we slept late and eventually made our way to Market Street for a movie. There I first encountered a homosexual, of whom there were many. Soldiers, very young soldiers, were sought out by these individuals and it was a frightening experience. We finally went to the ferry pier where a boat departed every hour on the hour. Harvey went aboard immediately. I walked up and down that pier for hours until the last ferry was due to leave for Angel Island. Something was holding me back until the last moment. I knew that once I stepped aboard that ferry I was in the

Philippines, and there was no turning back. The thought of being seasick for weeks to come almost prompted me to miss the ship. Fearing the consequences of desertion more than my seasickness, I went aboard.

Two days later we again boarded the *Grant* to begin our journey. As the ship crept under the Golden Gate Bridge, all aboard stared up at this magnificent structure. Many aboard the ship were seeing the bridge for the first, and last, time. For one out of every three soldiers assigned to Corregidor when we arrived in the Philippines, it was the last time they would see their country. For those destined for Bataan, two out of three would die. The bridge ultimately became part of our everyday prison life. With each passing year of captivity we lost more hope of returning anytime soon. From the expression "home alive in forty-five," it became "the Golden Gate in forty-eight." We began to believe it would take that long to get home, provided we were not killed by the Japanese.

The trip across the Pacific was uneventful, aside of the continued seasickness that plagued me from New York. Arriving one extremely bright morning in Hawaii, I marveled at the beauty of a place I had only read about. I never felt as peaceful at any time in my life as I did that morning. Not allowed ashore, we watched the bustle of activities on the pier. After several hours we put to sea again, our next port of call the island of Guam. Here General Wainwright and his aides went ashore in a motor launch and returned in several hours. Our next stop, the harbor of Manila in the Philippines late at night on 31 October 1940. The lights of the harbor were exciting to see. We were finally in the "Pearl of the Orient."

CHAPTER 4

PREWAR LIFE IN MANILA

Not allowed ashore until the following morning, for me it was a night to remember. The ship was at anchor and my stomach was almost back to normal. Staring at the multitude of lights surrounding us, I wondered what life had in store for me. After a forty-eight day trip of being sick every day, I was more than ready to go ashore.

The next day we reached the end of our journey when we were trucked by men of the 31st Infantry Regiment to their outdoor basketball court, a most modern facility in the midst of ancient surroundings. All those assigned to the infantry were gathered in formation for instructions and briefings. Corporals and sergeants from various companies of the regiment were gathered at the gym and soon barking out the names of new recruits assigned to their respective companies. I and a number of others were taken by truck across town where the second and third battalions of the regiment were quartered in an old Spanish cavalry post circa 1898. Assigned to Company F, I found myself with my buddy Alban Harvey, for which I felt very fortunate, under the "tender loving care" of our squad leader, Corporal Russell Cirrito of Brooklyn, New York. Cirrito was anything but tender, but I am sure I owe my life to his leadership. "Old soldiers" of that era were unusual people to put it mildly. He was responsible not only for our training but also for our table manners. He was, in short, "almighty." Fail to say "please" when asking that a plate of food be passed at the dining table, and you would find the plate dumped in your lap by the good corporal.

Attempt to "short-stop" a plate en route to one requesting that plate, and the same thing would happen. Yes, Corporal Cirrito ruled with an iron hand, but he made soldiers of recruits in a hurry.

Manila before the war was a soldier's paradise. Compared to the British Army in India of Rudyard Kipling's day, Manila was described as "our days of empire." Both officers and enlisted men sought assignment to those islands. While pay was low for the army of 1940 and promotions were very slow, soldiering in the Philippines had many advantages not found elsewhere in the army. The lowly recruit, paid twenty-one dollars for the first four months of his service, could look at that amount and see forty-two pesos, a tidy sum for prewar Manila. After the four months each recruit was advanced in pay by nine dollars more, for a total of sixty pesos. Armed with such an amount of money, soldiers could afford Filipino houseboys to do kitchen police, an onerous task in the heat of the Philippines; have their bunks made up every day to pass daily inspection; and have their shoes and other leather gear polished beyond description. Each infantry company had its own Chinese tailor. Each recruit was given a bolt of suntan material to take to the tailor where his uniform would be tailor-made. The uniforms fit so perfectly that each man looked as if he had been poured into it.

Most Filipinos working for American soldiers of that era had been unofficial members of the infantry regiment for years. Having a certain number of men in their charge brought these Filipinos a very good living, much better than the average Filipino outside the military. Their loyalty was unquestioned and many of them went into Bataan with the unit, remaining there until it fell. Many knew no other life than being a part of the regiment.

With many of his chores done for him, the infantry soldier was left to the duties of the garrison soldier of peacetime. The extreme heat and humidity lowered the Americans' energy level, and so a soldier's day in the Philippines consisted of reveille, followed by breakfast served by Filipino waiters, followed by unit drill or other military training. Such training was only permitted when each recruit satisfied the first sergeant that they had successfully completed the regiment's recruit training, which usually lasted eight weeks.

The company's sergeants and corporals insured that the recruits were ready before the first sergeant and company commander gave them their final inspection prior to becoming full-fledged members of the regiment. One of the last tests to be passed was moving one's rifle from right shoulder to left shoulder without touching the broad brim of the campaign hat issued only when a recruit was ready for full duty. Hit the brim and you returned for further recruit training. The campaign hat was without a doubt the pride and joy of each infantryman in the regiment. Attached to the front was the regiment's insignia, a polar bear with the Latin term *Pro Patria* (for country) emblazoned on the pin. The 31st Infantry Regiment had never served in the United States, being organized for duty in Siberia in 1917. When World War I ended, the regiment was reassigned to the Philippines and retained its identification with the Siberian polar bear.

Daily training ended at 11:30 A.M. and after cleaning up, a generous lunch was served. Enough for two meals, it contributing to our feeling of lethargy. Recognizing both the heat and the sluggish feeling, all men not assigned to guard duty in Manila were given the option: either have a siesta from one to 4 P.M., or leave the barracks. Siesta was highly thought of in those days, and anyone disturbing the siesta usually paid for it with a boot and a curse thrown at them. Those not wanting to sleep in the heat of the day (which usually meant lying under a mosquito net and sweating) would either go to town or spend the afternoon in the company dayroom playing cards or shooting pool. Usually it was the very young and newly-arrived soldier who opted for a movie or a stroll around town.

The barracks, though ancient, were completely "air conditioned." That is to say, no windows surrounded the sleeping quarters on the second floor. Slanted roofs came down partially over the opening which, in theory, was to allow the rain to run off. When heavy rains struck the area, which occurred often during the rainy season, water would come streaming in under the eaves. Looking out during one of those storms was an invigorating experience just to feel the coolness of the air after the stifling humidity normally present.

On the first floor were the company offices for the commanding officer, his first sergeant, and company clerk as well as rooms for the supply sergeant and company armorer. Also in "private rooms" were the company cooks, three to a room, and the mess sergeant located adjacent to the dining hall and kitchen. In this particular army cooks and mess sergeants were prized members of an infantry company, and the mess sergeant reigned supreme.

A good mess sergeant was a desired individual, as the morale of the unit rested upon his shoulders. Almost daily the mess sergeant would visit the local markets and purchase fruits and vegetables using funds allotted to him each month. Meats were shipped to the Philippines from either the U.S.A. or Australia. Also shipped from the United States was dried milk, which was reconstituted upon arrival at the company kitchen. A very poor-tasting milk was known to the soldiers as "mestizo milk" (named after persons of mixed breed) or half-and-half. Mestizos were usually very good looking, and, large numbers of them were located in Manila. It was my very good fortune to have known a mestiza girl just before the outbreak of the war, but unfortunately that event ended my relationship. Such mestizos were in a much higher strata than most Filipinos, and knowing one was a badge of good fortune.

Once a month, if the mess sergeant handled his funds prudently, a beer party was held for the company with any accrued savings. A conservative spending yet well feeding mess sergeant was a much sought after individual once his reputation was established. This often resulted in "raids" on the individual by other companies. Long before the Pentagon began issuing "balanced diets" orders for the military, mess sergeants had that responsibility. To my knowledge there was never one complaint about our mess sergeant. When the war broke out, he was taken from the kitchen and given a commission because of his length of service, as were other noncommissioned officers of the company. Assigned to a Philippine Army unit, he died in combat on Bataan.

Ordinary company assignments usually consisted of guard duties at various critical points in Manila when the battalion was not in the field. As a rule not more than a battalion at a time from the regiment's three battalions was "in the field." The usual practice was to be sure that one battalion remained in Manila at all times.

Soldiers selected for a particular day's guard duty would find their names posted on the unit bulletin board several days in advance. Their "houseboys" would also read the board and make sure that a perfectly starched uniform, polished leather gear, and high top shoes were placed near the bunk of the individual soldier assigned guard duty.

Assembling in the company area, the men selected would march in strict formation from the Estado Mayor barracks (home of the regiment's second and third battalions) to the headquarters of the 31st, and the battalion stationed in the Cuartel de España located in the Intramuros, the walled city of Manila, would march across town under constant scrutiny of the Filipinos who would gather along the route to watch the marching Americans. Needless to say, we were on our best behavior and the officer in charge of the detail ensured that we measured up to expectations. Marching as we did, one could not help but feel pride in being an American soldier stationed so far from his country. Philippine Army troops drilling on the lawn in front of the walls of the ancient city would stop their training to watch the Americans pass by. We were the "professionals" in their eyes.

Guard mount was held in the same gymnasium where we were first introduced to the 31st Infantry Regiment. Each guard member would compete for the coveted title of "orderly." Selection for same was based upon the individual's neatness, his uniform, and above all his rifle. Men going on guard duty would hone the stock of their rifle until it glistened as much as a highly shined pair of shoes. When presenting the rifle for inspection, the belt on the rifle had to snap hard and sharp to the point. The snap could be heard all over the gymnasium.

The one selected for orderly was assigned the post in front of the commanding general's office in Fort Santiago. Upon completion of his tour of duty he was given a two-day pass, free of all responsibilities. Guards were assigned to a post for two hours on and four hours off, hence four orderlies were chosen for twenty-four hours.

The remainder of the guard would then be assigned to various posts throughout Manila, including the piers where military and civilian boats docked. Other assignments had us in warehouses, coal yards, and fuel dumps where thievery was always a threat. It was not unusual for a sentry on guard duty to shoot and kill a would-be thief. Thieves were not highly thought of in those days. Another onerous task was "chasing" American prisoners from the regimental stockade to work details in the city. Should one prisoner escape from such a detail, the guard was told he would take the prisoner's place in the stockade. The provost sergeant in charge of the stockade made that very clear to new recruits assigned to this duty. We made sure that none escaped our custody.

A pleasant assignment however was guard duty at a pier where army transports docked. For me it was a touch of home to be so assigned. The ship had recently left the shores of California, and here it was sitting next to me. Usually one assigned to this duty could find excellent delicacies in the form of good dairy products aboard ship, treats unavailable in the Philippines. Such products were denied to us as Filipino cows were a source of tuberculosis. It was a special holiday in Manila when one of our transports arrived. Work was curtailed so that all interested could watch the ship come in. It was also a festive time when the ship departed, taking home those who had completed the required tour of two years.

On those occasions, one could witness Filipino women crying over the loss of a boyfriend going home. The tears I am sure were well meant, but within a short time, that same woman would be seen in the company of a new soldier friend, one who had probably arrived on the same ship as the departing friend. Yes, love was indeed grand in the Philippines. Venereal disease, which ran rampant, was a great threat to the health of all soldiers and sailors in the Philippines. To avoid the harrowing experiences associated with V.D., many soldiers would opt to live with one Filipino after he had her checked for disease. While the soldier only had few nights on pass that he could spend with her, he could depend upon his food while with her, have sex, and have his laundry done. All this for approximately twenty-five pesos (or $12.50). Those who could afford such an arrangement were fairly safe from disease. For all intents and purposes, soldiers and their "women" were married in spirit if not in fact.

This routine would usually be interrupted when the unit went into the "field" on maneuvers, or to Fort McKinley firing range nine miles outside Manila. Here we performed familiarization firing and occasionally firing for record. Training in the use of weapons was extremely limited due to the lack of funds appropriated for the army. Both ammunition and equipment were in short supply in an army of just over 300,000 men by 1940. Units in the States were worse off, using stove pipes as mortars, trucks made to look like tanks, and ordinary flour used to mark shell or bomb hits on those "tanks." For us in the Philippines it meant practicing machine gun firing without ammunition, using orange crates to simulate firing. A nice title for the training was "dry firing." One soldier would sit on a box which held a small target. A marker held in his hand would be moved over the target until the soldier with the rifle, looking through the sights, would call out "mark." Often times his "fire" was off the target, hence "dry firing." At no time do I recall ever throwing a hand grenade in practice, and when it came time to use one in combat I almost killed myself. If we were not fully trained however, it was not the fault of our regiment. It was the fault of our government, which gave a higher priority to Europe. We thus became "the expendables."

This was the daily routine in existence upon my assignment to the 31st Infantry Regiment (America's Foreign Legion) on 1 November 1940. It hardly seemed appropriate for a time that witnessed Hitler at war with France and Great Britain. While there were many "peaceniks" and those who wanted to remain neutral, many others saw our involvement in the European war as inevitable. The overall atmosphere prevailing in the United States at the time however prevented any real buildup in the Philippines. The Great Depression was still very much with us, and certainly no money was available to spend on reinforcing an army garrison in the faraway Philippines. The soldiers' days of leisure however were fast disappearing. In the Philippines, old-timers of the regiment were convinced that war with Japan was coming, and almost daily they pointed this fact out to those in training.

Most of the soldiers stationed in prewar Manila were regular army. All, with the exception of recently arrived reserve officers, had volunteered for the Philippines. Most were anxious for the assignment and did their best to secure such a "plum." A regular took great pride in the army, his unit, and the fact that he was a regular. Rarely did one hear a complaint from such a regular about his lot in life. He had asked for what he was doing and where he was. "Old soldiers" of that era usually requested one foreign tour of duty after another, going from the Philippines to Panama or Hawaii, with a short stopover in the States in between. Their money was usually worth more in those areas and the duty was much more desirable than at a Stateside post.

It was not unusual to see an old-timer coming down the gangplank of a recently arrived transport in Manila harbor, having just completed a tour of duty in another overseas port. Called "p.s. men" (previous service), the sight of these military journeymen coming into the Philippine command would usually put a first enlistment soldier into a nervous dither. He knew instantly that his chances for promotion had just grown slimmer. Easily recognized by the shade on the arm where stripes had been recently removed (obtained at his last assignment), the old timer was sure to get the first promotion available. Rank in those days belonged to the regiment, except for "first three graders" (staff sergeants and above). PFC's, corporals, and "buck" sergeants relinquished their rank upon leaving their overseas ports to return home.

For their personal protection, especially those who may have been overzealous in their enforcement of discipline while wearing the rank, such returning noncoms were given what was known as "saltwater warrants" which allowed them the retention, but not the pay, of their rank while aboard ship returning to the United States or another overseas port. It can be truthfully said that many of these corporals and sergeants needed such protection while aboard ship.

Prewar noncommissioned officers (corporals and above) oftentimes were harsh in their treatment of lower ranking soldiers. It was not uncommon for a noncom to take off the shirt indicating his rank and fight another soldier in an effort to prove himself in the eyes of all. As a result, many such individuals were intensely disliked. Should some of the aggrieved soldiers find themselves aboard the same ship as the returning noncom, it was always pos-sible that the noncom might not reach port alive, having been tossed overboard one night.

I went to the Philippines as a professional soldier, proud of my choice of the infantry, proud of my regiment, and even more proud of my fellow infantrymen. I am sure there were "better" regiments in the army than the 31st, but there was never a regiment with more pride and esprit de corps. There was a camaraderie among infantrymen that I never found equaled in other branches of ser-vice. Nor could such camaraderie ever be found in civilian occu-pations. I joined the army for excitement, but I was also looking for the security of a "home," and a place where I belonged. I found that in the army.

CHAPTER 5

AMERICA'S "FOREIGN LEGION"

As I mentioned previously, life in prewar Manila was truly pleasant. For officers and noncommissioned officers of the ranks of staff, technical, and first sergeants who were fortunate enough to have their wives with them, it was an idyllic life in the 31st Infantry Regiment, known as America's "Foreign Legion." This regiment was the only American infantry regiment never to serve in its homeland. Created in 1917 in Siberia as part of the Allied forces sent to that country after the withdrawal of the Russians from World War I, it adopted the Siberian polar bear as the logo for its regimental crest. The regiment was then sent to the Philippines to serve as garrison troops in those distant islands. In 1932 the regiment was dispatched to Shanghai, China, to protect American interests in that country. After a short time the regiment returned to Manila and remained there until the fall of Bataan, when it lost its colors upon surrendering.

Overseas duty in the Philippines in the thirties, and even as late as 1940, was often compared to the colonial era of British India. Wives of the regiment did little but maintain a busy social schedule. Domestic help was extremely cheap, and American women who normally would never know the luxury of having help with their household chores and raising children, suddenly found themselves hard pressed to do more than attend parties at the clubs open to them.

Unfortunately all these pleasant days and nights began to end starting in May 1941. As it became more evident that war was fast approaching the Philippines, orders were issued to return all military dependents to the United States. What had once been a holiday in Manila when army transports arrived, now became a tearful occasion of bidding farewell to one's family as they embarked for home. Meanwhile, those who stayed behind went about their duties of preparing for both war and the forthcoming independence of the Philippines, due in 1946. While the United States had been a colonial power for forty years in the Philippines, the Tydings-McDuffie Act of 1934 had granted the country independence. Even in today's "different" Philippines a good number of Filipinos still look back with nostalgia on the "days of empire."

In 1940, Americans stationed in the Philippines without wives confronted one of man's oldest medical problems, venereal disease, which was widespread in the Philippines. Needless to say it was a subject never mentioned by the army recruiter. Should American personnel find themselves infected with gonorrhea or syphilis, they could look forward to a period of quarantine in a hospital ward with the large black letters VDJ painted on the walls. Treated as if they had leprosy, military patients would go to any extremes, but one, to avoid hospitalization. Education programs were unheard of in those days, and the only "prevention" consisted of a "shot" after exposure, or what the military thought was exposure.

In a small attempt at prevention, members of the 31st Infantry Regiment returning to their barracks after a 1 A.M. curfew would summarily be taken to a dispensary, located within the confines of the Estado Mayor, home of the regiment's second and third battalions. Here they were administered a shot in an unmentionable place, whether they had sex or not. In addition they would then be confined in an adjacent jail cell, sans mosquito net, and told to sleep on a mattress only. These cells were located on the banks of the Pasig River, so the mosquitoes had a field day. The following morning a company officer would appear to obtain his men's release.

Such a situation is exactly what happened to me upon returning from midnight mass, on Christmas Eve in 1940. The midnight service was held in the army's Sternberg Hospital chapel and it ran late that evening. No explanation satisfied the corporal of the guard, who was called to the front gate when I returned to the barracks at 0115 A.M. Christmas Day. The humiliation of that evening has been unforgettable. My "sex education" was completed that night, and I made sure from then on that I was safely in bed when the magic hour of one struck. The following Christmas Eve found me attending church in the small town of Balanga, Bataan, and hardly concerned about bed checks. My concern that evening was to live to see the dawn of Christmas Day.

The upshot of this very prevalent problem in the Philippines was that young soldiers and sailors often simply "shacked up" with a Filipina for whom the American had paid for a physical examination for venereal disease. Unfortunately, this setup could only be afforded by better paid soldiers, certainly not by the recruit who had to take his chances with the local prostitutes. As a result it was not uncommon to see a very young soldier—as young as sixteen, who had lied about his age—being transported from the maneuver fields to an army hospital for periodic treatment.

Rampant also in the Philippines in 1940–41, especially in Manila, was homosexuality; only no one identified it as such. It was a sort of "passive" homosexuality. The soldier, fearful of venereal disease, was certainly not a homosexual by choice. The very same soldier who would consider such a relationship normal in Manila would most likely have nothing but disgust for the "queer" soliciting him on the streets of San Francisco.

Newly arriving Americans were shocked by such relationships. Old soldiers openly bragged about their "binny boys," a name derived from the Tagalog word "binabae." Being shown the photograph of a Filipino male by an old timer was my introduction to the Philippines. Yet no one dared call the soldier who had a binnie a "queer"; nor did a soldier who engaged in a homosexual act consider himself a deviate. However, such relationships were in the great minority. Most soldiers sought sexual gratification among the many, many prostitutes frequenting the many, many bars of Manila. To avoid disease most soldiers, when sober, frequented bars they were fairly sure were controlled by the management. Many bar owners provided a "stable" of prostitutes, and one of the girls would spend time with a soldier at a table and then lead him to a room in back or above the bar. To ease the patron's mind on the subject of VD, the owner could usually produce records to show that his "girls" had a recent checkup by a doctor. For those who did not trust such medical reports, there was always the unpalatable alternative of chastity. Many bar owners, to attract military clients, would offer sex "on the arm," so one could sign his name for the sex and then pay on payday. It was not uncommon to see a Filipino "pimp" at a company headquarters on payday waiting to be paid for the sex tab his clients had run up. Many such pimps were openly cheated when a name they produced for a company commander investigating their complaint of nonpayment turned out to be a Hollywood star such as Tyrone Power or Spencer Tracy.

American women in the Philippines were extremely scarce. Such women were either wives of officers and enlisted personnel, or nurses. In either case, they were considered untouchables. Contrary to the movies, American enlisted personnel rarely if ever had contact with such women. It just wasn't done! "White women" were placed on a pedestal in the Philippines. The military class system prevailed, and fraternization rarely occurred. In mid-1941 the subject of white women became academic. They were all sent home.

A standing remark of that time was, "when the Filipino women begin to look white, it is time to go home." In all fairness however, Filipinas are attractive women and numerous marriages between Americans and Filipinas became common, especially after the end of the war. Also very attractive and sought after, were the "mestizas" of Manila. This group of women, half-Spanish and half-Filipino or a similar mixture of European and Filipino blood, were outstanding in their beauty. This handsome ethnic group generally remained to themselves, feeling vastly superior to both pure Filipinos and Americans.

While Manila was considered idyllic by many, the climate was not. Temperatures in the city were generally in the nineties with extreme humidity most of the year. Some relief from the oppressive heat came with the rainy season between July and October. While the rain dissipated the heat somewhat, the humidity jumped by leaps and bounds. Air conditioning of course was unknown at that time as far as the soldier was concerned. All the army barracks in prewar Manila were built in the days of Spanish occupation of the Philippines. The Estado Mayor barracks had been quarters for the Spanish cavalry stationed in Manila. (One could swear that the smell of horses still perfumed the barracks.) The barracks were two-level with overhanging roofs and absolutely no windows. The slope of the roof was supposed to keep the rain from coming into the upper floors where the sleeping quarters were. However, when severe storms struck, the soldiers' cots would be moved away from the walls and the mop-up crews would go to work.

Neither the roof nor the windowless walls deterred the mosquito. Because of the dangers of malaria and dengue fever, no one was allowed to sleep without mosquito netting completely enclosing their bed. To do so was to invite a court-martial. Each night after crawling into his bunk, each soldier would go to great lengths to insure that his netting was tucked in. My first night's sleep under the net brought to mind visions of Kipling's India.

Duty for infantry soldiers in prewar Manila was mainly of a security and a ceremonial nature. Two reasons were behind the lack of more vigorous field training, other than our annual three weeks spent in the jungles south of Manila. First and foremost was a lack of funding on the part of the United States that would allow such training. Firearms training was also restricted due to a tight fiscal restraint placed upon the army by Congress. Once a year for a two week period our regiment, battalion by battalion, would be taken to the firing range at Fort William McKinley. Here each soldier was required to qualify with his weapon. Although the newer Garand M1 rifle had already been developed and was in the hands of the army, we were still qualifying with the single bolt action Springfield rifle of 1903. The Garand was a semiautomatic rifle capable of firing nine rounds before reloading, while the Springfield was a single action, five round weapon. Old time officers preferred the "reliability" of the Springfield and kept the M1 in cosmoline. As a result, true familiarization with the M1 came about only when actual combat broke out. During the fighting on Bataan, the M1 proved itself over and over by producing firepower which the Springfield could never match. Strangely, when the Japanese finally took Bataan they destroyed the M1's while preferring to keep the Springfields. They also were armed with a single bolt action rifle and opted to keep the Springfields still in the hands of many Fil-American soldiers.

The second "hidden" reason for limited training was the oppressive heat. The option of siesta for all military personnel up to July 1941 was mandatory. All training had to end by 11 A.M. All units were turned to their barracks, allowed one hour to clean up and then lined up for noonday "chow," a most sumptuous meal, which usually produced a state of lethargy. Most men then returned to their sleeping quarters, where they had the option of going to sleep or leaving the barracks within fifteen minutes. Silence would then descend on the companies until a bugle call at 4 P.M., awakening everyone in order to prepare for dinner. For me and other newcomers to Manila it meant either an afternoon walk in the hot sun, a game of cards, or a game of pool in the company dayroom. Those with money could visit one of Manila's modern theaters on the Escolta, the Broadway of Manila.

Despite the failure of the American government to provide adequate funding for an active training cycle, the 31st Infantry carried on its limited training program as well as could be expected. Upon the regiment's return from either the field or the firing range, the "thirsty-firsters," as the men of the regiment became known (referring to their penchant for Manila's fine San Miguel beer), would make haste to do the town in a fashion of their choosing.

Manila was a city of bars and many houses of prostitution. An alternative, however was the one and only Army-Navy YMCA, where pool tables and bowling alleys could be found. Both were usually empty because most soldiers did not opt for such mundane entertainment. Payday of course was filled with excitement. Every soldier had to appear in his best uniform before the company commander, who would dole out in cash the G.I.'s monthly pay. It was a required experience as it usually was the only time the company commander got to see his individual soldiers. Reporting therefore became a procedure to allow this review of the individual. A young recruit felt he was appearing before royalty. Sitting alongside the company commander was the first sergeant, another of the "anointed ones" of the army of that era. He too was probably seeing "his" men for the first time in a month. We feared his comments the most.

Payday gambling commenced with the paying of the last member of the company. With a large army blanket spread on the pool table in the company dayroom, monthly salaries soon were exchanging hands. Hundreds of dollars were won and lost in one day with numerous old-timers returning to the States with more money than they needed. Usually the gambling continued aboard ship and long journeys at sea usually produced big winners. I recall one crap game played in the ship's refrigeration area on the top of a casket of a returning Filipino. I was always convinced that he did not mind the game being played on his "chest." Filipinos are inveterate gamblers who will gamble on anything.

Each payday—which fell on the last day of the month—proved to be a bonanza for Manila's bar owners and prostitutes. Manila was the playground for the army and navy and what few Marines could be found there. The bars also provided monthly headaches for the local military police. The M.P.'s could always count on losing personnel the first three nights of the new month as they attempted to quell nightly fights while the money lasted. Five nights after payday, Manila would settle back to being a peaceful city. Certain soldiers became well-known for their bar-wrecking abilities and their reputation spread throughout the city. Worse yet were drunken encounters between army and navy men, who had a particular dislike for each other.

Rivaling these contests were the battles between the infantrymen of the 31st Infantry Regiment (us) and any artillerymen visiting Manila from their post on Corregidor, who were easily distinguished by the piping on their campaign hat, a bright red. It became a simple matter to pick a fight, common around paydays in Manila. After the military police ended the fracas, the contestants would pay for the damage and usually end up in their unit's jail, or in a "hold tank" maintained by the military police in Manila. The heat of course was often the fuse that ignited the fights. For example, one pay night in a bar in Manila I saw a fellow infantryman take an artilleryman by the head and try to flush it down a commode in the men's room. We stopped him before he drowned him with the constant flushing, however.

Along with the heat came skin problems. Despite all attempts to avoid exposing our skin to the sun, none really gave complete protection. A fungus I picked up in early 1941 still causes some discomfort to this day. Upon contracting this skin rash on my chest, I visited our army medics who laughed at this so-called "problem." Taking matters into my own hands (literally), I followed the advice of an old timer and applied Sloan's liniment to the area. Unfortunately, the itch had driven me to such a point that I did not bother to read the instructions on the bottle. Rubbing it into my skin (which I later learned was not the way to apply Sloan's), I practically set my skin on fire. The itch had now been replaced by a tremendous burning which I could not ease. Remaining in an ice cold shower directly sprayed on my chest brought some relief, but only after a few hours.

Dengue fever, malaria, yaws, and other diseases rarely known to most Americans became part of our daily conversations, as many of us were affected by them. Loneliness was often a major problem, especially among very young soldiers away from home for the first time. Such loneliness often resulted in suicides and attempted suicides. During my first Christmas in the Philippines (1940) I witnessed my first suicide. A young recruit who had come to the Philippines with me placed the muzzle of his loaded rifle into his mouth and pulled the trigger. That has lived in my memory ever since. Not too much attention was paid to such episodes by the army in those days, as homesickness was an accepted part of a recruit's life. No counselors were on hand for such depressed individuals.

While the days of peace slipped away, the war in Europe soon began to cast a shadow in the Far East. As General Wainwright in his autobiography wrote, "the sparkle went out of Manila in the spring of 1941. War was coming and we all knew it." So as 1940 rolled into 1941 "our days of empire" faded—forever as it turned out. By late spring 1941 war with Japan became a daily topic of conversation. This talk also brought a feeling of haste and inadequacy pushed along by old-timer sergeants who saw the war signs not seen by the young. Our training took on a greater meaning,

but in a frantic way. We could not do enough with the time allotted us to prepare for a war that was surely coming. The enemy was
no longer a "make believe force" or "the aggressors." Our enemy
was now Japan.

About the spring of 1941 I decided I could not wait for the war
to come to the Philippines, and inquired about joining the war in
Europe. Mustering up the courage to visit the British consul's office in Manila, I visited that gentleman to offer my services. (I can
still visualize the magnificent portraits of King George and Queen
Elizabeth hanging in his office.)

At that time an American soldier could "buy out" of the army
for two hundred and fifty dollars, a tremendous amount for that
day. Where I could raise such an amount never entered my mind.
I think I had hopes that the British might pay. Of course it was
always possible to win a large amount of money at the monthly
gambling table, but with my luck that would never happen. I don't
recall ever winning in my few attempts at gambling. It was all academic, however. The consul was extremely kind and let me down
gently by saying "you will be in it soon enough." I went back to my
barracks with a feeling that I had tried, and just had to wait for the
war to come to me.

The Philippine Islands had prospered and grown. American
occupation had resulted in modern roads, a school system (previously unknown), and basic sanitation systems, another innovation.
With the American military bases in the Philippines came more
jobs and a great amount of American money in developing those
bases. During the period of American occupation, it is generally
conceded that Filipinos became more dependent upon Americans than a country about to become independent should have
been.

Filipinos, generally speaking, like Americans. Rarely did we ever
see an anti-American attitude. Most Filipinos believed in the power
of the United States to support and defend them. To the Filipino
of 1940 it was inconceivable that any country was stronger than
the United States. Given this impression, the Filipino was reluctant to take on the responsibility of independence. In my thirteen
months of prewar life there, I never encountered a feeling that the

Philippines would be better off as an independent nation. Many Filipinos looked forward to independence with mixed feelings of pride and trepidation.

Forty-five years later, when revisiting the Philippines, I still found this attitude among many Filipinos. They were never anti-American, despite the "ugly American" there as well as elsewhere in the world.

Near the end of 1941, I found myself assigned to Fort William McKinley. My new duties were with the 12th Military Police Company, American Platoon. While the unit was part of the famous Philippine Scouts, made up entirely of Filipino enlisted men who were part of the American army stationed in the Philippines, our duties were to police the American troops stationed at the fort. The corps of military police did not exist at that time, so these assignments were given to other units stationed in Manila, such as 31st Infantry Regiment.

The stark difference between Manila and Fort McKinley became readily apparent. Fort McKinley was the home of the Philippine Division. General Wainwright commanded the division. This division, destined never to see action as a division, consisted of the only really trained units in the Philippines. As such, it was used piecemeal in the form of companies and battalions to support the Philippine Army.

Among the units of the Philippine Division were the 31st Infantry Regiment and the 45th Infantry Regiment (P.S.), all Philippine Scout enlisted men with American officers. That makeup applied for all Scout units. Other Philippine Division units included the 57th Infantry Regiment (P.S.) and 23rd Regiment (P.S.). Other P.S. units were the 24th F.A. Regiment, the 14th Engineer Regiment, 12th Quartermaster Regiment, the 12th M.P. Company, the 12th Signal Company, the 12th Medical Company, and the 4th Vet. Company. Non-division and attached units of the Philippine Scouts when the war broke included the 26th Cavalry Regiment, 43rd Infantry Regiment, 86th and 88th F.A. Regiments (P.S.); the 59th, 60th, and 91st Coast Artillery Regiments (P.S.) located on Corregidor; the 200th Coast Artillery Regiment (U.S.), a New Mexico National Guard unit just arrived; the 192nd Tank Battalion, a National Guard unit from several states recently arrived; and the 194th Tank Battalion (U.S.), also from several states in the Midwest and new to the Philippines. The 803rd Engineer Battalion was also freshly arrived and from several states. The 808th Military Police Company (U.S.) was assigned to police Manila for years before the war. Some of the above units arrived as recently as two weeks before the war's outbreak.

The subsequent casualty loss of the 200th AA unit on Bataan put the greatest burden on any one state, New Mexico. Hardly a village, town, or county in New Mexico escaped the loss of a soldier in the battle of Bataan or in captivity. It is now a recognized fact that these men were ill-prepared for what faced them in the Philippines. Arriving in Manila still clad in winter uniforms issued them prior to their leaving the States, they came down the gangplanks overloaded with winter gear. That they gave a good account of themselves on Bataan can be attributed to their own individual fighting spirit, not to any training received.

While most of the Philippine Division was scattered about Manila, the "heart" of the division was located at Fort McKinley. While preparing for war these troops led quiet lives at one of the most beautiful army posts of the day.

No finer soldier ever wore a uniform than the famed Philippine Scout. Proud of his profession, his regiment, and of being a member of the United States Army, the Scout was the envy of all Filipinos. Scouts were known to spend twenty and thirty years soldiering. Upon retirement, they continued to live at military bases in the Philippines. These men excelled in every combat situation they found themselves in during World War II. To have been a member of a Philippine Scout unit has been my proudest military achievement.

Upon arriving at my new unit in McKinley, I soon discovered that my primary duty was to be part of a security detail "for a rogue Philippine Scout, of the 14th Engineers (P.S.)."

This officer, a Captain Rufo C. Romero, a graduate of the United States Military Academy caught in a sting operation trying to sell maps for $25,000 to a fictitious Mindanao Sultan with pro-Japanese leanings, was being kept in a padded cell at Fort McKinley's hospital after his trial. His security consisted of a twenty-four-hour watch outside his cell door. We were required to look through an opening in the door every ten minutes to preclude any possibility of suicide. He was not allowed visitors other than his wife, and she was never permitted to be alone with him at any time. Inasmuch as her high living led to his becoming a traitor, that was probably just as well.

An eight-hour tour of duty assigned to that detail consisted of playing the role of father confessor, psychologist and jailer all rolled into one. Romero was more than eager to discuss his situation. In those days no one was concerned about the possibility of a guard being brought into court and repeating anything that Romero said.

Each day of his trial he had been taken under extremely heavy guard to a nearby temporary courtroom and returned immediately after the day's proceedings had ended. Married to an extremely beautiful woman, living in prewar Manila, Romero had found it difficult to support her in the lifestyle to which she aspired. Being very despondent and lonesome after his initial confinement, he would often talk of the events and circumstances that led to his plight. Scorned by every Filipino in or near Fort McKinley, he truly was a pathetic individual and almost childlike in his behavior.

After several weeks of his trial, the jury, consisting of American and Filipino army officers from various units, found him guilty. Then began the long wait for appeals to go through and a determination as to where his sentence, would be served. Upon hearing the verdict this young, bright officer virtually fell apart, running the gamut of remorse, self-pity, hate, and suicidal moments. He was finally placed aboard a U.S. Army Transport ship in July 1941 and sent to a military prison in the United States. Most of his security detail had been through an emotional wringer. Romero spent the entire war in prison and was released in 1950. Romero died in 1985, an embarrassment to West Pointers. The war soon erased any knowledge of his wife, but those of us associated with her during her husband's imprisonment felt that she could handle herself quite well in any situation.

On 27 July 1941, General MacArthur was designated commanding general of all United States Forces in the Far East (USAFFE).

This famous soldier had come to the Philippines before in 1935 after retiring as chief of staff, U.S. Army, in Washington, D.C. Then Philippine president Manuel Quezon had named MacArthur as the commonwealth's first field marshal of the Philippine Army. He offered MacArthur this prestigious title in return for his anticipated services in training the Philippines armed forces. Thus, MacArthur became the United States' first field marshal.

When assigned as commanding general USAFFE in 1941, MacArthur had been recalled to active duty with the rank of lieutenant general despite his retired rank of full general. Washington, giving overall command to MacArthur, was acting in accordance with the Tydings-McDuffie Act which provided for Philippine independence ten years from the signing of the act on 24 March 1934. The act specifically allowed the United States "to maintain military and other reservations and armed forces" in the Philippines. and stipulated that the President of the United States would have authority "to call into the service of such armed forces all military forces organized by the Philippine government."

The Philippines are made up of some 7,000 known islands in a 1,200-mile-long archipelago, approximately 500 miles from the Asiatic mainland. Situated in the "geographic heart of the Far East, the islands lie along the trade route of Japan and China." Oil from the East Indies, so vital to Japan's war machine, was also within easy striking distance of Japan.

A major problem MacArthur encountered early in his attempt to train the Philippine Army was the variety of more than sixty-five dialects spoken by Filipinos. While the dialects had certain similarities, it was not possible to train a Philippine Army unit using a native language. On many an occasion—before and during the fighting in the war—English became the only means of communicating with the Filipino. Tagalog, considered the national language, was spoken mostly by the Filipinos from central Luzon, the major island of the Philippines. It was not chosen as the national language however until 1937. Inasmuch as 27 percent of the Filipinos spoke English, brought about by 40 years of American occupation, it proved to be the best choice of language for training the new army.

Lack of a common language was detrimental in fostering these military units' esprit de corp and cohesiveness. Inability to communicate also had a negative effect on the unit's ability to fight as a unit. MacArthur, fully aware of the numerous problems inherent in his task, once called the Philippines "the key that unlocks the door to the Pacific." Fully confident that given support by Washington he could keep the key, he set about to defend the islands.

Meanwhile, back in Washington, General George C. Marshall, U.S. Army chief of staff, felt that MacArthur's demands were great while the supplies available were limited. Marshall feared that reinforcements and supplies sent to the Philippines would leave the United States "in peril" should Great Britain fall to the Nazis. While the United States was stalling for time, Japan made a move that brought the Filipino situation clearly into focus. Japanese forces occupied bases, air and sea, in Indochina on 22 July 1941, thus further threatening the position of the United States in the Philippines. With this situation, the United States was galvanized into action.

Beginning in August 1941 the U.S. War Department began to think that "possibly, just possibly" the Philippines could be defended, and it hastily began to ship men and materiel to that outpost. Large shipments were soon assembled on the west coast of the United States destined for the Philippines. Unfortunately it was a case of too little, too late.

MacArthur however was fully convinced that he could defend the islands, though he based this confidence upon a Japanese timetable of attack in April 1942 or later. Meanwhile the Japanese, feeling the strangling effects of an oil embargo by the U.S., Great Britain, and the Dutch, had other plans. While peace talks between the United States and Japan were taking place during the first few days of December 1941, Japanese military forces moved into attack positions throughout the Pacific.

At the outbreak of the war, United States forces in the Far East consisted of about 120,000 men. This was made up—primarily— of Philippine Army troops who had never fired their weapons, who were poorly equipped, and poorly trained, and recently inducted into the service. They were totally unprepared for war. As part of the forces in the Philippines, approximately 23,000 Americans were stationed either on Corregidor or at military bases in or near Manila. With the exclusion of the Philippine Division stationed mainly at Fort William McKinley and made up of U.S. Army Philippine Scouts and one American infantry regiment (31st Infantry Regiment), most of these Americans were new arrivals to the Philippines. They, too, were poorly trained National Guardsmen newly inducted into federal service shortly before the outbreak of the war. Considering their lack of training, these guardsmen gave a good account of themselves on Bataan.

Adding to their problems, in most cases these reinforcements arrived only a few weeks before war broke out. Stepping off the army transports (most of which were converted luxury ships of the President Lines) into a ninety degree heat, wearing their stateside winter uniforms, with sweat dripping profusely, they were ill-prepared for both the climate and what was to come.

If ever American army troops were unprepared for what awaited them, it was the men of the 200th Anti-Aircraft Regiment from New Mexico. Along with the 200th, came Guardsmen from the 192nd and 194th Tank Battalions, assembled from California, Minnesota, Illinois, Kentucky, Wisconsin, and Ohio. All of these units gave their very best in the defense of Bataan, along with the regular U.S. Army regular troops, in a losing cause, and all were given the U.S. Presidential Citation three times in a four-month period, more than any other U.S. Army unit during World War II. Never had so much been accomplished by so few with so little.

CHAPTER 6

WAR CLOUDS GATHER

Upon completion of my assignment at Fort McKinley, I returned to my parent unit, Company F, 31st Infantry Regiment. Our company training soon began taking on a more serious note than at any time since my arrival in the Philippines. Gone was the leisurely pace of previous months. Much of our training took place in what was known as "the sunken gardens," an area immediately outside the walled city of Manila which at one time in history must have been a moat. Since the shortage of ammunition restricted the actual firing of our weapons, we resorted to "dry firing" which cost nothing. Each day would see soldiers lying on the ground in the prone position, sighting their weapons in on paper targets fastened to wooden crates, while a second soldier sitting on the crate would mark the target on command of the one doing the so-called firing.

Bayonet drill had a definite purpose, with dummies identified by our sergeants as "the Japs." Our noncommissioned officers (noncoms) exhorting us to greater efforts in our training began to register. I recall one sergeant in particular, a Sergeant Austin, telling his charges that we were on the verge of war with the Japanese and we had best prepare for them. Sarge was an "old hand." As each day of our training closed, men of the second and third battalions would form up in platoon-size units and march proudly back to their respective companies in the Estado Mayor, the headquarters of both battalions located along the Pasig River. Marching in cadence through the streets of Manila with many Filipinos watching, we would pass Philippine Army soldiers and various college ROTC units drilling. Dressed in coconut fiber helmets and tennis sneakers, they were doing their best to get ready for the war we all now knew was coming. Their training consisted of learning the fundamentals of marching, or close order drill as it is called in the military. I am sure these greenhorns felt that being a soldier consisted of knowing how to march on a parade ground.

As we Americans marched toward our barracks and dinner, nearly every one of us felt that Japan would be making a huge mistake to take on the United States Army. Such was the pride of youthful soldiers. Unfortunately we were wrong in our estimate of the enemy. We were led to believe that Japanese soldiers were nearsighted and could not shoot straight, that they were inferior soldiers compared to Americans. Arriving back at our barracks each day, we were convinced that we could beat anyone. Estado Mayor barracks, home for Spanish cavalry when Spain controlled Manila, was eventually burned to the ground by the Japanese when they were being cut to pieces in 1945 upon the return of the American forces under MacArthur.

In early June 1941, the 31st Infantry Regiment was put on a state of advanced alert in anticipation of a Japanese attack. Various companies of the regiment were put on the rooftops of the tallest buildings in the city to learn aircraft observation and identification. Lightweight machine guns were placed on the rooftops as anti-aircraft defense. Gone was the slow pace of 1940 Manila!

Army Air Corps personnel arrived about the same time as the Guardsmen, with a number of their units without aircraft. Bombers destined for these units had only made it as far as Australia when war broke out. This lack of aircraft destined for the Philippines combined with the destruction of the fighters at Clark Field on the first day of the war left the ground forces without air support for the entire Bataan-Corregidor campaign. It may be said however that the failure of the bombers to arrive was a mixed blessing. For surely they would have also been destroyed on the ground like those already in the Philippines. Without question MacArthur had under his command the largest gathering of U.S. aircraft, at that time, within the American military. The story of the destruction of almost all American aircraft at the outset of hostilities has not been fully told. This shameful blunder, placed squarely at the door of the United States, led directly to the debacle in the Philippines. While Pearl Harbor was caught by surprise, why were Philippine airfields, eight hours after the Hawaiian disaster, also caught in the same predicament? True, it was a command by MacArthur that Japan must make the first overt hostile act before American forces could respond. But the catastrophe at Clark Field was unforgivable.

The lack of planes and the destruction of aircraft in the initial attacks eventually made ground troops out of all Air Corps personnel. They too however were totally unprepared to become infantrymen. Basic training of enlisted men before the war did not include infantry training for Air Corps personnel. As a result these men were completely unqualified for the role thrust upon them.

Normally the barracks remained quiet in the morning in consideration of those sleeping after being on night duty. However, at approximately 0800 hours (8 A.M.) 8 December 1941 (7 December in the United States and Hawaii), I was rudely thrown out of my bunk when others in my unit turned my bed upside down. Having come in one hour previously after being on duty from 11 P.M. the night before, I had fallen into a sound sleep, my last such luxury for nearly the next four years.

That fateful morning the barracks noises I heard in my sleep should have alerted me that something was very wrong. No one ever disturbed the sleep of those on duty all night. It just wasn't done. But war had finally come to the Philippines, and life would never be the same again for any of us.

When fully awake, a somber understanding of what was happening rid me of any desire for further sleep. Radios turned up full blast blared out the news of the attack on Pearl Harbor. Don Bell, our local American radio broadcaster, was giving us the latest news of what had happened in Hawaii. Everyone listened to Don Bell religiously. He was Manila's Walter Cronkite in 1940–41. We learned for the first time exactly where Pearl Harbor was. To my surprise, I found out that this was the very same harbor our ship had steamed into in October 1940, and which I thought was the most beautiful sight in my trip from New York to the Philippines.

While most Americans are aware of the "day of infamy" and the deaths of 2,200 Americans at Pearl Harbor during that attack, many are unaware of the fatalities that occurred in the Philippines eight hours later. Japanese forces had launched air attacks on Clark Field, Nichols Field, and Cavite Naval Base that same day. Hundreds of Americans and Filipinos were killed or injured by attacks that took place after we knew about Pearl Harbor. The Asiatic Pacific Fleet was almost totally destroyed and the entire air force in the Philippines was decimated to such an extent that we had no fighting aircraft to combat the Japanese.

Two days later I received orders to report to Headquarters and M.P. Company, Philippine Division. I was returning to what had formerly been the 12th M.P. Company (Philippine Scouts), an American platoon recently combined into a Filipino/American unit assigned to Brigadier General Maxon S. Lough of Palo Alto, California. He had assumed command of the division when General Wainwright was moved up to a corps command on Bataan. It was great to see faces I had known previously, but I truly missed my initial friends of Company F, 31st Infantry Regiment. While I visited the old company several times on Bataan, both on duty and on my own, I had a deep feeling for such people as Alban Harvey and Bill Hough who had enlisted with me. They felt I was fortunate to be in a headquarters company assigned as a liaison officer riding a motorcycle. But I was not so sure.

Chapter 7

FIGHTING ON BATAAN

Historians have long since recognized how ill-prepared for war the United States was in 1941. While we had unshakable confidence in our country and the inevitable triumph of the American military, we soon began to realize how poorly matched we were against Japanese forces in the Philippines.

Lieutenant Henry G. Lee, Headquarters, Philippine Division, a noted poet of World War II, who was not only my platoon leader but my friend, described it best in July of 1941. In a letter home he said, "our criticisms are not for the boxing commission that makes the matches, but for the man who sends us into the ring in a worn out pair of shoes." Lee, an amateur boxer before coming into the army, succinctly summed up our dilemma in the Philippines. This fine officer and gentleman was destined to survive the fighting on Bataan, the horrors of two prison camps, and the sinking of one prison ship en route to Japan, only to die aboard a second "hell ship" anchored in Takao Bay, Formosa, which was bombed and strafed by American aircraft in 1944. The irony of his death from friendly fire hurts keenly every time I think of it.

As early as the spring of 1941 the expected fall of the Philippines was an anticipated fact to the man who "sent us into the ring in a worn-out pair of shoes." In March 1941 the policy of "Europe first" became the object of our "boxing commission," namely the U.S. War Department, Chief of Staff Marshall, and the President of the United States. Every effort was made to build up the British defenses against Hitler while merely giving lip service to us in the

Philippines. In the summer of 1941 however, Washington changed its thinking about the defense of the Philippines and began to ship some men and supplies to the islands. The crucial question however was: would such help arrive in time? Months of communications between Marshall and MacArthur had finally found the right ears. This after years of denying reinforcements to the Philippines. That the Philippines could have survived a sneak attack by the Japanese until help arrived from the United States is highly questionable in light of the Pearl Harbor disaster. Still, when one considers how quickly the United States recovered from that, the effective defense of the Philippines seems at least more plausible. Who knows? Too many factors converged into the picture in those fateful early days of the war.

At the outbreak of the war in the Philippines, the United States had a formidable army, on paper at any rate, to defend that country. In fact, the Philippine Army, equipped with ancient World War I Lee-Enfield British Army rifles, never fired by them before, and wearing only coconut fiber helmets, were a poor match for the battle-hardened Japanese. Most Filipino soldiers got a surprise when first firing their outdated rifles. While the recoil was very noticeable to an American, it was twice as severe to the smaller-sized Filipino. Looking somewhat like the ragged army found in American history books describing Washington's army at Valley Forge, these men were issued blue fatigue uniforms very visible in the jungles of Bataan and tennis shoes that soon wore out after a number of forced marches. They also had very little support from their artillerymen, who also had not fired their weapons before Bataan. Even though almost totally untrained, these soldiers did as much as they could with what they had. Lacking equipment, food, and ammunition, they were still the mainstay of each main line of resistance drawn up by the American generals. On repeated occasions these troops broke under fire and fled to the rear, only to be gathered together and once more placed in the front lines. At the end these men were mere shells of their former selves. With their morale shot, they had finally had enough and the Japanese broke through. American soldiers on Bataan had sincere allies in the Filipinos, who placed their trust in the United States only to learn later that they were considered expendable along with their American comrades-in-arms. I think it fair to ask: were American soldiers that much better, really? What if the American were in the shoes of his Filipino comrade? Would the American have performed as well? It's a fair question.

The number of 120,000 Fil-American forces on Bataan has always been controversial. But it seems acceptable that approximately that number of men were in the peninsula when the fighting started. This figure at any rate usually shows up in reports written today. It becomes confusing when one reads the operations report on the Luzon Force for the period 22 March–9 April 1942 submitted to General Wainwright, dated 29 January 1946 when Wainwright was commanding general, Fourth Army, San Antonio, Texas. That report, which included 26,000 civilians who fled to Bataan before the Japanese onslaught, indeed indicates a force of 120,000 fighting men. Hence, if these figures are accurate, the number of the defending forces on Bataan would be reduced to 94,000 men, a number still in excess of the attacking Japanese forces. The presence of the civilians on Bataan was unplanned for and also unwanted. On 1 April 1942, eight days before the fall of Bataan, with only a week's supply of rations available, the United States was feeding 15,000 to 18,000 civilian refugees in four evacuee camps. This "siphoning" of food to noncombatants through the four months of fighting was to play an important role in the deaths from starvation and disease (malnutrition) of the Fil-American forces, both on the infamous Death March, and in the prison camps to follow. To allow such a situation to occur was another major blunder on the part of those responsible for the move into Bataan. Inasmuch as General MacArthur was awarded the Congressional Medal of Honor for his role in the withdrawal into Bataan, he then must also be held responsible for the civilians that had to be fed from military supplies. This factor is not usually mentioned in reports on the Bataan debacle, but it is unfortunately a fact.

I owe a lot of what follows to my platoon leader, Lt. Henry Lee. As previously indicated, Lee survived the fighting on Bataan and we shared the same prison camps until my separation from him in October 1942. Until then I would gather with him and other men of our unit in an attempt, on Lee's part, to establish some morale among the men. At one such gathering Lee told us he was writing a complete account of the unit, with several citations included, for use after the war. He urged those of us whom he was recommending for awards to "follow up" on these recommendations in the event he became one of the unfortunate ones "not making it."

Shortly after the war I contacted Lee's dad, Thomas R. Lee of San Mateo, California. While glad to hear from me, he also told me of what had befallen Lee. He told me that his son had buried his manuscript and citations beneath a barracks in the Cabanatuan prison camp, our second Philippine camp. They were written in a child's copy book. All of Lee's writings, along with a number of poems he had written in that camp, were uncovered by Lt. John W. Lueddeke, Signal Corps, when the camp was liberated by elements of the 6th Ranger Infantry Battalion on 30 January 1945. Five hundred eleven prisoners of war, all that remained of the thousands of Americans in that camp, gave testimony of what had occurred there. One prisoner indicated where Lee's papers were buried. While looking for a diary, which was never located, a unit history, several citations for men in his unit, and a number of poems were found. A war correspondent of the *Saturday Evening Post* soon started the poems on their way to publication. Shortly thereafter Lee was acclaimed as the finest poet of World War II. While Lee never saw his poems in print, his other papers made their way to his family. The poems later saw the light of day in the magazine and in a leather bound book entitled *Nothing But Praise*, a title chosen by Lee while in prison. The title was taken from a quotation made by Secretary of War Stimson after Bataan's fall: "We have nothing but praise for the men of Bataan." Here again, Lee was expressing his bitterness for the "boxing commission."

Found with Henry Lee's poetry and unit history were letters recommending citations for three men of the company. Inasmuch as I was one of those named, and remembering my promise to him to follow through, I learned that my particular recommendation was written on the back of Lee's will. It was years before the will was released to Henry's father by the courts. Immediately afterward, Mr. Thomas Lee, Henry's dad, sent me a copy of the citation recommendation, and I initiated action through the Department of the Army. Alas, the army's red tape still existed, and I was informed that I needed corroboration of the incident in order for an award to be made. Of all the men in the advance platoon of Headquarters Company, Philippine Division, I was sure that I was the only member alive. Forty-five years later I met Elmer Parks of Fletcher, Oklahoma, a fellow member of my unit. I, at this late date, have not attempted to obtain this award as it is now more than fifty years after the incident. During my army career of twenty years I received a number of decorations and citations. The loss of any of them would not bother me as much as losing the citation recommended by Lieutenant Lee.

Our company was organized early in December 1941 just prior to the war. It was comprised of Philippine Scouts from the old Headquarters Company, Philippine Division, and the American platoon of the 12th M.P. Company, Philippine Scouts. Both units were stationed at Fort William McKinley now the site of the American cemetery in the Philippines. Due to the war the reorganization of the unit was never fully completed.

Certain NCO grades which were to be transferred out of the company remained with it throughout the war. This created an excess of NCO's, which resulted in very few wartime promotions. An example: the company had two first sergeants, a Scout and an American. This "doubling" of rank followed through to the rank of private first class, with the morale of both Filipinos and Americans less than what it should have been. Despite this, it was a rare incident when Filipino and American did not share each other's lot. Both had extreme pride in their unit. It was one of the few times—if not the only time—in American military history when Philippine Scouts and American enlisted men belonged to a Philippine Scout Unit.

All of the company officers however were Americans, from other Scout units. Major James Ivy, headquarters commandant, Orville E. Hutchings, Lt. Henry G. Lee, and Lt. Orville Olson were assigned to the unit. Lee was assigned as CO of the security platoon, protecting Brigadier Maxon S. Lough, commanding general.

Of the Philippine Division, it should be mentioned again that

upon Wainwright's promotion, at no time did it ever function as
one unit under its own commanding general. Because it was comprised of the only trained regular army units of the Bataan defense
force, its line outfits were usually under the command of corps or
USAFFE itself. Used as mobile shock troops and reserves, only
two times in the battle for Bataan did a large element of the division operate under its own commanding general. The first time
was during the battle of Abucay, and the second was during the
last days of the Japanese breakthrough on the Orion Line, the last
major line of resistance.

The tenth of December (9 December in the U.S.) found our
company working on the paper reorganization. At about 11 A.M.,
we moved outside the barracks anticipating a Japanese air raid.
We began digging foxholes, setting up field kitchens, and camou-
flaging vehicles and equipment. We were destined to never again
sleep or eat as a company from that day on. When told to start
digging, I immediately set to the task at hand until I discovered
that the sun-scorched earth was so hard as to make progress almost
impossible. I am sure that had I been given a second chance to
continue, I most certainly would have done so. But as it was I
decided to postpone this errand. Shortly after this foolhardy decision, enemy aircraft appeared overhead attacking nearby Nichols
Airfield and Fort McKinley. As the Japanese planes came in to
drop their bombs and strafe the area, I realized the folly of not
finishing my foxhole. I crawled under a cement culvert in front of
our barracks and waited. The concussion of the bombs made my
head bounce on the concrete above me, leaving me dazed and
cursing my laziness. From that day on I never failed to complete
digging of a foxhole.

The story of the "unprovoked attack" on Pearl Harbor has been
told many times. That the United States was caught with its proverbial pants down is an understatement. Details of that attack
need not be retold here. Suffice it to say however that given the
time between that attack and the subsequent air strikes on the Philippines, our military command had ample time to avoid what had
befallen Pearl Harbor. While according to MacArthur "we had
only one radar station operative and had to rely for air warning

largely on eye and ear," the fact remains that we in the Philippines
had almost six hours after the attack on Pearl Harbor to prepare
ourselves for their certain arrival. At 9:30 A.M. on 8 December 1941,
American reconnaissance planes from Clark Field north of Manila reported a flight of bombers over Lingayen Gulf even further
north of Manila. Why were American planes not sent up to intercept and fight?

At 12:35 A.M. the Japanese air attack on the Philippines struck at
Clark Field, the home base of our fighters, catching a number of
of the planes like sitting ducks on the flight line while the pilots
ate lunch. One pursuit squadron and two bomber squadrons were
smashed on the ground. The American air force in the islands
never recovered from this blow. How it came about is really a bigger mystery than the surprise attack on Pearl Harbor. Blame for
this debacle was never established, while responsibility for the
Hawaiian disaster was laid at the doorstep of Admiral Husband
Kimmel and Lieutenant General Short of the U.S. Army. Following that rationale, MacArthur should have been held responsible
for these similar attacks in the Philippines. Did Major General
Lewis H. Brereton, commanding general of the air force in the
Philippines, indeed recommend that American planes strike Formosa, where Japanese planes launched their strikes against the Philippines, before they had made this attack? MacArthur denied that
such a recommendation was ever made to him. Would such an
attack have been successful—if approved—given the weather conditions over Formosa? Well, it was precisely the poor weather conditions which caused the Japanese to think they had lost the element of surprise when they finally arrived over bases in the Philippines! Imagine their elation at finding the Americans completely
unprepared for their attack. MacArthur insisted that an air strike
on Formosa "would have been suicidal" given the Japanese strength
there. Regardless of the outcome of a raid that never took place, it
was just as "suicidal" to have our fighters lined up at Clark Field
when the Japanese struck. We leave the final decision on the failure to take protective measures to the historians. One clearly established fact emerges—Fil-American forces in the Philippines
were doomed after the total destruction on Clark Field. The Japa-

nese enjoyed total air superiority from that day on, and their aerial umbrella over Bataan prevented maximum use of Fil-American artillery. Despite this, the 155 mm cannon in place on Bataan still managed to devastate many Japanese army units attacking Fil-American positions.

Pearl Harbor will always be remembered as a colossal failure to take protective measures to prevent an attack. Both Admiral Kimmel and General Short saw their military careers end in disgrace, while neither was to blame. The failure of those in Washington has never been exposed, and so the field soldier ends up paying the piper's tune. The same can be said of the debacle in the Philippines.

With the attack on Nichols Field and Fort McKinley, near panic ensued. A Philippine Air Force 0-52 recon plane painted red with a white diamond on its tail flew over McKinley. Every rifle, pistol, and machine gun opened fire on the plane. The unfortunate pilot, incorrectly thought by some to be Jesus Villamor, who became Philippine air hero of the war, bailed out over McKinley along with his observer. Despite gunfire aimed at them, they managed to make it to the ground, only to be "captured" by the American and Filipino troops doing the shooting. During the Japanese attack on Nichols Field near McKinley—under construction to handle B-17's—enemy planes were soon strafing the barracks we had recently vacated, with shrapnel flying everywhere from small bombs. The few American aircraft that managed to get into the air were soon dispatched by the Japanese.

On 10 December 1941 we received orders to head for a place none of us had ever heard of before, Bataan. Around 10:30 P.M., we cleared Eagle Gate at Fort McKinley, with many of us wondering somberly "would we ever see it again?" Driving all night, we witnessed the chaos of those experiencing war for the first time. Manila had lost all semblance of order and control. As we sped through the dark city streets under blackout conditions we could see Filipinos and Americans breaking into American auto dealers' showrooms and driving cars out through the broken windows. Eventually, after fueling them, the cars would end up in a military convoy headed for Bataan. It became quite common to see an American driving a brand new automobile on Bataan during the early days of the fighting. This "luxury" soon came to a screeching halt when the gas ran out. It was only a question of time before fuel became a very precious commodity.

Panic was supreme in Manila when the city was evacuated. Rumors had "Jap parachutists" being dropped near McKinley. Squads were formed and we fanned out over the countryside looking to repel the invaders. But all these rumors were just that, and we returned without seeing one Japanese soldier. There is every reason to believe that such rumors were created by what were then known as Japanese "fifth columnists," a term borrowed from the European theater. With frayed nerves we also investigated a report that the BBB (Balintawak Beer Brewery) was a hotbed of Japanese armed to the teeth, all of whom were plain old civilians the day before. While some war materiel was found at that brewery, rumors of Japanese soldiers lurking behind the walls turned out to be a hoax. Unfortunately, despite orders to the contrary many lights were in violation of the blackout order, and periodically American forces would shoot out these lights, innocent or otherwise. No one stationed in the Philippines at the outbreak of the war has ever doubted that Japanese living in Manila were assisting their attacking countrymen, and they resorted to any measure to aid their oncoming troops.

Soon the daylight of 11 December found us between San Fernando and Lubao, caught in a stream of two-wide bumper-to-bumper traffic. We watched for an air raid which never came. But had the Japanese bombed the convoys that night and the next day the units would have been decimated. Adding to this nightmare were thousands of Filipinos fleeing Manila on foot and in every conceivable means of transportation, from pony-drawn wagons to Cadillacs. It was truly a miracle that we were not attacked by the Japanese. If they were aware of our movements, and it is probable that they were, why did they ignore us? Our company finally bivouacked in the town of Hermosa, in Bataan Province on Luzon. Soon the military police platoon of the Philippine Division was busy attempting to bring order from the chaos created by so many vehicles driving with almost no lights into Bataan. Due to a shortage of trained M.P.'s, individuals of that platoon were assigned to crossroads for traffic control for days on end without relief or food. I spent three days with another soldier moving division after division through our intersection leading into Bataan. To find something to eat, one of us took turns foraging for food while the other kept traffic moving. Inasmuch as the Japanese had landed in the north, every unit that had gone north to intercept them was now beating a hasty retreat into Bataan, with the Japanese attempting to close the trap before they did so. Finally one of our company officers came by and apologized for our having spent three days at that one intersection. It seems that the CO had forgotten about us and only relieved us when the movement into Bataan was complete. Upon returning to our unit we were greeted like men coming back from the dead.

During the three days at our post we experienced several air raids on trucks moving through our position. These scattered raids resulted in few casualities. Not too long after being assigned to our post, two guns and crews of the 200th Coast Artillery (Antiaircraft) Unit appeared at our road intersection and offered their support. We accepted, only to find that the guns attracted more Japanese than we had seen prior to their arrival. We soon asked the gun commanders to relocate to avoid drawing fire at that point. It was much easier to concentrate on moving traffic without those guns acting as honey to a bee.

Bataan for myself and twenty-seven others of my unit assigned to the forward CP (command post) of the Philippine Division was a constant series of air raids, shelling, and infantry fighting against infiltrating Japanese. Our division commanding general, Maxon S. Lough, was an extremely brave and competent soldier who firmly believed that a general's place was with his troops.

Each decision by General Lough to move to a new position as the lines began to edge south on Bataan was an adventure in itself. Enemy infantry would often come within 150 yards of the general's tent, held off by a thin skirmish line of military police acting as infantry. On several occasions the general in his sedan, with his security platoon close behind, would disappear from sight just as the Japanese emerged on the road we had just taken. During such nights awaiting a move we would find ourselves formed into a perimeter defense around the CP, listening to the Japanese coming closer. Daylight usually brought the order to move out to another location.

While I had a number of close calls on Bataan during the fighting, the afternoon of 29 January 1942 remains my most vivid memory of the fighting. On that day the division had established forward command post in a mango grove 100 yards off the Pilar-Bagac Road, a line of resistance formed after the battle of Abucay. We had moved to this location the day previously without any incident. The 29th however saw continuous air raids on our position. We were not the primary target of the Jap Zeros, however. Instead, the dive bombers were attracted to a large convoy of Philippine Army troops loaded in civilian buses brought from Manila as transportation for that division. The buses, open to allow egress from both sides, came to a sudden halt when Japanese dive bombers appeared. These buses, crowded to the hilt with human cargo, also carried all sorts of equipment and baggage on their roofs.

When they stopped in front of the division CP, chaos ensued. Filipinos fled the buses, anticipating the whistle of bombs. I and another member of my unit attempted to keep the vehicles moving by waving a pistol in the drivers' faces, but we found we had little effect on the mass exodus. Their fleeing, while certainly understandable, could not have come at a worse time. Gathered together at our CP were a number of generals from various divisions attending a meeting with the Philippine Division commanding general only a hundred yards from the road. One bomb could have decimated the Bataan Defense Force had it landed in that CP. While I and my partner attempted to keep the convoy moving, we soon abandoned that idea and sought cover as Japanese aircraft dove towards the targets. Every available "safe" spot was occupied, and when my partner dived into a latrine slit trench I refused to follow. I fell to the ground alongside our units' motorcycles and, with no explanation whatever for my actions, suddenly decided that my position wasn't too safe. Making a dash for cover, I ended up under one of the buses just abandoned on the road! Looking up, I saw a flight of nine Jap Zeros diving at what I was sure was the bus I was under. Hurtling down towards me was a gathering of "black baseballs," which later proved to be 250-pound bombs. These soon exploded near the bus convoy, hitting several of the buses. I became suddenly aware that I could no longer hear after the explosions. While the planes were circling for a second run, I quickly realized that I was part of their target. I ran into a field containing a number of bomb craters from the attack. Diving headfirst into the nearest one, I landed on a man who later turned out to be a doctor. While I couldn't hear a word he was saying to me, I did manage to read his lips when he said "you dumb son of a...." I got his message. Back came the Zeros, and soon a number of buses were hit and burning. Besides being unable to hear, I found myself with the shakes—which I have always attributed to my recognition of my stupidity when I selected the bus to hide under. The doctor, a true Southern gentleman, took a flask from his hip pocket and gave me my first taste of Canadian Club. It brought instant relief, but since I had never drank anything stronger than beer, I found the taste unpleasant. Later, I promised myself that the first bottle of liquor I would buy would be Canadian Club. It really did the trick in settling my bad case of the shakes.

While the liquor worked its magic, the Japanese flew off. We assembled around the buses to assist with the wounded and the dead. Looking at the bus under which I had taken refuge, I saw the damage inflicted by the bombing. The seats, made of leather, ran the width of the bus and every one was slashed as though someone had taken a knife to it. All the tires were flattened, and no windshield or rear glass remained.

Looking at the spot where I had initially decided to "take cover" near a motorcycle, I discovered a Philippine Army soldier. He was dead, and was in a kneeling position leaning backward as if attempting to rise when he was hit. A large chunk of shrapnel was embedded into the back of his head, and it was lodged in such a manner that no blood flowed from his wound.

I have always believed that this young Filipino soldier saw me leave the position and felt that the spot was safe; why else would an American have chosen it? Philippine Army soldiers placed great faith in their American counterparts, and they would follow newly

appointed American second lieutenants not much older than themselves into battle without question. Emulating this American cost
one Filipino soldier his life.

As for me, I had been struck by shrapnel in the helmet. While it
was a glancing blow, I was never aware of it until treated by the
doctor in the bomb crater. All my personal gear and equipment
left on the side of the road had been destroyed and I soon found
myself taking new equipment from those killed in the raid. While
I would have welcomed being relieved from duty that day, a shortage of personnel necessitated that I remain in my position. We
shortly rounded up the troops who had fled the buses and got the
division on its way. Remaining on duty gave me ample time to see
clearly the folly of my ways during the raid. I resolved not to repeat
them.

As early as 6 January 1942 most troops on Bataan went on half
rations, and on 15 March this ration was again cut in half. The
half ration was hardly an American diet. It consisted of rice and
canned salmon or tuna twice daily. We on Bataan were beginning
to starve. Japan's honor would not permit General Homma, the
Japanese commander, to allow us to starve ourselves into submis-
sion. Instead, Homma was instructed to inflict a severe military
defeat on the defenders of Bataan in order to impress the Filipino
populace of Japan's determination of ridding the Philippines of
American colonialism. Had the Japanese allowed us to starve, they
would have saved countless lives, American, Filipino and Japanese alike.

Bataan was known to be one of the most heavily malaria-infested regions in the world in 1941. I believe this fact was considered by those planning the defense of Bataan years before the battle
itself. Surely any enemy following Fil-American troops into
Bataan — with shortened supply routes — would soon fall victim to
the disease. This of course was based on the assumption that the
Fil-American forces would have an ample supply of quinine to
offset the deleterious effects of the disease. Such "thinking" back-
fired and soon, due to a critical shortage of quinine, Filipinos and
Americans became victims of malaria. At one point during the
fighting, medical reports indicated that more than 70 percent of

the defending forces came down with the disease. Nor were the Japanese troops spared either. They also found malaria depleting their combat strength.

Living and fighting in the jungles of Bataan became a day-to-day effort at survival. Sleeping nightly on the jungle floor had to be the most uncomfortable daily experience, next to being hungry.

On one particular night in late March 1942, I found myself sharing an army "pup tent"—a small tent made up of two shelter halves. Each individual soldier carried a shelter half and he would then team up with another soldier, whereupon they would erect their tent at night. This particular evening had proven eventful.

Earlier, before going to bed, I had discovered a large "lump" under my shirt. Putting my hand inside the shirt, I realized that whatever it was, it was alive! Without thinking, I ripped it off my body and discovered it was a leech of some sort. In my haste to remove it, I had left the head in my side. Going to our medical detachment nearby, they removed the head and told me that had it remained in my body I could have had a very serious fever.

I soon fell asleep thinking of that incident, but during the night I felt a large object crossing over my legs. Not moving, I turned on a flashlight to see a large boa constrictor sliding the rear portion of his body off of my body. As soon as the snake cleared the tent, sliding under the edge of a shelter half, I jumped up in time to see it disappear into the jungle. My tent partner at that time was one Fred Pavia of New Jersey. He never woke up until he felt me jumping out of the tent.

About 11 March 1942 we learned that General MacArthur had left the Philippines from Corregidor under orders of the President. While most understood the necessity of his leaving, it caused a huge drop in morale. I think it was at that particular time that the thought of losing the fight with the Japanese began to sink in.

Nevertheless, we continued our daily duties. We also began to build shelters in the very tall trees found in Bataan. The idea was that the rainy season was shortly to commence, and to withstand the heavy rains we needed to "live" in the trees. But the tree houses were never used. The Japanese also knew the rainy season was due and prepared their final assault to finish us off.

The following is the text of the Voice of Freedom, broadcast from Corregidor, announcing the fall of Bataan. It best summarizes the spirit of Bataan.

"Bataan has fallen. The Philippine-American troops on this war-ravaged and bloodstained peninsula have laid down their arms. With heads bloody but unbowed, they have yielded to the superior force and numbers of the enemy.

"The world will long remember the epic struggle that Filipino and American soldiers put up in these jungle fortresses and along the rugged coast of Bataan.

"They have stood uncomplaining under the constant grueling fire of the enemy for more than three months. Besieged on land and blockaded by sea, cut off from all sources of help in the Philippines and in America, these intrepid fighters have done all that human endurance could bear.

"For what sustained them through all these months of incessant battle was a force that was more than merely physical. It was the force of an unconquerable faith—something in the heart and soul that physical hardships and adversity could not destroy! It was the thought of native land and all that it holds most dear, the thought of freedom and dignity, the pride in these most priceless of all human prerogatives.

"The adversary, in the pride of his power and triumph, will credit our troops with nothing less than the courage and fortitude that his own troops have shown. All the world will testify to the almost superhuman endurance with which they stood up until the last in the face of overwhelming odds.

"But the decision had to come. Men fighting under the banner of unshakable faith are made of something more than flesh, but they are not made of impervious steel. The flesh must yield at last, endurance melts away, and the end of the battle must come.

"Bataan has fallen, but the spirit that made it stand as a beacon to all liberty-loving peoples of the world cannot fail."

In this message was a hope expressed to the Japanese that they would recognize the efforts of other soldiers and treat them with the respect they deserved. It was not to be.

On 9 April, Bataan fell at last. Over sixty thousand prisoners were in the hands of the Japanese Army. In Manila, a Japanese Army order was issued to the effect that.... "every troop which fought against our army on Bataan should be wiped out thoroughly, whether he surrendered or not, and any American captive who is unable to continue marching all the way to the concentration camp should be put to death in an area 200 meters off the highway." (Extract from *Dawn of the Philippines*, page 14, by Nobuhiko Jimbo, colonel, Japanese Army.)

CHAPTER 8

THE FALL OF BATAAN

Bataan's fall began with starved, emaciated, disease-ridden Filipinos and Americans, without equipment, short on ammunition rounds that were not "duds," attempting to stem a thoroughly modern, well-equipped Japanese Army. By 23 March 1942 the surgeon of the Bataan Force (a name given to all defenders of Bataan in a reorganization of those forces dated 12 March 1942) indicated that our defensive efficiency had been reduced more than 75 percent during the final weeks before the collapse. According to him: "This was due to malnutrition, avitaminosis, malaria and intestinal infections and infestations." By 1 March 1942 many individuals had used up their ability to fight disease and were deteriorating rapidly physically. By 1 April our combat efficiency was approaching zero. The half rations inaugurated on 6 January (in terms of energy units) averaged 2,000 calories that month, 1,500 calories during February, and 1,000 calories in March. The nature of the terrain of Bataan, conservatively estimated, required an energy output of from 3,500 calories to 4,000 calories per day. The end was inevitable.

Filipino and American foraging parties hunted constantly to add to our limited rations by killing any animal, snake, or livestock that wandered into their paths. Some of the more fortunate troops had their daily ration supplemented for a very short time by the horse meat from the 26th Cavalry. General Wainwright, an old-time cavalryman, was heartbroken the day it became necessary to kill the three personal horses he had brought with him on the U.S.A.T.

Grant in October 1940. Rumor had it that he would not allow others to do the killing, and that he did the deed himself. When the horse meat disappeared, carabaos—the Filipino beasts of burden—were next. Unfortunately, these water buffalo were few in number, having already been eaten or hidden by Filipinos. Eventually, we found ourselves eating monkeys, iguanas, or any animal at all that strayed our way. While I was willing to eat iguanas or snakes, a skinned monkey looked too much like a human baby for me, even in my starved condition.

The supply of quinine was never adequate on Bataan. By 1 March, 500 daily malarial admissions entered our field hospitals. By 1 April the rate of admissions for malaria climbed to 1,000 soldiers daily. At the same time, over 12,000 patients were hospitalized with all types of dysentery. Nerve fatigue due to the constant shelling and aerial bombardment became more prevalent. Bataan had no "quiet area" to which sufferers could be evacuated. Every area on Bataan was subjected to constant enemy bombing and shelling.

A greater number of front-line troops had no shoes or underwear. Raincoats became almost nonexistent. There was no replacement stock and no reserves had ever been established by the military on Bataan. With prewar plans for the defense of Bataan already in place, such a lack of supplies and materiel was inexcusable on the part of the "Brass." Surely the phrase "The Battling Bastards of Bataan; no mama, no papa, and nobody gives a damn" was clearly applicable.

Beginning on 15 March 1942, hostile aerial activity grew in intensity each day. Both front-line and rear area troops were on the receiving end of heavy daylight bombing and intense nighttime shelling. It became unsafe for anyone to leave his shelter even to relieve himself. Instead, five-gallon cans were used in the relatively safe holes, or in the stumps of the huge banyan trees so numerous on Bataan. This devastating enemy firepower increased daily. In order to empty the containers used as "portable toilets," an individual would wait for the enemy artillery battery to zero in on our position to fire. Four rounds of shellfire would bracket the area in a diamond-shape pattern. Shortly after all the rounds landed, the "volunteer" would jump out of our shelter and hastily empty the container. We had a fairly good supply of coffee to keep us up and alert against enemy infiltrators. We quickly consumed that coffee, only to find we had to get rid of it into those cans very quickly.

On 3 April 1942 at 9 A.M., the reinforced army of General Homma began its final assault on what remained of the Fil-American positions. One hundred ninety-six heavy artillery pieces ranging from 75mm to 240mm began their barrage on the line of resistance where the Japanese hoped to break through. At the same time Japanese planes dropped sixty tons of explosives on the same sector of the line. Japanese infantry then seized the opportunity to strike the shell-shocked Filipinos and Americans.

The heavy enemy fire continued for six consecutive hours while incendiary bombs were dropped by the Nipponese air force. The jungle literally burst into flames. Troops panicked and ran to avoid being burned to death. "Cover" was burnt away, leaving the ground as barren as no man's land of World War I. Japanese troops began pouring through the abandoned positions on a three-mile wide front, and the beginning of the end for the defenders of Bataan was at hand. On Good Friday, 1942, amidst the onslaught of Japanese, a Catholic chaplain appeared in our hastily erected position and offered Absolution to those Catholics wishing to avail themselves of it. I and other Catholics sincerely believed this would be our last chance to receive the Sacrament of Communion before meeting our deaths. Each one of us wanted to make peace with God since we felt we would soon be with Him. Immediately after, the Japanese renewed their firing for eight additional hours. No man in the area could lift his head out of a foxhole. When that barrage ended, men left their positions, walking like zombies. Easter Sunday saw all denominations at prayer in very brief services, while Japanese aircraft bombed and strafed everything in sight.

A counterattack on 6 April ordered by General Wainwright, who could not have been aware of the condition of the men on Bataan, failed, and Fil-American troops began their retreat before being encircled. My unit eventually made its way down Bataan's west coast to a point known as Signal Hill on Mt. Bataan. It was here, after eating for the first time in four days, that we learned that our commanding general, King, had ordered a surrender. I emphasize that we were surrendered. I know of no individual soldier who surrendered on Bataan or had any intention of doing so. Later, in our first prison camp, O'Donnell, General King made it clear to his men that he and he alone had surrendered and that his decision to do so was his responsibility alone. I can still see General King at that meeting, with tears in his eyes, explaining his act and imploring those around him to feel proud of what they had accomplished. While the main body of our troops made their way through the mountain to a prisoner-of-war enclosure, I and several others went further up that mountain, thinking the Japanese would settle for those who had reached the enclosure in an airstrip off the National Highway.

On the following day a fellow soldier, Corporal Elmer Parks, and I were ordered to return to the surrender site and search for supplies which remained there. Making our way down the hill in a half-ton Dodge truck with an open cab (Elmer was driving and I was riding shotgun), we came upon an immensely large tree so common in the Philippines and Bataan. From behind this tree sprang a Japanese soldier with rifle and fixed bayonet. The Japanese soldier did nothing but stand in front of the tree for what seemed minutes, but could not have been more than 75 seconds. Elmer had stopped the truck and we both stared at the Japanese and then at each other. We were both armed with a .45 pistol and an M1 rifle, and we thought of shooting him and then turning tail back up the mountain. Finally the Japanese motioned for us to get out of the truck. He then indicated that we should drop our pistol belts. For some reason, common sense told us what to do, and upon dropping our belts and making no hostile moves toward the Japanese an additional fifteen to twenty more Japanese soldiers emerged from the heavy jungle bordering the road. Hiding there, they had hoped we would fight so they could kill us and thus not be saddled with prisoners. This patrol had given us the opportunity to die gloriously in the true tradition of the Japanese warrior. (Many times after that day, both Parks and I wished we could replay that scene.) We were alive however and the war for us was over. So we thought, without the faintest idea that ahead of us lay the misery, degradation, suffering, and deprivation of the Death March, "hell ships," and the prison camps of the Philippines and Japan.

CHAPTER 9

WHY BATAAN FELL
Anguished Questions

Numerous questions concerning the battle of Bataan have been asked by many historians. How could the final attack on Bataan's last line of resistance end so quickly? The Japanese launched their final offensive on Good Friday, 3 April 1942, and for all intents and purposes, the battle was over on 7 April due to the terrible condition of the defending forces as I have already described. The date of 3 April was no coincidence, since that date has great significance for the Japanese. It is the anniversary of the death of Emperor Jimmu, who, according to legend, held the first throne of Japan.

How could an army that had held the Japanese at bay for almost four months collapse so suddenly? Why, asks Louis Morton's U.S. official history: *The Fall of the Philippines,* did an army evaporate into thin air in a matter of days? It seems too simplistic to say that Fil-American troops were totally exhausted, sick, and hungry and were with only one day's rations remaining. Of the soldiers available to defend Bataan at the final breakthrough, 24,000 were sick and wounded in the field hospitals. Obviously, these above were all contributing factors. However, for the full story one must look elsewhere, to the larger picture.

How could MacArthur, with six years to prepare the Philippine Army, knowing what would come in the event of war, waste such precious time by failing to adequately train the Filipino soldier? In fairness to MacArthur, it must be pointed out that Washington

failed to support him. Nevertheless, when war finally came, the
U.S. government found the Philippine Army a green, untrained
outfit attempting to do battle with battle-hardened Japanese veterans of the China campaign.

Why, knowing the locations of the Japanese landings in advance,
as MacArthur did, did he make only a feeble attempt to prevent
them? Numerically the Philippine Army at the landing sites far
outnumbered the Japanese. Why send the Filipinos north to intercept the Japanese and then pull those troops back into the Bataan
Peninsula almost immediately after the Japanese had landed?
Shortly after these troops took up their defense positions at Lingayen
Gulf, the newspapers of Manila screamed headlines proclaiming
that the "Philippine Army had repulsed the invasion." In reality,
untrained Filipino soldiers, led by inexperienced and ill-trained
officers saw objects floating in the water offshore which they believed to be the invasion force. They opened fire on this "force,"
which turned out to be floating flotsam. Finally, sanity prevailed
and orders were given to cease fire. When the smoke cleared and
no enemy was seen, a "huge victory" was claimed. Several days
later, the Japanese landed without encountering any meaningful
resistance.

Why did Filipino and American troops (as well as the American
public) believe that they were greatly outnumbered by the Japanese on Bataan, when just the opposite was true? U.S. Army Intelligence had some indication of Japanese troop strength. U.S. officers did nothing to dispel this myth, thereby contributing to the
"hopelessly outnumbered" feeling of troops defending the Philippines. While it may have sounded heroic to Filipinos and Americans to read about "heavily outnumbered defenders of Bataan,"
such talk also contributed to a general climate of fear and inadequacy of the Philippine Army fighting in Bataan. No more than
10 percent of their officers and enlisted men were considered "combat ready" when war erupted in the Philippines. As for the 13,500
Americans on Bataan, they too in general were poorly trained and
unprepared for combat. The vast majority of these men (10,000)
had not spent even eight months in the Philippines before the
war. Like the Filipino, the American was also ill-equipped. The

very few modern weapons in his arsenal had arrived only a month or so before the war. Thus, ammunition for the newly arrived weapons was in extremely short supply. What ammunition was available turned out to be mostly duds. When mortars were used, approximately 20 out of every 25 shells failed to detonate on impact.

As mentioned previously, Filipino troops were armed with the British World War I Lee-Enfield bolt-action rifle. The "kick" of this rifle was so pronounced that the Filipino's shoulder was constantly bruised severely. While hardly comical, one could see a Philippine Army soldier firing his rifle for the first time and being thrown off balance backward from the rifle's recoil.

Just prior to the war, most Americans received the new Garand M1, semiautomatic rifle. This weapon produced far greater firepower than the old Springfield .03. The M1 went on to provide American infantry units with superior firepower compared to the Japanese .27 caliber single-action rifle. Unfortunately, many units had kept these rifles in cosmoline and issued them only after the war began. Old infantrymen were dedicated to the old Springfield which had a far greater record for accuracy than the new unproven M1. The upshot was that many American soldiers fired M1's for the first time only when in actual combat.

Why were the warnings received by MacArthur's headquarters of the Japanese flights of bombers heading for the Philippines ignored? What lay behind MacArthur's policy to let the Japanese "commit the first overt act," despite their attack on Pearl Harbor eight hours before? Why antiquated munitions for obsolete weapons in the American arsenals in the Philippines? Why a lack of adequate food and equipment on Bataan, when it was well known to the war planners of that day that defense of Corregidor was to deny the Japanese access to Manila Harbor, and that the defense of Bataan was necessary to the defense of Corregidor? Why wasn't Bataan, a malaria-infested area, adequately stocked with quinine? The questions of American ineptness from a command level go on endlessly, from the outset of the war until Corregidor's fall.

The bitterness over such blundering was carried by American officers into the prison camps, and the same could be said of the enlisted men, less informed though they were than their officers.

The officers, without physical work to do in the prison camp, had ample time to rehash the actions, or lack of them, that led to their imprisonment. To say that many were disgusted with MacArthur and his staff would be an understatement. Eventually, after condemning nearly everyone concerned, the final blame settled on MacArthur. Many officers including MacArthur's classmates and peers felt that he had blundered badly in his assessment and planning. Could this burden of conscience explain MacArthur's subsequent obsession to return to the Philippines?

General Wainwright later was to comment "we had been sold down the river" in the Philippines. In a paper written in prison camp, General William E. Brougher, commanding general of the 11th Division, Philippine Army, used those exact words to describe the feelings of the imprisoned general officers. Author-historian Duane Schultz in his book *Hero of Bataan* quotes General Brougher's essay on the generals in the Philippines being "committed to a hopeless task from the beginning." Why? Perhaps what occurred was just a colossal military blunder. There was no fairness or common sense in committing a small group of Americans to such a hopeless task in which they had little chance to succeed. Nor was it right to commit thousands of ill-trained Filipinos to their deaths. Who had the right to sentence 20,000 Americans to an enterprise that would involve them in endless suffering, tremendously cruel hardships, death, or a hopeless future in a Japanese prison camp? Who takes the responsibility for saying that no other option was available? Didn't any one of them realize and object to the fact that their plans were effectively sentencing the men of the Philippines to sure failure, defeat, and death? Or, as it turned out, worse, namely rotting in a prison camp, or going down to the bottom of the ocean when their "hell ships" were sunk by American naval forces? Again, quoting from Brougher, "A foul trick or deception has been played on a large group of Americans by a Commander-in-Chief and a small staff who are now eating steak and eggs in Australia. God damn them."

The blame however goes beyond MacArthur and his staff. Those in Washington gave little, or certainly not much, thought to the Philippines. They were too worried about Europe to be concerned with the Philippines. And this, long before the outbreak of the war. Responsibility for the Philippines debacle began with President Roosevelt and his policy to support England first. Much of Roosevelt's thinking however came from his military advisers who felt the Philippines were a lost cause anyway in the event of war, and that supplies and materiel should not be wasted in that part of the world.

This second-class treatment was evident with the assignment to the Philippines of General Wainwright. Considered too old for a major Stateside assignment, he drank too much and needed a cane to help him walk. Wainwright was an ideal candidate to spend what little active duty time he had remaining in a nice quiet post somewhere, one that did not rank too high in any war plans of the day. Since he had good "efficiency reports," what better place to put an "old war horse" out to pasture than the Philippines? Given his position and the lack of support from Washington, and knowing full well he had been "sold down the river," Wainwright gave his one opportunity to enter the history books his best shot. That MacArthur had little faith in Wainwright's military ability was evident. While loved by his men, Wainwright was not the type of military leader the United States needed in World War II.

While some writers of today firmly feel that MacArthur's departure from the Philippines to Australia in March 1942 did not have a deleterious effect on the troops remaining on Bataan, other "brass" left behind in the Philippines did feel it was an act of desertion. Enlisted men felt he had run out on them, and while the officers kept their feelings to themselves, after their capture many of them expressed the same feelings. MacArthur, after arriving in Australia, made his famous promise: "I shall return." But every man in the Philippines felt that the promise—as far as they were concerned—could never be kept. Japanese propaganda leaflets dropped daily on Bataan made that fact very clear. The leaflets depicted the Philippines as being completely surrounded, with no chance of anyone or anything getting through the Japanese blockade.

Verification of those leaflets came very fast. While MacArthur in a broadcast to the men of Bataan and Corregidor had promised hundreds of ships and planes, no one—and the horizons were watched daily—ever saw anything resembling a boat or plane coming to the rescue. Most defenders of Bataan and Corregidor will go or have already gone to their graves with the firm conviction that they were truly "sold down the river," and for better or worse they place most of the blame for their fate on MacArthur.

For myself, I do not blame any one particular person or group. Instead I attribute America's largest surrender of military forces to a foreign foe to a combination of errors too numerous to mention. As a survivor, I firmly believe that those of us unfortunate enough to be in the Philippines at the outbreak of the war were victims of circumstances and destined to suffer the insufferable, to bear the unbearable, and to live or die as preordained.

Chapter 10

CAPTIVITY BEGINS

Winston Churchill, taken prisoner during the Boer War in South Africa, wrote of his captors some forty years later, during World War II, "You owe your life to his humanity, and your daily bread to his compassion. You must obey his orders, go where he tells you, stay where you are bid, await his pleasure, possess your soul with patience." While Churchill was certainly describing the basic rules of being a prisoner of war, he had done so not knowing what it meant to be a prisoner of the Japanese. The common decencies of civilized people holding captives were completely ignored by the Japanese. As evidenced by the death rate, at no time in modern warfare has an enemy mistreated its prisoners on such a grand scale as did the Japanese, a fact long since forgotten by most but above all, and ironically, by the Japanese themselves.

Americans have always taken their freedom for granted. Freedom to most Americans is just a word, and while we often read of others losing their freedom, it is of no great concern to us. Along with a lack of knowledge of what freedom really means, it seems to me that we also lack knowledge of what being an American means. Some of us become aware of it only when going abroad, and we cannot wait to return to this country, even after a short absence.

With the capture of Elmer Parks and myself on 11 April 1942 on that mountain road on Bataan, we found ourselves searched and stripped of all personal effects. As each item was taken from me, I received a blow on the side of my head as a receipt. I guess that was the Japanese way of saying thank you. Parks fared similarly.

While the beatings took place, I readily recognized that the Japanese language in itself was very threatening. Their style of speech always included shouting at the top of their voices. That was as threatening as a blow to the body, especially when one did not know what they were saying. To this day a Japanese will often shout in a menacing fashion when talking to an inferior. The Japanese soldier of World War II could not talk to a subordinate without shouting, which was usually followed by a beating. In a short time most Americans were bullied by the Japanese voices alone, as were lower ranking Japanese soldiers.

While the American military has never allowed corporal punishment for infractions of military rules and orders, the Japanese soldier knew nothing except this type of punishment. In the American army, a minor rules violation could lead to forfeiture of pay or restriction to barracks. For the Japanese soldier it meant a beating at the hands of a higher ranking soldier. It was not uncommon to witness a one-star private—next in rank to a recruit—being beaten by a two-star private, our equivalent of a PFC (Private, First Class). Of course, this method of Japanese army punishment continued up the line. A three-star private could beat on a two-star private, corporals beat three-star privates, and so on. The recruit with no stars on his shoulders had no one to beat other than a prisoner of war. Fortunately not too many of that rank guarded prisoners of war. To this day I am fascinated by Japanese businessmen who are bullied by a higher ranking civilian in a training session offered by a major corporation in Japan. Such dialogues conjure up, in former prisoners of war, the image of a Japanese soldier about to "talk to them."

Americans, totally unaware that such form of punishment was the "norm," could not accept this humiliation. It went against the grain to stand at attention as was required while someone beat on you. A Japanese, after taking a thrashing from a superior, would dutifully bow and thank the one who had just beaten him. In the early days of captivity most Americans and British would attempt to show the Japanese how tough they were by continuing to stand erect when hit. They soon learned that in order to shorten the beatings, it was best to fall down after the first blow. The Japanese "ego" would then swell, thinking he had just knocked down a big Caucasian, and he would walk away strutting like a peacock.

This punishment did eliminate a lot of paperwork found in the

American code of military justice. Unfortunately, the tactic of falling down when hit was not a guarantee of avoiding further abuse. The booted foot or a club often continued the assault.

Not too many Japanese knew how to punch as an American did. It was not part of their makeup. This shortcoming however was soon remedied when some Americans taught them how to punch. Of course these "teachers" were usually rewarded in some manner by the Japanese. I soon learned that they could do little damage to me with their hands, but they could do a lot of damage when they used an oak club shaped like a samurai sword. These "swords" were carried by every guard in the camp. They didn't have the rank to carry a real sword, so their wood swords inflated their sense of importance.

When Parks and I were taken down Signal Hill by four of our captors—more dragged than walked—Parks and I soon passed our headquarters commandant, a Major Ivy. We saw Ivy tied to a tree and punctured with so many bayonet holes we could not count them. Ivy, a huge man, was not the type to absorb a beating without fighting back, and he must have fought back, resulting in the atrocity we saw. Major Ivy was a fine officer and his death was the first one I witnessed after my capture. It is not difficult to bring the image of his body back in my mind. It will always be there. One of my biggest regrets was that there were not many Jim Ivy's to handle his men in captivity. He was a soldier in every meaning of the word. Years after the war I contacted his widow to see if she was aware of the circumstances of his death. Apparently someone else had seen her husband that day and had told her what happened. I was thankful to be spared that role.

Shortly after reaching the bottom of the mountain, we were forced to stand at an opening in the hedges lining the road. A Japanese hand felt our collar in the darkness that had just settled in and then pushed us through the opening into a large field filled with thousands of prisoners, American and Filipinos. Wondering why the Japanese were feeling collars, I waited by the opening to see what happened. I soon had the answer. Each officer wearing any rank on his shoulder would be bent over and unceremoniously kicked in the rear end to propel him through the opening in the hedge. Here for the first time I witnessed the degradation American officers would endure. This was to become common practice in the years ahead.

Many officers and noncommissioned officers, corporals and sergeants, had not worn their rank in combat for fear of becoming a target for the numerous Japanese snipers who infiltrated our lines. After the surrender they put their rank back on, believing they would be treated as officers as dictated by the Geneva Convention. Instead, they found out very quickly that they were held in supreme contempt by the Japanese for having surrendered.

CHAPTER 11

THE BATAAN DEATH MARCH

During my first night of captivity I soon lost contact with Elmer Parks. I would not see him again for forty-four years. Not until I visited Fort Sill, Oklahoma, for a regimental reunion did I even know that Elmer had survived. The enclosure we were put into was a huge field, part of an airfield bordering the National Road outside the town of Mariveles. Thousands were already assembled there from the two previous days, guarded by Japanese soldiers. Because of the tremendous number of prisoners (I later learned there were approximately 85,000 of us), it became almost impossible to locate anyone from my own unit. It was also possible that members of my unit had been brought to that assembly point and already began their march north out of Bataan.

Finding a place to lie down in an attempt to sleep was almost impossible. Every inch of ground in that field contained an American or Filipino soldier. Sleep for me that night meant sitting in a crammed area near an open trench latrine (toilets). The stench was unbearable, but the opportunity to relax for the first time in days offset the odor. All night we could hear the curses of someone stepped upon by another on their way to the latrines.

When dawn broke the following day the Japanese gathered together about 500 Filipinos and Americans, including me, and we began our march up the Bataan Peninsula, having no idea that we were beginning a march that became one of World War II's most notorious atrocities.

In all the years since the infamous Bataan Death March, I always hoped to read an account of it that really conveyed the feelings that I had experienced as part of it. I have yet to see such an account. The reason is simple. No one, including myself, can ever adequately describe the conditions that existed during those days. Suffice it to say that all those making the march, had they known what they would experience, would have chosen to continue to fight even if it meant their deaths. Far better indeed to die as a soldier than survive as a slave. Not just any slave, I might add, but specifically as a slave of the Japanese Imperial Army.

Upon rising from sleep, most people look for breakfast. That first morning was no exception. Hunger had been part of our existence for several months, and we hoped to be fed as prisoners of war. Such thoughts were forgotten as we were immediately forced to march almost as soon as we got up. I found myself in a group of Filipinos and Americans without knowing a single person around me.

Some had their own food with them that first morning, and soon set about eating it while others watched in stony silence. Nothing to worry about, we thought we would most certainly get something to eat pretty soon. We soon found out that was not going to happen for many days. As we began our long upward climbs on what was then known as the zigzag trail, we could look down and see thousands of our comrades slowly making their way up that road. Our climb continued for what seemed endless miles upward and through what was without a doubt the most difficult terrain of the entire march.

A heavy white dust created by numerous Japanese trucks flying up and down that one road leading to Mariveles and the jumpoff point for Corregidor had settled on the marchers, giving them a ghost-like appearance. The dust became so thick we found ourselves constantly spitting it out of our throats and mouths. Being the dry season in the Philippines, no rain had fallen for a long time. Soon our noses were also clogged, which made breathing during our upward climb even more difficult.

As each Japanese truck passed by Japanese inside would lean out with a rifle or long stick and attempt to knock the hats off those marching. The fact that heads were inside the hats made it more of a sport for them. Truly the little sons of Nippon had their fill of fun that day. Only a few were successful in that macabre spirit, however, as we learned to duck at the right time as the truck went by. When a blow did land on target it usually sent the recipient reeling to the side of the road, if he was not knocked unconscious. To add insult to injury, literally, the conquerors engaging in this "sport" were not front-line troops but rear echelon soldiers.

Seeing the enemy for the first time as we made our way over one particular stretch of the road, I saw Sergeant Florence Hardesty of my company in a sitting position alongside the road, dead. While it became the norm to see dead men along the road, it still came as a shock to see one I knew so well. Sitting upright, still in the throes of rigor mortis, he reminded me of the chalk white statue of Abraham Lincoln you see in postcards in the Lincoln Memorial in Washington, D.C. Just as white and cold as the statue was this kindly "old soldier" who had taught me the fundamentals of riding a motorcycle before the war. Covered with a heavy blanket of white road dust, his appearance was almost comical. He appeared to be watching a play unfolding in front of him. The players were of course those who straggled by in front of him.

The harsh reality of what was taking place soon settled in on all of us. Not knowing one person with whom I was marching, I soon became a loner. Most of us were in the same situation. I am convinced however that it was the intent of the Japanese to ensure that units were not kept intact. A group of individuals unknown to each other would prove less troublesome than a cohesive military unit. Our conquerors knew this.

As we made our way along the highway we learned our first Japanese word, "q-kay," or what sounded like that. Japanese interpreters soon explained that it meant "take a rest." This was not done for our benefit, but theirs. They were almost as tired from walking up the zigzag trail as we were. Our "q-kay" meant we sat in an open field while they searched our belongings for anything they wanted. Required to lay out everything we possessed so it could be easily seen, including our headgear, we soon became aware of their intention to have us sit in the sun at the hottest time of the day. Our first "sun treatment" was upon us.

Anyone found in possession of anything Japanese—and that
included propaganda leaflets they had dropped on Bataan during
the fighting, urging us to surrender—would be marched away, never
to be seen again. What happened to them was never known but
before they were marched away they were given a beating in front
of the other prisoners. The fact that all Americans, at least, had
been warned prior to the surrender to rid themselves of anything
Japanese, failed in many cases to register. When first warned about
this, I buried a Japanese soldier's diary and some propaganda leaflets that I had collected. I always regretted the loss of that diary as it
contained sketches from a Japanese soldier's impressions of all the
action he had witnessed, from his unit's landing at Aparri in northern Luzon until just before he died for his emperor on Mt. Samat
in Bataan. Returning to the place where I had buried it some years
later, I found out what the tropical climate of Bataan can do to
anything placed in the ground for any length of time. My treasure
was nothing but soil.

Needless to say, the first time I was searched I was happy not to
have that diary on my person. I did witness one American who had
photographs of a Japanese soldier's family on his person. He was
immediately executed on the spot by a squat ugly Japanese corporal. The means of death: a pistol shot to the head. Undoubtedly he
must have forgotten that he had the photographs in his wallet.
Others also ignored the orders to dispose of these items and paid
the ultimate price for their souvenirs.

During the march it was quite common for us to be sat down in
an open field for up to three hours. The sun would beat on us
until we would be dripping sweat merely sitting still. This "sun
treatment" was a calculated effort at torture by the Japanese. It
happened every day of the march from the beginning at Mariveles
to the railroad station town of San Fernando. For me, that was
nine days of treatment. How many times can one be searched?
What could be left on an individual after so many searches?

As night fell every day of the march, we learned there would be
no food or water for any prisoner, but we watched our guards enjoying their evening meals and waving their food in our direction.
On the second night, as on the first, space for sleeping was so lim-

ited we found ourselves fighting one another for a place to lie down. Tempers were at the boiling point under such conditions.

A detail of prisoners including me was selected by the Japanese to dig latrine trenches. The diggers were allowed to lie near where they dug. This was not as positive as it may sound, as many prisoners had begun to feel the effects of dysentery and there was a constant stream of traffic to the latrines. Some too ill to make it any distance soon relieved themselves where they sat or lay. Such sick and extremely weak men would find themselves kicked and cursed at by their less ill comrades. The word "bastard" could be heard all night when one of those attempting to reach the trench would step on someone attempting to sleep. At no time during the march did I ever see a commissioned officer, American or Filipino, attempt to bring some semblance of order to this chaos. This total absence of military discipline was my first real shock as a prisoner of war. I had always looked to commissioned officers to assume command and take action when necessary. Here for the first time I recognized that even the officers were interested in only one thing: survival.

At the crack of dawn each day our guard detail—some walking, others riding bicycles—with shouts typical of Japanese soldiers, hurried us back on the road again without food or water. As the sun grew hotter in intensity, those who had gone several days without water reached the breaking point. Soon Americans and Filipinos broke ranks and ran to artesian wells near the road. The guards, incensed at this breach of conduct, ran after them and beat them with clubs and rifle butts. Those too weak to rise after the beatings were bayoneted where they had fallen. Some were still alive after the bayoneting, and shots would ring out ending their misery. This brutal reaction by the Japanese curbed for a while any onlookers' thirst.

While the Japanese would not permit prisoners' breaking ranks to obtain a drink from a well, they didn't mind those who drank from puddles of water along the side of the road. Water had accumulated from a brief shower the night before, and a carabao, or water buffalo, had wallowed in the mud at the bottom of the puddle in an attempt to cover itself with a coating for protection against flies and mosquitoes. After the carabao had left these "wallows," the mud would settle to the bottom. Thirst-crazed prisoners, seeing what appeared to be water, would dive headfirst into the puddle and lap up what certainly was not potable water. To see a human being lying on his stomach with his head in a puddle of water reminded me of a cat lapping up milk from a saucer.

Many marchers knew that these puddles were places for mosquitoes to lay their eggs, and disease-carrying flies were in abundance. Their warning to those who drank this water fell on deaf ears. Thirst had driven many marchers beyond the point of accepting advice. Men such as myself who had soldiered in the Philippines for some time before the war had some training in water conservation. Infantry units on maneuvers in peacetime had stressed this aspect of survival in a jungle situation.

On each day of these prewar exercises in the field, every soldier returning to the bivouac area had to empty his canteen in front of his first sergeant. Water had best come out, or one faced a session with that sergeant. On only one occasion did I drink my entire canteen of water. My first sergeant, George Evans, was an old hand with most of his duty served in the Philippines. He made sure I would never commit that "offense" again. Evans was the best at reaming a soldier I ever met. On the Death March I blessed him repeatedly. He was destined to die in a prison camp within two years. All during the march I would wait until I saw a well near a village when we stopped. Many times the rush of prisoners to the well would prohibit me from completely filling my canteen, but regardless of how much I got I conserved it until the next well. Obtaining water at "authorized" stops was permitted. Unfortunately no one took charge of such efforts and bedlam usually ensued. This could have been avoided if we were still a disciplined force. We were not. Once I had my water I would put some in my mouth, move it about to quench the dry mouth, swallow a little bit of it, and then spit the remainder back into the canteen. Hardly dining in accord with Emily Post's book on etiquette, but it saved my life. At no time on the march did I ever allow myself to run out of water, despite my urge to take deep swallows as others did.

By the third day of the march, most respect for commissioned officers was gone. Any officer giving a command was totally ignored to the point of embarrassment. While much will be said later about the lack of military discipline among American enlisted men in Japanese camps, I can say here that the commissioned officers contributed to this condition. All ranks had been lied to when the promise of help from the United States turned out to be a falsehood. MacArthur in a message to the troops insisted that "men and planes are on the way. You must hold out." When such help failed to materialize, all ranks began to see "the big lie." Years later senior American officers in prisoner camps cursed MacArthur and everyone in Washington, blaming them all for what had befallen them. The miseries of the Death March just brought the anger and breakdown in discipline to the surface.

There were those officers, few in number, who by virtue of their training and individual personalities continued to act as officers were expected to. Sad to say, a great number of others, looking to survive at any cost, threw off the cloak of civilization and reverted to their animalistic instincts. Many such officers survived the war, while many who acted in an exemplary manner died in prison camps or aboard "hell ships" going to Japan or Manchuria. This condemnation of commissioned officers is not directed at any individual. Rather, it is directed to the corps of officers as a whole. Later I would be commissioned a second lieutenant and higher. I would serve for twenty years of continuous service. I had learned how not to be an officer in prison camps, probably the best training any officer can receive.

The failure of this country to recognize the shortcomings of such officers in the early days of World War II eventually brought about a similar situation during the Korean War, and this necessitated the Uniform Code of Military Justice to spell out how an American soldier of any rank was to behave if captured. No code can totally regulate human behavior, but it serves a guide in the most trying days of a soldier's life. That there was a breakdown in discipline in the Korean War is evidenced by the large number of Americans who went over to the North Koreans. Many never returned to the United States. Somewhere we failed them before they entered captivity.

In the case of the officers and noncommissioned officers captured in the Philippines, many deserved a court-martial for their
actions. Yet very, very few were ever held accountable in all the
excitement of victory and the postwar feeling that there would be
no more wars. All was forgiven. One sergeant was tried for treason
and justly so. His sentence was then commuted by President Eisenhower. To see, as I did, a full colonel who had been a despicable
and cowardly major in camp attempting to convince others after
the war of his bravery was hard to swallow. He made it a point to
tell those who knew him best how they should go after the Japanese in court. Again this was hard to swallow.

One aged colonel had somehow broken both his legs during
the march. When I first saw him he was lying alongside the road
pleading for help. I later learned that he had been left there by
four carriers the night before. A number of prisoners were asked to
help, but continued to walk by pretending not to hear. Embar-
rassed by this indifference on the part of so many, I agreed to be a
bearer. It took about two hours to obtain four volunteers, and soon
we began our laborious task of carrying the injured man.

Time dragged and the stretcher became heavier with each passing hour. About midday we asked for others to replace us. No one
offered to help, so we original four continued the journey, praying
for nightfall. When we stopped for the night, two of the four bearers slipped away in the dark. Two young officers who knew the
colonel came along however and filled the vacancies, and we set
off for another day of carrying our burden when we were hardly
able to carry ourselves.

At the close of that day I was utterly exhausted. I knew that night
that I could no longer carry that stretcher and survive. My basic
instinct of survival took over. Leaving the area where the colonel
lay, I joined a group leaving early the next morning. Did that officer live to see the end of the march? I never found out, but I
doubt if he did. My leaving him however has always bothered my
conscience. Officers, especially, carried all sorts of gear out of
Bataan. As each day passed one could see the side of the road
strewn with such gear. I recognized a lieutenant's riding boots one
day. The next day his suitcase which he attempted to carry. The

day after that I saw him, dead, along the road.

No man under a roasting sun with very little water can be expected to be a good samaritan. Other marchers jeered us when we had volunteered to carry that stretcher. Hundreds of men had been asked to help that colonel, yet all had ignored the request. Yet, individually, no one can be blamed for refusing to help. Their own physical condition was bad enough. Collectively however, any organization in our ranks could have provided relief for the man on that stretcher. Here for the first time I realized that my fellow prisoners, generally speaking, were not going to help anyone but themselves. Then and there I learned just exactly what the expression "every man for himself" was all about.

Days of marching slipped by without any food or water from our Japanese captors. Instead there were bayonetings and shootings for those who broke ranks to obtain either. Six days into the march we were again instructed to "q-kay" while the guards searched our possessions. My possessions, incidentally, were nil. I walked out of Bataan with the clothing on my back and nothing in my pockets. All I carried was a water canteen on a web belt. On one occasion the individual in front of me spread his blanket out on the ground. From his backpack he brought forth various types of food — cans of Spam, powdered milk, and other items I had not seen in months. They were all there within reaching distance staring at me like pieces of jewelry. I could only assume that the owner of such a supply had either made purchases from the many civilian Filipinos running alongside us offering such wares for cash, or he had been well supplied on Bataan. Being totally penniless, I was reduced to begging the man for some of his food. He looked at me as if I had two heads and totally ignored me. I could not blame him, but given the opportunity — while he was busy with a Japanese guard — I stole a can of Klim powdered milk, which I later discovered was only half full. I make this "confession" without reservation and would do the same again, if all things were as they were that day. That half can of milk kept me alive for the first eight days of the march. We finally reached the town of Lubao, and it was here that I received my first food from the Japanese. Had I known what was in store for me in that town I would gladly have passed

up the "meal" and kept walking. Upon my arrival I was told along
with the others that we would be fed the next morning. Crammed
into a warehouse made from sheet iron—formerly owned by the
National Rice Company and used for storage—we found ourselves
roasting in a veritable hell.

As we arrived at the warehouse men were shoved in until there
wasn't an inch of room remaining. The building literally bulged
at its seams, somewhat similar to a subway car at rush hour in Tokyo or New York. After the last man was squeezed in, the windows
and doors were secured from the outside. Without a doubt several
thousand men were packed into a building that at most could con-
tain only several hundred. Soon the stench became overwhelming. Tremendously hot and with practically no air, men who were
not too ill soon became very ill. The smell of human waste became overpowering. Men sick with dysentery relieved themselves
where they stood as there was absolutely no place to lie down.
With no designated area for a toilet it was academic where the
poor unfortunates relieved themselves. Between the stench of the
building, the heat, and oppressive humidity, plus standing up all
night, I thought for sure I would go mad. Each hour of the night
dragged by, and it turned out to be truly a night in hell. As dawn
broke the windows were opened from the outside and never did
fresh air ever smell better. Those fortunate enough to have died in
the building were taken unceremoniously to an open pit that had
been dug during the night and thrown in. Some turned out not to
be dead, but were so close to it the Japanese felt it didn't matter.
Several rifle butt blows to the head of the victims soon took care of
that little detail. The dead then had earth thrown over them, but I
am positive that a number of them were still alive. Scores of both
Filipinos and Americans were buried there that day.

That morning, amidst the stench of the men and the warehouse,
we lined up outside and were issued a handful of rice from a steaming cauldron set up by the Japanese. Inasmuch as I had lost my
mess kit (a soldier's plate) and my canteen cup along the march, I
offered my two hands cupped together. The guard laughed at me,
said something I did not understand, and dumped the very, very
hot rice into my palms. To avoid burning my hands any further, I

gulped down the small amount in a single mouthful, burning my mouth and my stomach in the process.

The denial of food and water by the Japanese during the entire march was in my opinion deliberate. Those Japanese put on trial after the war for atrocities committed on the march claimed they were unprepared for such large numbers of prisoners. The question never asked of these Japanese however was why they prohibited the Filipino civilian populace from feeding and providing water to those marching. That is exactly what the Japanese did, and I am sure this rationale was the deciding factor in the sentence meted out. However, the commanding general of the Japanese forces, Homma, paid the supreme price of death by a firing squad while those truly responsible such as the guards themselves walked away free. The acts of kindness displayed by the Filipino people was truly "one for the books." They constantly tried to feed us all along the way, often risking their lives. Their decency and caring are unforgettable.

Near the town of Lubao I witnessed an act of barbarism I have never forgotten. As we were walking along I noticed an American sergeant lying extremely close to the road, fast asleep. His group had stopped for a break and was gathered in a field by the road. As our group approached him I noticed a Japanese tank bearing down on the sergeant's body. The tank driver making a positive effort to come as close to the edge of the road as possible, ran over the soldier. The man was instantly crushed to death, his body pressed into the earth. Each succeeding tank, about four or five of them, veered off the road and deliberately crushed the body further into the roadway. When the last tank had passed one could see the headless corpse's outline in the road. The Japanese tankers went out of their way to have fun that day by running over a lifeless body. It is fair to say that no Japanese ever paid for that crime, witnessed by a number of Americans and Filipinos.

Finally my group of marchers reached the town of San Fernando in Pampanga Province. The nine days that I spent on the march had been a grueling and terrifying experience. Days filled with endless sun burning into your very being. Constant shouting and beatings, and seeing outright murder committed before one's very eyes. San Fernando was a railroad junction, and Japanese plans called for shipping their prisoners by rail from this town to our first prison camp. The prisoners, unaware of such plans, were again stopped at sundown. We spent another night and day without food or water. Most prisoners arriving in my group were dispersed to several locations near the railroad station. My group was forced into a schoolhouse until the building could hold no more. The building was packed like a can of sardines, but I got lucky that night as one of those who could not be fit into the building. We were left outside in the schoolyard. For those forced inside it was a repeat of the tin hell at Lubao. As foul as the air was, it was still better than what men were enduring in the school building.

The next morning I was not so lucky. To feed those who had been in the school, the Japanese needed the schoolyard to set up a field kitchen, so they dispatched those of us in the yard to the rail-road station without food. We sat on a concrete platform at the station waiting for our "fed" comrades to join us. After about a two-hour wait in the sun, all prisoners were formed into groups of one hundred and loaded into freight train boxcars. The cars were similar in construction and as old as the French 40-and-8's of World War I. Some were made of metal, others wood. My "luck" again came into play. As the wooden car filled up, I was among the first to enter the next car, made of steel. Certainly the wooden cars were not as hot.

Metal or wood, the journey turned out to be a nightmare for everyone. I later learned, after the war, that not all those captured on Bataan were forced to make the march. A number were taken out of Bataan by Japanese trucks. Others who were captured in northern Bataan Province only had to make a two- or three-day march. Yet to this day I have yet to meet anyone from Bataan who admits to riding out of that place, or of being fortunate enough to spend only two days walking. Everyone claims to have been among the vast majority of those who spent five, six, seven, eight, and even nine days walking. The duration was determined by where one was captured.

Our car soon became so filled with bodies that no one could lie down. Most of the prisoners, excluding myself, had dysentery. As a result, human waste was soon all over the floor. Being among the first put into the car, I found myself pressed up against a wall. That was somewhat of a benefit as I could lean against it. Our assigned guard, overcome by the stench of the car, decided to ride on the roof of the other car. To insure the security of his prisoners he then locked the door. The only air to penetrate these hellhole conditions came from several small openings along the roof. In a short time the men in our car bordered on madness. Civilized behavior became a memory. Any resemblance to human beings and disciplined soldiers had vanished even before the train got under way.

The train made several stops on its four-hour journey, and when it did the guard would open the door. Finally, an act of kindness, or was it fear that the train would arrive with a carload of dead men?

When the train stopped, the Filipinos from the immediate area — who somehow knew the train's cargo — would throw food at the open doors of the cars. While several guards objected to this, others allowed it. Unfortunately however, those at the door seized all the food thrown and passed none back to the rest of us. Each stop was a repeat of the previous one. Those fortunate to be in or near the door made sure that any food they caught was consumed on the spot. My fellow Americans in the front of my car believed in self-preservation, and damn those behind them. This act would be reenacted endlessly in various ways during our captivity.

Near the end of the train ride our guard decided to leave the door open after a stop. By this time he realized how bad the conditions in the car were. Those near the door opening who had to eliminate — especially after their recent feeding — were held by the hands by others in front while they defecated regardless of where the train was. If not for the grimness of the situation it was almost comical. Here was a trainload of soldiers passing through Filipino barrios (villages) with some of its passengers being held with their naked bottoms mooning outside the car and spraying a watery excrement over stations and unfortunate Filipinos standing near the railroad tracks.

Near the end of the journey from San Fernando to Capas, Tarlac, more and more Filipinos gathered along the route of the train as it

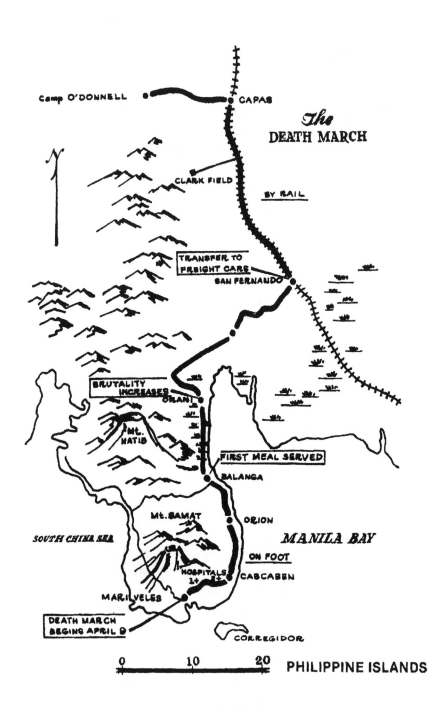

moved through their villages. Many efforts were made by these very kind people to get food to the prisoners. Often such acts resulted in a rifle butt applied to the head. While I did not receive any of the food (which I attribute to my selfish fellow Americans), I remember with gratitude the kindness of Filipinos who went out of their way to feed us.

Those strong or lucky enough to get food however soon became more bully-like. On one occasion a fight broke out, resulting in one American being thrown from the train. What happened to him remains a mystery but I shed no tears over him. He was one of those at the doorway who refused to pass any food to the rear. In fact, I distinctly remember how pleased I felt at the time he was thrown off the train.

After about four hours of a snail-like pace our train ride ended in the small village of Tarlac, about forty kilometers from our point of origin, San Fernando. Each car discharged its passengers, at least those who could walk. A number of men had died in the cars. Many died standing up as they could not fall down. They were laid along the side of the train. I never learned what happened to them but most likely they were carried to the camp's cemetery. Here again, prisoners milled about with no organization until the Japanese came along, screaming as only they could, while beating the prisoners into some form of order.

Once again we were on the march. Everyone however was very grateful to be out of the airless infernos of the railroad cars. At least now there was some degree of morale visible. We all welcomed the opportunity to breathe once again. With our thoughts on those who had died in the cars, we began our last stage of the march. Only eleven kilometers remained before we reached our final destination. Not aware that the march was about to end, men again began seeking food and water from any source.

Again the Filipino civilians attempted to help all those marching. Men, women, and even children would leave five-gallon containers of water alongside the road. Japanese guards would deliberately kick them over rather than allow prisoners to drink. Growing weaker with each passing day, and after the experience of the boxcars, men took even greater risks to obtain water. By this time many felt it was better to be shot or bayoneted than go without the water so close to them. Many who tried to get water paid for that with their lives. We passed several Filipino soldiers, one of whom had been beheaded, lying dead alongside the road. The Japanese warriors had again proved their mettle as warriors, and so, for me, the Bataan Death March passed into history. The date was 24 April 1942. I had been on the march ten days.

Could the Bataan Death March have been avoided? The answer is an unqualified yes! General King, commanding general of Fil-American forces on Bataan, knew full well the desperate physical condition of his men. In his meeting with Japanese sent to negotiate his surrender by General Homma, King repeatedly described the high percentage of his men in poor condition. Prior to surrendering King had ordered his trucks saved for the express purpose of transporting his men out of Bataan. He offered this transportation to the Japanese repeatedly, but they refused to talk about it. Finally King asked: "Will you not just assure me that my men will be well treated?" The Japanese colonel in charge drew himself up and said loftily, "the Imperial Japanese Army are not barbarians." No survivor of Bataan will ever question the fact that the Japanese were to a man "barbarians."

CHAPTER 12

CAMP O'DONNELL

Around noon, with the sun at its peak, we came upon a large, flat area devoid of vegetation. The scorched earth sent heat waves rising in front of us. It was desolation, plus. On the ground on both sides of the road were partially completed Philippine Army barracks. These "barracks," an assortment of native huts, were raised off the ground as was most Filipino housing in the rural areas. We had finally arrived at Camp O'Donnell. Before the war this area was meant to house one of the many Philippine divisions being called to active duty. While never used, these "barracks" were now destined to hold approximately 45,000 Filipino and 9,300 American POWs.

Camp O'Donnell—"the Andersonville of the Pacific"—was to be the burial site for about 25,000 Filipinos and 1,537 Americans. The march out of Bataan had taken thousands of lives. It has been conservatively estimated that between 5,000 to 10,000 Filipinos and about 700 Americans perished on the march itself. With no accurate records to support these figures, they can only be considered a "guesstimate" based on the number of men in Bataan at the time of the surrender compared to the number arriving at O'Donnell. Of the deaths at O'Donnell, the camp's records revealed that the American deaths occurred within forty days of their arrival! As many as fifty were buried each day. For Filipinos the situation was even grimmer. Their death rate reached 500 a day for a period of time.

Because of its brief history as a prison camp, very little has been written about O'Donnell. As a result, Americans are unaware of this hellhole. To every American and Filipino who survived the equivalent of the "black hole of Calcutta," it was the nearest thing to hell on earth. Because of the tremendous number of deaths in that camp, the Japanese thought best to move the prisoners to another camp. So on 6 June 1942 most Americans were moved to Cabanatuan, another Philippine Army division prewar camp. To woo the Filipino population over to the Japanese "greater east Asia co-prosperity sphere theme," Filipino soldiers were gradually paroled after a meticulous recording of their families and home address.

The second prison camp for Bataan's American survivors, Cabanatuan, is better known. While that camp remained in existence until February 1945, it recorded almost 3,000 American deaths. Ninety percent of those who died at Cabantuan died in the first ninety days, and it must be emphasized that they were men from Bataan, not Corregidor.

I have returned to O'Donnell after the war several times since first leaving there on 5 July 1942. Nothing there indicates that it was ever the site of what was probably the most hellish prison camp for Americans in our history. The only remembrance to those who died there is a massive seven-foot-high cement cross. This has a history all its own. In 1985 during one of my visits to the camp site I found the cross on a lofty windswept spot inside an American communications area. Nothing was near it for miles except the high towers used to transmit intelligence data.

Upon our arrival at the gate of the installation, an American Marine initially refused us access because of the sensitive nature of the site. While we awaited permission to enter I had the opportunity to speak to the sentry. He had absolutely no knowledge of either prison camp O'Donnell or the cement cross we wished to visit. I could accept this lack of knowledge from most any civilian. But a military person stationed on the very grounds of the site of so many war dead? Here was an American soldier, thousands of miles from home, stationed where thousands of prisoners of war had died, many perhaps from his home state, totally ignorant of the site's history. I was aghast. It was almost like a sentry being posted in Arlington National Cemetery who did not have the faintest idea that it was also the location of the Tomb of the Unknown Soldier!

Subsequently we were taken to the cross, finally visible after thirty years of being buried in the very tall cogon grass of the Philippines. In 1945 the cross was discovered by American graves registration troops exhuming the remains of American prisoners who had died in O'Donnell. When found it was believed, by even General MacArthur himself, that the Japanese had erected the cross. It was then allowed to become overgrown and deteriorate over the years. Finally, an O'Donnell "graduate" on a tour of the area discovered it in the grass which had grown to twenty to thirty feet high. Once discovered, it became a regular stop for American tourists visiting there.

In late June 1942, I along with a number of other American prisoners worked on a detail building that cross. My involvement consisted of pouring concrete into a form. The next day I was taken off that detail and reassigned to the burial detail. The cross was eventually inscribed with the words: "O'Donnell War Personnel Enclosure. In memory of the American dead, 1942." At the base of the cross is the inscription "Omnia Pro Patria," which coincidentally is the motto of the 31st Infantry Regiment. However, it may not be a coincidence. There were a number of 31st Infantry Regiment men on that work detail. Who was responsible for the wording no one can say. One thing is known; the word "prisoner" was not used as an act of defiance.

Colonel John Olson (U.S. Army Retired) was the camp's adjutant during its existence. Many of the records now in American hands are a result of his notes and records. Later, Olson wrote a brief article entitled "A Sack of Cement," a catchy title with the inference that only one sack of cement was used. My memory however is that a number of sacks were used. Olson in his book *O'Donnell: The American Andersonville of the Pacific*, is under the impression that the cross was not built before he left there on 5 July 1942. However, I also left on the same date as Olson and I know the cross was already there at that time.

That the cross was there prior to 5 July 1942 is verified by Camp O'Donnell's graves registration officer, Captain A. L. (Duke) Fullerton. In his report dated 8 August 1942, submitted to the commanding officer, Cabanatuan Prison Camp, Fullerton wrote: "a concrete monument in the form of a cross is installed in the space between plots 'O' and 'C'. On July 5, 1942, the undersigned made the 1461st. Internment at Camp O'Donnell and received order of transfer to Cabanatuan...." Fullerton, Olson, and I all left on the same day.

Years after the cross was discovered, Olson began a campaign to bring the cross to the U.S. I recall his attempt to have the American defenders of Bataan and Corregidor agree to support a move to do so. The membership, made up of two-thirds Corregidor survivors, chose to leave the cross in the Philippines. Soon it became apparent that the American military would be forced to vacate all military sites in the Philippines and thus the future of the cross would be in jeopardy. Many American veterans of Bataan asked both their Filipino counterparts and the Philippine government for their approval to send the cross to the U.S. This request was met with the questionable argument that the cross was a part of Filipino history. In view of the fact that the cement was Japanese and the labor American, that argument to me did not hold water. Shortly after the volcano Mt. Pinatubo erupted, almost burying Clark Field and nearby O'Donnell in ashes, the cross was brought to this country by a number of people, headed by John Olson. The cross now rests at the home of the Museum of American Prisoners of War at Andersonville, Georgia, where Northern Civil War prisoners were held by the Confederacy, a most fitting place. Those of us from Bataan will always be grateful to John Olson for his dogged determination to bring the cross to this country. At this writing, the site of O'Donnell is a huge housing area sheltering the many victims of the volcano eruption.

Today a monument erected in memory of the Filipinos who died in Camp O'Donnell has been erected by the Philippine government at the camp site. Philippine officials would welcome a similar monument to the Americans who died across the road. The problem, of course, is money. The Philippines look to the United States for funding such a monument. It is highly unlikely that there will ever be such a memorial.

At Cabanatuan one can find a most beautiful memorial to the

three thousand who died there. If not for efforts of graduates of the United States Military Academy at West Point, odds are there would not be a marker there as well. A group of Americans led by Major General Chester Johnson, West Point, class of '37, are responsible for the construction and maintenance of this monument. Surrounded by a steel fence to protect the site, so very necessary in the Philippines these days, stands an altar-like monument under flags of the United States and the Philippines. It is truly a reminder to visitors of what happened there in 1942–45. Ninety percent of those who died there were men of Bataan and most deaths occurred within the first ninety days of the camp's existence.

While both Camp O'Donnell and Camp Cabanatuan saw suffering, death and misery, Cabanatuan in general fared the better of the two camps. Men from Bataan arrived there in June 1942 after the horrors of Bataan and the Death March. The meeting of the Corregidor survivors who had been taken to Cabanatuan after their surrender with the Bataan survivors who had preceded them in that camp was a shock to those from Corregidor. The appearance of the disease-ridden Bataan-O'Donnell survivors came as a complete surprise to the men of Corregidor, who had arrived in captivity in much better shape than the Bataan veterans. The men of Corregidor had not known the torture, starvation, and disease of their fellow Americans from Bataan. That they were lucky enough to escape the misfortunes Bataan men endured was to their benefit, but the horrors visited upon Bataan men need to be separated from Corregidor's experience. At least this was true until June 1942.

To further establish the difference between the two groups of prisoners: one out of every three Corregidor men died while in captivity, while two out of three Bataan men failed to survive prison camp. Such statistics—gained by comparing unit strengths both before and at the end of the war, clearly support the fact that Corregidor men entered their first prison camp in relatively good health, and thus withstood their internment much better than their comrades from Bataan. It was in Cabanatuan that Corregidor veterans first experienced the "mercy" of their Japanese captors. Captured on 6 May 1942, the Corregidor survivors were held on the island for two weeks while they waited for American forces in the southern islands of the Philippines to comply with their commanding general's order to surrender.

Two weeks after their capture they were loaded on ships and taken directly to Manila, not Bataan as some noted historians have written. There they were compelled to march six miles through the streets of Manila by the Japanese in an effort to humiliate all Americans in the eyes of the Filipinos. Just before reaching the city prison of Bilibid, one American officer succumbed to a heart attack, the only victim of Corregidor's surrender up to that point.

I was actually very impressed with the Cabanatuan camps when I first arrived there 5 July 1942 from O'Donnell. Some degree of organization was apparent there compared to O'Donnell, where there was practically none. I was more impressed with the healthy looks of my fellow Americans captured on Corregidor. While hardly a picnic, Cabanatuan was a vast improvement over O'Donnell. Future historians may one day point out the tremendous differences between the two prison camps—who survived and how they survived.

A news article published in the *Las Vegas Sun* dated 24 April 1983 sums up the difference between the two groups. "Corregidor troops had not endured the hardships of the battling bastards of Bataan during the fighting. As a result, they were in far better shape to survive three and one-half years of imprisonment. Of the approximately 9,000 American Death March survivors, only 2,000 are alive today and rapidly diminishing year by year. Their death rate is seven times higher than for the average American."

No one who arrived in O'Donnell in April 1942 after completing the march can ever forget the greetings of the Japanese camp commander, a Captain Tsuenyoshi. An overage officer undoubtedly passed over in the promotion plan of the Japanese Army, he possessed a burning hatred for Americans. While many memories of a Japanese prison camp may have faded with the passage of time, no soldier who ever listened to Tsuenyoshi's welcome speech has ever forgotten not only what was said, but how it was said. Americans and Filipinos were separated: Filipinos on one side of the road and Americans on the other.

As each group arrived in O'Donnell, the Americans were made

to sit in the blistering hot sun for hours to await the camp commander's official welcome. Here again, yet one more body search of each prisoner took place. Even at this late stage some Americans were found in possession of "contraband" and taken away. After the search, a pint-size Japanese officer wearing riding britches, a sun pith helmet, and a very white shirt, with highly polished black boots, mounted a small box. He stepped up on the box for the express purpose of being higher than the lowly prisoners before him. I found very few Japanese officers and noncommissioned officers who did not stand on a box when addressing American prisoners. Anyone who saw the movie *Bridge on the River Kwai*, has witnessed an exact copy of the Japanese commander played in the film by Sessue Hiyakawa.

Many prisoners of O'Donnell remember him more for his speech, however. Tsuenyoshi delighted in spending at least thirty minutes eating his lunch in front of the starving prisoners before going into his act. His speech was always the same. To every group arriving, he spit out the words "Americans" and "British." Further, he shouted that Japan would destroy both countries even if it had to fight a "hundred-year war" to bring about their defeat. Many of us in attendance ridiculed such remarks, but in view of Japan's prosperity today long after the war and domination of so many American interests, one has to wonder if he knew something we didn't. The Japanese lobby today in the United States gives many the feeling that Tsuenyoshi may yet be correct. Tsuenyoshi made it very clear that we were not prisoners of war but captives of the Imperial Japanese Army, and as such they could do whatever they wanted with us. He scorned and ridiculed us for becoming captives, saying "you don't deserve to live." His remarks about our status as captives proved to be correct, as they did what they pleased without any fear of consequences. If ever a Japanese showed his hatred for his captives, it was Captain Yoshio Tsuenyoshi.

After the speech we were assigned to our barracks. Made from bamboo poles and held together by rattan strips, the barracks were double-deckers with nipa thatch roofs. Elevated off the ground to avoid the rains that were soon to flood the camp, this would be home for me for several months. Americans who had never slept

on bamboo soon developed ulcer-type sores on their thin, emaciated bodies from the beds. As exhausted as the marchers were,
they welcomed the chance to sleep on anything. Soon after my
arrival at O'Donnell, I was assigned to work at one of the "mess
halls," a misnomer if ever there was one. Some buildings in camp
were yet to be completed, and the Japanese selected one of these
as a place to serve food, another misnomer. Missing half a roof, the
kitchen I was assigned to soon proved to be my living quarters as
well as my work place. It also came close to being my death place.

While an enlisted prisoner had to work on some detail providing he was "well," he also had to abide by all rules of being a prisoner. To obtain water other than for cooking purposes, one had to
get in the drinking water line opened only according to Japanese
timetables. In my area one water tap served several thousand men.
Lining up to get drinking water was analogous to a lottery or to
betting on the horses. The odds of getting any water before the tap
was shut off for the day was extremely small. It depended on the
number of prisoners in line ahead of you. Nevertheless, we all
took our chances and lined up for the precious fluid.

One day while waiting in the extremely hot sun, a certain air-
man, later to be considered a "hero"(sic) in his own book, went to
the head of the line—with hundreds waiting—carrying a five-gallon can—and yelling "making way for the hospital's water detail."
Obtaining the water under this guise, our "hero" would then go
behind a barracks and split the water with his cronies while others
waiting in line went without when the tap was shut off.

This was one predator who would survive. This story, told today,
has in fact provoked a laugh or two, as I actually heard when it was
told at one of the American Defenders of Bataan and Corregidor
(ADBC) conventions. In truth, this one selfish act may have cost
the lives of several fellow prisoners. This individual used the same
ruse time and time again, and in later years had the gall to admit to
it in writing. How many men died as a result of this selfishness will
never be known. Water, a lifesaving commodity in the Philippines,
was ten times more valuable to dehydrated men who had marched
for days with little or no water. That men would kill for a drink of
water is an understatement, as future happenings were to prove.

My experience with this predator "hero" continues to burn me every time I think of it.

Shortly after my assignment in the kitchen, where I kept the fires burning under huge pots, I found myself suffering a severe attack of malaria with chills and fever for several days. While I did have my first case of malaria during the fighting on Bataan, I was fortunate at that time to be given some quinine by our medics, and that shook it off. But now, dragging myself up off the dirt floor which I called my bed, I made my way to the so-called hospital. Early in O'Donnell's existence, all prisoners knew that if you entered that place as a patient you would not come out alive. Speaking to a medic—at least he called himself one—I asked for some quinine which, I will admit, was like asking for gold. I still remember him telling me none was available. Yet sitting on a box which the medic used as a desk I could see a bottle of quinine. Living on that medication on Bataan, while the supply lasted, it was easy for me to recognize. When I asked what was in the bottle, I was told "that's my private stock, not the hospital's." And then came his fateful words: "available for a price." Having had no money for months, I was hardly in a position to buy anything. After describing the illegitimacy of the medic's birth to his face, I made my way back to the kitchen floor where I lay down, hoping for the best. That I was having a bad attack was obvious. Yet fellow Americans working in the kitchen had absolutely no concern for my impending demise. They had seen too much death and dying to give a thought to another person leaving this world. One kind soul however, did throw some empty rice sacks over me to help ward off my severe malaria chills, which by now had become violent and were tearing through me.

Malaria attacks often affect one's hearing, and soon I heard muffled—as though they were far away—yet distinct voices asking about my condition. It sounded like they were short of help and looking to replace me. Comments such as "he's had it…leave him alone, he's finished" did little to encourage me when I finally realized that I was the subject of the conversation. After two days of feeling unbelievably ill, a friend from my unit, Fred Pavia, whom I had shared a pup tent with on Bataan, came into the kitchen looking for me. When he learned of my illness, he left, assuring me he would be back. True to his word, Freddie returned several hours later with some quinine, which he admitted stealing from the same medic who had refused me. I was to never see Fred again. A month after giving me the medication to save my life, Fred died from malaria himself and without anyone to help him survive. Returning to the Philippines in 1986, I learned of Fred's fate from records at the American cemetery outside Manila.

The quinine Fred stole did the trick. I was up and about in several days but no longer a member of the kitchen staff. Too many "healthies" wanted the job. I have been and will always be eternally grateful for the kindness of Fred Pavia. All I knew about Fred was that he was from New Jersey and we were assigned to the same unit on Bataan. I fault myself that I did not attempt to learn of his fate after the war. Reading his name on the list of those who had died in O'Donnell made me regret my second failure to at least contact his family to express my thanks to them for their son's kindness.

The reason I never went to the "hospital" for treatment I have mentioned before. Conditions there were beyond description, though later I will attempt to do just that. Suffice it to say that anyone entering the place voluntarily signed his own death certificate. Visiting a friend there before my illness convinced me that I would prefer to die outside that hellhole.

After recovering from that particular bout of malaria, I soon joined the main body of prisoners. Here I became a regular on the burial detail. I say this despite Colonel Olson's contention in his book *O'Donnell: The Andersonville of the Pacific*, that men "were occasionally assigned to such duty." Numerous prisoners such as myself were assigned to this onerous detail repeatedly, both at O'Donnell and Cabanatuan, because there were so few of us "healthy" men in both camps. You were considered "healthy" if you could walk upright and did not have to run to the latrines as a dysentery patient. Each time I was selected by the administrative officers, I would report to the hospital's "St. Peter's" ward or "zero" ward," names given by the prisoners to the ward where the dead were gathered for burial. Some modern day writers of this period of American prisoner-of-war life state that the "dead were buried."

I, and others on this detail, will state unequivocally that some were still alive among the dead piled high beneath the trap door of zero ward. Anytime the medics believed a man had died, they would drag the corpse to the opening in the floor and drop the body through. There they would pile up until the burial detail came along and removed them. They were, in all truth, stacked like cords of wood.

Picture if you can a large bamboo and nipa covered "building" raised off the ground about eight feet, enough headroom to walk under it to gather bodies for burial. Above in the ward lay numerous patients, mostly stark naked, lying in their own excrement with hordes of huge black flies completely covering their bodies. The flies were even in the mouths, ears, and eyes of those men, as they lay gasping for life. Maggots could be seen in the open wounds of the prisoners. Many wounds were body sores caused by a lack of sufficient flesh on parts of the body touching the bamboo floors. American medics hardly paid them the slightest attention. While it is true that medical supplies were almost nonexistent, the medics could at least have provided some care. The medics, including the doctors, ignored the dying men during the first two months of the camp's existence. They could have at least tried to keep the place clean. Instead they were concerned only with their own survival. It was truly a scene from Dante's Inferno.

Only in July were doctors brought to O'Donnell. These American doctors had been fed and treated fairly well while at hospitals on Bataan, treating Japanese as well as Fil-American captives. They brought some degree of order to the hospital. Shocked by what they saw upon their arrival, they set about to clean up the place. Coming from a field hospital where the Japanese had given them medication for their patients, they brought what they could carry. More important: they brought badly needed medical discipline. They themselves had missed the march and as a result still had some civilized behavior about them. Also, they were in excellent health compared to the medical personnel who had made the march. Upon capturing the field hospital on Bataan, apparently the Japanese were pleased to see how their men had been cared for while they were prisoners of the Americans. To show their appreciation, they provided food and medicine to all those at the hospital.

One, Captain Harold Immerman, former commanding officer of the 12th Medical Battalion (PS), stated the following: "This morning we started work on the so-called hospital, the dirtiest, filthiest mess I have ever seen, patients included. We scrubbed, bathed prisoners, etc. Several died while we were doing our work. This is a chapter of my life that will always be unbelievable." Years later I became very good friends with Dr. John Browe, a neighbor. John was one of those medics who arrived in O'Donnell with Immerman, and he agreed fully with his CO's assessment of conditions at that horror show.

Every day we reported to the hospital for the burial detail we would assemble under the trap door where between fifteen and twenty-five bodies awaited us. To repeat, slight movement was visible on the part of some of the dead. Ignoring those we thought were still alive, we would strip whatever personal effects might still be on their bodies, such as shoes, mess kits, and dog tags. Periodically some type of clothing would be on the body. This too was saved and placed in a pile for future use. Shoes were extremely valuable.

Dog tags identifying each individual were taken from around the neck and placed on the big toe or put in the mouth of each victim. Finding a way to carry the bodies meant hunting for anything solid and big enough to hold one. In many cases the stretchers were doors from various buildings. As soon as enough bodies had been taken from the pile to form the designated number allowed in that particular burial detail, we set off for the "cemetery." As we left the ward, other prisoners would sift through the pile of personal effects for any item that would help them survive.

Burial details usually consisted of about twenty-five dead bodies on the "stretchers," each carried by four fellow prisoners. Soon the column was stretched out with Japanese guards screaming at the bearers to "Speedo, speedo!" jabbing them with their bayonets to ensure compliance. They didn't care for this detail either. The bodies, still covered with their own bowel movements, attracted swarms of huge flies to the stretchers. Bearers, weakened from their own disabilities, complained about being forced to carry the bodies, knowing full well they had to be buried. Those dying in the early days of O'Donnell were mostly victims of the train ride from San Fernando to Capas and from the march itself.

As the death rate steadily mounted to almost fifty a day, the Japanese designated a cemetery area several hundred yards from the hospital. To the stretcher bearers it seemed miles away. Burial detail became more difficult with each passing day.

On one detail I was assigned as one of the four carriers, using a door as a stretcher, when suddenly we were under a tropical downpour. While it had been raining for several days, the element of weather never interfered with Japanese plans for burials. I always felt better off when I was selected as a bearer as opposed to a grave digger, especially in such rainy weather. To attempt to dig a huge hole in the ground in pouring rain, as I had occasion to do one day, was an impossible task. Each shovel brought up mud that stuck to it with each attempt to dig. On this particular day, without any gear resembling a raincoat, we set off for the cemetery soaking wet. My position was the front left bearer of the stretcher.

Dressed in an army suntan uniform of the day, with shirtsleeves cut off at the elbows due to wear and trousers cut off at the knees for the same reason, and with no socks or shoelaces, I soon found myself attempting to avoid large puddles in the dirt road. Forced to walk through one puddle, I felt my left shoe sink into the mud. Dreading the thought of losing my shoe, I stopped walking, to the screams of my fellow prisoners to keep moving. Actually they were screaming obscenities at me for slowing them up. I then attempted to pull my foot from the mud where it had stuck. To do so, I reached down to hold my shoe while I lifted my foot. I forgot I was holding a stretcher of corpses enormously bloated from wet beriberi. (There are two kinds of beriberi. Dry beriberi affects the heart, while wet beriberi causes bloating from a buildup of body fluids.) With my movement, I tilted the litter and the bloated corpses rolled off and landed on me. As one body hit mine, a part of its tightly stretched skin burst, spraying me with a foul-smelling body fluid. Cursed some more by my fellow prisoners, we put the bodies back on the stretcher and proceeded to the cemetery. I can, to this day, still recall that horrible odor which remained on my body for days. There was no way to take a bath in that place.

Upon arriving at the cemetery, we saw that the digging detail sent out earlier had dug several large, but not deep, holes in the ground. We then brought the remains of a human being and unceremoniously dumped his body into the grave. The sound of bone cracking against bone was quite common as one body was thrown atop another. Once rid of our burden we assisted in throwing dirt on the corpses. Heavy rain made the shovels ten times heavier than normal with the mud clinging to them. The most heart-wrenching part of this sickening detail was to witness the bodies of American soldiers, many still boys, resting in shallow graves with part of their arms or hands still protruding above the mud thrown over them. Those doing the shoveling cursed the dead as they stood in the pouring rain, anxious as hell to get the hell out of there as soon as they could. No graveside services were held, despite some stories to the contrary. At least, not on my burial detail. Most chaplains were too concerned with the living to care about the dead. Throughout the early days of my captivity I was always puzzled by this lack of concern on the part of the "men of the cloth." I am sure there were exceptions, but I did not see them in O'Donnell.

On 4 July 1942, the day before I was to depart O'Donnell for Cabanatuan, an incident occurred which has remained vivid in my memory for over fifty years. An army major named Horton, left behind as the senior American officer when the main body of prisoners left O'Donnell on 6 June 1942, gave instructions that a special meal was to be prepared for the officers in order to celebrate the Fourth of July. While this party has been written about by others, none have mentioned where the "goodies" came from. They consisted of powdered milk and sugar taken from the sick prisoners to the "officer's mess." The Japanese had only days earlier left those treasures for the sick and dying. In order to make sweet camote pies, milk and sugar were needed. The camote (koh-moh-teh) which resembles a sweet potato and is found in abundance in the Philippines, was served to prisoners as a vegetable. For a drink to accompany the pies, an ersatz coffee was made from slightly burned rice. While this incident has been denied by fellow officer-friends of the major, I can swear to the event, possibly along with others who survived. The ingredients for this "party" were taken from the sick and dying to satisfy one officer's attempt at playing the role of commander. Enlisted men, aware of this incident, soon despised our friend the major for his actions. His moment in the sun as it turned out was to be short-lived.

When the next day dawned, 5 July 1942, the major was part of my detail going to Cabanatuan, and I became very aware of his whereabouts for several weeks to come. In Cabanatuan he became just one of many field grade (majors to lieutenant colonels) officers in that camp. Ironically, he had been promoted to lieutenant colonel and was unaware of the promotion at that time. I have always admired West Point graduates and had always wanted to go to the academy myself since my days in high school. I admire the academy's graduates for their training, their love of country and their pride in themselves and our army. This man however was a disgrace to West Point, failing in his duties to his men and to his country. Most West Pointers live by their oath. He did not.

My barracks in Cabanatuan was on a street leading to the open slit trenches of our latrines. I had the opportunity to see our major make many visits there. For shortly after his arrival at Cabanatuan he came down with a severe case of dysentery and his trips to the latrines became more frequent each day. Eventually, he took to lying on the ground near the latrines to expedite his trips. A week or so after he decided to lie there, I no longer saw him on my daily trips to the latrines. When I next saw him I was on the burial detail and found him among the dead. Several of our burial detail members had been with me at O'Donnell on 4 July, and we were completely without sympathy for him. At this time, the Japanese were allowing officers to be buried separately from enlisted men. Our burial group arrived at the unanimous decision that this officer had "screwed" the enlisted men in life and in retribution should spend eternity with them. That decision made, our officer had his dog tags removed and placed on an enlisted man whom we buried in the single officer's grave. We then threw our friend the major in with the enlisted men. When reading this today I am somewhat contrite over my actions of that time. In all honesty however, I fully supported what was done and, given the same circumstances that existed then, would do it all over again. To those who died as a result of being deprived by this predator officer of the milk and sugar intended for them, I say "that was one for you fellers." While I came to despise many officers and enlisted men in prison camp, this particular officer holds an unenviable place in my list of fellow prisoners who were despicable predators.

How pervasive were prison camp predators? Those surviving today will claim they were few in number. I state the opposite, emphatically. Medication sold by medics—and I include doctors— was a way of life (and a means of sustaining their own lives) at O'Donnell. I know of numerous cases where soapy water was sold as medicine to unsuspecting prisoners in order to turn a profit. Survival at the expense of fellow prisoners became routine at O'Donnell and Cabanatuan, on "hell ships," and in every prison camp on the Japanese mainland or in Manchuria. It cannot and should not be brushed aside with the easy term of "relatively few." (Americans were not alone in such behavior; the same applied to Filipinos in O'Donnell.)

How many prisoners died as a result of their fellow man's greed and desire to survive at all costs will never be known, but a safe assumption is hundreds of men and perhaps thousands. American POWs continued to make a profit off fellow prisoners regardless of where they were held. Those fortunate enough to have money or the ability to obtain money lived that much longer and probably owe their lives to the predators.

Officers who had checking accounts in Stateside banks would pay their fellow prisoners for whatever food or medication they could obtain. Enlisted men who had the opportunity, denied officers, to be involved in "outside work details" charged exorbitant prices for items they brought back into camp at the end of the day. Food and medicines were soon made available to these men by the Filipinos living near the camps. They, too, were quick to "make a buck."

One enlisted man, in his own published book, admitted to leaving the Philippines for Japan with nearly $100,000 in cash and checks obtained in a period of six months. I have often wondered how good such checks were and if they were ever cashed after the war. Ironically, this one predator lost the entire amount while aboard a Japanese transport en route to Japan.

Shortly after the infamous "July 4th Party," I found myself among that group of approximately 400 American prisoners who had remained in O'Donnell being transferred to Cabanatuan. Left behind in early June when the major group of prisoners was transferred to Cabanatuan as a "service group," our job had consisted primarily of burying those who were too ill to be moved and subsequently died.

During my stay at O'Donnell—where I remained longer than 99 percent of the Americans held there—I never believed I would leave that camp alive. The suffering that took place there is beyond imagination. On one particular day a severe toothache almost drove me insane. Seeking any relief, I sought out what was supposed to be an American army dentist. He had absolutely no interest in helping me. Finding a friend who was willing, I allowed him to pull the malignant tooth out with a pair of pliers, sans anesthesia of course. The pain of the tooth was far worse than the pain of extraction.

As late as 1951, I still had parts of the tooth's roots surfacing to the top of the gum. At that time that I distinctly remember an army dentist giving me a dental examination for my commission as a second lieutenant telling me "you don't have officer's teeth," a reference to the dental condition brought on by my years of neglect as a prisoner of war. Needless to say I found that remark ironic, as I did not know officers had different teeth from enlisted men.

When it came time for me to depart O'Donnell, I would have gone anywhere to escape what I had witnessed for ten weeks. Others more fortunate than I, I thought, had left the camp for work details in other parts of the Philippines. Some of the other camps, I later learned, were just as bad as O'Donnell. Leaving, we thought we had escaped a death sentence. Well, for some this was true, but for the majority of Bataan men in O'Donnell it was just the opposite. Yet, boarding trucks for Cabanatuan, we were all very glad to escape the hell that was O'Donnell.

CHAPTER 13

CABANATUAN PRISON CAMP

Immediately after my arrival in Camp Cabanatuan, I was again assigned to either the grave digging detail or the burial party, carrying our dead to the cemetery. I assumed from this assignment that they were seeking "experienced people," based upon my duties in the previous camp. Within a month of my arrival, however, I came down with a case of dengue fever and a recurrence of malaria. Having had dengue fever before the war, I readily recognized that ailment's symptoms. While food was about as poor at Cabanatuan as at O'Donnell, I had no desire to eat, feeling as sick as I did. I was unable to eat for days. If I had had money I might have been able to buy "delicacies" from the "black market" flourishing in camp. Those of us without money were compelled to eat a watery substance issued three times a day known as lugao, a native word for watery rice. That "food" always reminded me of the gruel of the Charles Dickens classic *Oliver Twist*, with us saying "more please" whenever we had the opportunity. I unfortunately was unable to swallow this "food," and I began to physically go downhill rapidly.

Into my life came Charles Augustinelli of Pennsylvania. "Gus," as he was known to his few select friends, was in my barracks and foresaw my impending demise. Recognizing that I had to eat, Gus managed to obtain some extremely hot dried Filipino peppers. Dried in the sun, they became hotter than a jalapeno pepper of Mexico. Gus coaxed me into taking a bite, and when coaxing did not work, he forced the pepper into my mouth. Quickly finding my mouth on fire, I did anything to cool it off. I had taken only a small bite of that pepper and its incendiary effects were unbelievable. The lugao didn't taste half bad after that pepper. For several days Gus would literally force me to take a bite of the pepper, followed by an immediate downing of anything resembling food!

In a few days my health improved, and I am sure I owe my life to one Charles (Gus) Augustinelli. Soon I was back on the burial detail or whatever the American administration of the camp decided for me the next four months. During this period I witnessed an incident which, as an American soldier, I have always been ashamed of and which I have given considerable thought to over the years since the war ended.

Three American officers, one army and two navy, attempted to escape from our camp. We later learned that they were acting on orders received through the grapevine to attempt to escape. Their particular services were needed at home. The escape took place just outside my barracks, which was at the end of a row of barracks nearest the wire fence erected around the camp. At this particular point stood a Japanese sentry tower containing a Japanese soldier. On the inside of the fencing patrolled an American prisoner of war, placed on duty there by our American administration to keep watch over the inside of the camp. It must be pointed out here that this was in the early days of August 1942 when no restrictions on escaping had been placed upon any prisoner by American authorities. To escape from captivity, if possible, is the duty of every captured military person.

Sitting by the side of my barracks facing the fence, I noticed three Americans walk by outside it. Since the Japanese had posted signs warning prisoners to remain at least 25 yards from the fence, I felt that something was up. The three men shortly disappeared from my sight in the tall cogon grass outside the compound, and almost immediately I heard a loud outcry from one of the Americans patrolling inside the fence. His continuous cry of "halt" and "sergeant of the guard" created a commotion, and the Japanese guard in the tower also started calling. In a short while a detail of Japanese soldiers came running to the scene, seized the three men, and led them away.

That evening every American prisoner was forced to walk past the three, who were tied to individual posts, and made to strike each officer with a pole supplied by a posted Japanese guard. The failure of any American to strike a hard blow upon each of the three resulted in the Japanese guard hitting the reluctant striker. Dozens and dozens of Americans, unable to get away from that area, were forced to beat their fellow Americans. Soon all three men were bleeding profusely. After the last American in line had accomplished his beating, the Japanese guards, numbering a dozen or more, began their continuous beating of all three men. Those men remained tied to their poles for several days without food or water. When taken down, they were led into the tall grass area and a number of shots rang out. The officers were never seen again. Why any American would aid in preventing these escapes has always sickened me. Those men would not have been caught without the American guard, acting on American orders, sounding the frantic alarm.

This escape attempt led to a Japanese policy of "ten men death squads" for all prisoners. Each man was assigned to such a squad with the knowledge that if one escaped, the other nine would be put to death. Such escapes did occur and the Japanese carried out the executions of the other squad members. Lt. Kermit Lay was one of the first officers to have his men sign a sworn statement that if anyone escaped and caused the death of anyone else, that those signing the statement would follow through after the war to ensure justice. Lay's statement "if anyone of the second platoon, fifth company, building [no.] escaped and caused the death or punishment of any remaining members of the group, that individual responsible would be later apprehended at the expense of and efforts of the remaining members and punished by either army or civilian court as the group sees fit." These statements were then sworn to before a "G.B. Gross, Major, Infantry, Adjutant, Group II, American Prisoner Headquarters." A copy of a statement, dated 18 August 1942, may be found appended to this book.

Such "death squads" became standard in Cabanatuan while I remained there. The common expression of that time was "if you are going, let me know." The system however proved fairly successful as very few wanted to knowingly cause the death of others. Escapes did occur and men were shot as a result. On one occasion shortly after the attempted escape of the three officers, Japanese guards called the Americans to attention and had them turn their eyes toward the road that ran through the camp. Carried by a Filipino was a bamboo pole several feet tall, atop of which sat the head of a would-be escapee caught and beheaded by the Japanese.

What I have always remembered about my time in Cabanatuan was a beating that I endured there. Let me quickly point out that the beating was not administered by the Japanese but by a fellow American. It happened this way. Shortly after my arrival in Cabanatuan I met an old friend named Hinds who was assigned to the same barracks as I was. Hinds and I first met in a Manila bar during one of our payday "nights on the town." A very quiet, small individual, you would not know Hinds was around.

Shortly after our reunion in Cabanatuan, Hinds and I were sitting and talking when another prisoner came up and joined the conversation. Soon he began to deride Hinds for his missing teeth, knocked out by a Japanese rifle butt during our march out of Bataan. Hinds became upset and wanted to physically fight his agitator when I put my neck out and said "just consider the source, Hinds, and ignore him." The person to whom I referred said to me "For two cents I would knock your block off." Without a moment's hesitation I reached into my pocket and gave him two cents that I happened to have. He fulfilled his part of the bargain. Challenging me outside, he proceeded to "knock my block off" and I had to defend myself. I guess I forgot that I had just gotten over an attack of malaria and I was as weak as the proverbial kitten.

In addition, my opponent had just come into Cabanatuan from the hills, where he claimed to have been a guerrilla, but turned himself in rather than have the Filipinos do it for him. He had been well-fed and apparently was not sick. In addition to being in excellent health, it turned out he had been a professional prizefighter in Philadelphia, fighting under the name "Kid Lindy." I am sure that if the fight had not been stopped by spectators he would have beaten me to a pulp.

During the four months I spent in Cabanatuan I never failed to recognize a man captured on Corregidor as opposed to one taken on Bataan. Healthier and heavier than their fellow Americans from Bataan, it was usually this group who participated in the camp shows put on periodically. To have the energy to do so was beyond the capability of most Bataan survivors. Some Corregidor men had brought their musical instruments with them from the island. On top of this, most "good jobs" in the camp were filled by Corregidor men since they had arrived before Bataan men. Thus the latter, much more ill, were left to do the dirty jobs.

Kitchens in the camp had "bird colonels" (full colonels) acting as mess officers, a job considered so menial in peacetime that not even lieutenants were ever assigned to the task. Colonels, believing that "rank has its privileges" (RHIP in military jargon), took over the jobs of dealing the food out. One brazen colonel in charge of one of the mess halls erected a sign above the entrance: "Fitch's Kitchen quit your Bitchin'." Fitch was a full colonel who became a general after the war. I have to admit that one thing this general had was experience in running a mess hall in a prison camp. Not many generals could lay claim to the same talent.

It was not long before my malaria returned. Going to "sick call" (a misnomer if ever there was one), I found myself being treated by a Dr. Bleich from Buffalo, New York. (Bleich was to survive the war and, twenty-five years later, could recall our meeting.) This very honest gentleman was to tell me that no medication was available—this time it was true—and he recommended that I immediately apply for a work detail being formed to go to Japan. The good doctor reasoned that I might get lucky and find some medicine in Japan. He also opined that at least I would have a change of climate which might help me. (I can't believe he had any idea of how much of a "change in climate" I had in store for me.) Nonetheless he maintained that my chances for survival would be better in Japan or Manchuria as, in his words, "You are not going to make it here." I never questioned Dr. Bleich's advice, as I survived. But I often wonder how many of those he gave the same advice to eventually died of pneumonia in the mountains of Japan. Before leaving his care he did give me some ordinary charcoal for the diarrhea (dysentery) also plaguing me at the time. Surprisingly, the charcoal mixture worked and I only had malaria to worry about. Dysentery patients in camp were readily recognized by their black mouths, a result of eating charcoal from the kitchen fireplaces.

Following the doctor's advice, I sought out the officer assigned to gathering a detail for Japan. At that time however, I had no idea that the ship might go somewhere other than Japan. I later learned that a second shipload, put together at the same time, was destined for Manchuria. Apparently the Japanese were beginning to feel the pinch in manual laborers and were eager to get as many "healthy" prisoners aboard their ships as they could. "Volunteering" as I did was a welcome relief for the officer responsible for making up the roster. Most prisoners preferred to remain in the warm climate of the Philippines. Their unwillingness to leave the Philippines continued for the next three years. In the back of the minds of most was the thought that they stood a better chance at liberation by remaining where they were. Putting together such rosters often reminded me of the British Navy's "pressing" of men into service during the American Revolution. While the "reluctant" were correct in their assumption, all but approximately 500 prisoners were eventually shipped to Japan, Manchuria, or Korea. For those "pressed into service" to Japan who did not want to go, a trip to the hospital could usually produce a stool specimen from a dysentery patient for a small sum of money. This dysentery-infected stool was then offered as evidence of one's inability to go. This ploy generally succeeded in keeping them off the list in the early period of our prison life. The irony of such procrastination however eventually unraveled. Those leaving the Philippines in 1943 and especially 1944 lowered their chances of survival as a result of attacks by American submarines and airplanes which grew in strength and intensity with the passing of time. Many who deliberately staved off going to Japan or Manchuria earlier went to the bottom of the Pacific later when their ships were sunk. Almost five thousand Americans lost their lives this way.

Before leaving Cabanatuan on 30 October 1942 en route to Bilibid Civil Prison in Manila (a staging area for all prisoners going to Japan or Manchuria) I had my last opportunity to visit with my platoon commander, Lt. Henry Lee. He was one of the very

few officers who maintained his integrity, courage, and responsibilities to his men. Lee often gathered his men about him in an
attempt to keep up their morale. I know of very few officers who
could compare to him.

The saying "the good die young" is certainly applicable to Lieutenant Henry G. Lee, Infantry, U.S.A. Lee was among the last officers to leave Cabanatuan and he had the misfortune to be aboard
the ill-fated *Oryoku Maru* when it was sunk by American planes
from the U.S. carrier *Hornet*, after a previous day of constant strafing and bombing failed to sink the ship. Swimming ashore, the
survivors were assembled on the beach where they remained for
several days. On 27 December 1942, Lee boarded another ship,
the *Enoura Maru* which was sunk on 9 January 1943 in the harbor
of Takao, Formosa. Lee perished aboard this ship from bombing
attacks by American aircraft. Survivors of that bombing were placed
aboard a third ship, the *Brazil Maru*. Conditions aboard that ship
were so bad that the death rate averaged twenty-five to thirty men
a day. Of the 1,609 who had started from Manila, fewer than 300
arrived in Japan on 29 January 1943 after forty-eight days of con-
tinual horror from inside and outside the ship.

I ask the reader's indulgence as I repeat my reminiscences on
Lieutenant Lee. Lee was acclaimed the best poet to emerge from
World War II by the *Saturday Evening Post*, which eventually
printed all of his poems. Lee buried his poems prior to leaving for
Japan, and they were subsequently found when the 6th Rangers
liberated that camp 30 January 1945. Also buried with his poems
was our company history and three citations for men of the unit,
including me. Unfortunately the citation did not surface until 1948,
when Lee's father, Thomas Lee, obtained the will from the courts.
My citation was written on the back of his will. Attempts to obtain
the decoration failed when I was told by the army that the awards
board for that period had been disbanded and I would need cor-
roborating evidence to secure it. Inasmuch as three people were
present during the incident involved and two of them had died, I
never received the award. This has always bothered me because
Lee had told me of his actions and instructed me to follow up on
his recommendation. In a way I feel that I let him down. He was

the one man, during combat, that I was ready to follow anywhere.

For those who remained in Cabanatuan life slowly improved from late 1942 until the departure of the last group of prisoners for Japan. For the 511 prisoners who did stay behind it meant early liberation on 31 January 1945. Food supplies in the camp from late '42 on were augmented by an organized buying system from outside sources. It was increased again by Red Cross supplies that came into camp, along with Filipino help in the form of money. Life became very livable in the camp from all reports. I heard later that the death rate dropped dramatically with issues of food and medication. But what had just begun shortly before my departure soon developed into an unwanted situation: homosexuality. When the stomach is empty, food is of paramount importance. But once the stomach no longer craves food, a sexual appetite reappears in the young male. A medic at Dr. Bleich's "sick call" was the first alert I had that there was such a thing in camp. This Navy corpsman, known as "Queenie," was the talk of the camp. Obviously on better rations and able to secure the little medication available, Queenie was raring to go. From talking with Cabanatuan inmates who joined my camp in Japan in 1943 and 1944, I further learned that homosexuality was indeed rampant. A number of Queenies had surfaced in Cabanatuan.

Leaving Cabanatuan on 31 October 1942 with hundreds of volunteers and "forced volunteers," most of us were glad at the prospect of escaping the tropical heat of the Philippines and the diseases the islands had brought us. In a few hours we found ourselves in the city of Manila, home for some of us, with plenty of pleasant memories. Taken through the streets of Manila, we recognized many of our peacetime haunts. With this came the bitter realization of the depths to which we had fallen in less than a year's time. Our pride, like a pecan, took a severe beating that day.

We finally arrived at Bilibid Prison, an ancient civil jail used to incarcerate Filipino criminals. An old Spanish penitentiary, it had been closed before the war due to its deteriorated condition, and the Filipinos felt was unfit for human occupation. Reopened by the Japanese in 1942, the prison, located in the heart of Manila, became a prison for Americans. (In 1995 I had the opportunity to visit Bilibid. It was still in terrible condition and overcrowded with Filipino prisoners. It still had not been renovated.)

Eventually destined to become a hospital (a sure misnomer) for American sick and wounded, it had become a "starts area" for prisoners about to embark on prison ships for Japan, Manchuria, and even Korea. During my seven-day stay at Bilibid I was fortunate to have some dental work done, which allowed me to spend three years in Japan without the need for a dentist. During my stay in Japan I witnessed numerous prisoners suffer from toothaches so much that I blessed my good fortune at getting dental care at Bilibid. Those unfortunates with dental problems would resort to knocking their heads against a post to obtain some relief. A simple toothache with no relief in sight could make a grown man cry like a baby.

Upon my arrival in Bilibid we were informed that there was a dental clinic available for those leaving for Japan and that we should take advantage of it. I was shocked by what I saw upon entering the clinic. Transferred intact from Corregidor was a dental team of several officers and enlisted men. Dressing in starched white coats, they looked like they had just arrived from the United States. They were even wearing their clean navy uniforms underneath their coats, including ties! It was an almost unbelievable sight after experiencing O'Donnell and Cabanatuan. The Japanese, extremely conscious of their own special dental needs—and they had many— had transferred that dental unit intact to Bilibid. The dental team had complete freedom to function without any Japanese guards present. The equipment in that clinic was an even bigger surprise. One could easily believe he was back in a fully equipped army dental clinic, only in this case all the personnel were Navy, taken on Corregidor.

When my turn came, after a long wait, I was ushered into a (long unseen) dental chair and the dentist went to work. In less than the thirty minutes allotted to each patient he filled two teeth and extracted two. It felt as if I was on an assembly line. Needless to say I was more than appreciative of the work done. Leaving the clinic, I went to supper where, for the first time since my capture, we had meat on the menu. We had mutton soup that night. With the condition of my mouth I had a terrible time attempting to eat a very meager portion of the meat. For years after that, I remembered the mutton I had to give away due to my inability to chew. Attempting to swallow tiny pieces of mutton almost resulted in my choking to death. I could not even describe the taste, as my mouth had absolutely no taste. This turned out to be the only real meat offered me for the next three years.

In Bilibid, my group leaving for Japan was organized into sections of one hundred. Three American officers, one major and two captains, became part of this unit. The assigned major, Alan Corey, was one of the many reserve officers who had arrived in the Philippines just prior to the war. As the officer in charge of my group, he proved his ineptness at supervision on several occasions. I was destined to be under his command for almost two years. All of the prisoners headed into cold country that November had the common sense to ask for warmer clothing. At this point most of us were dressed in rags, with only remnants of a khaki shirt cut off at the elbows, khaki trousers cut off at the knees, no socks, and very little remaining of the laces in our shoes. While the major promised us warm clothing, he did not say where or when we would get them. He ruled out our request for better shoes, though the pairs we had were obviously worn through. In both camps we could usually find a better pair of shoes than those we were wearing by searching among the corpses awaiting burial. Those who did not found themselves almost barefoot, with toes often protruding out the front of the shoes.

The next day we boarded the *Nagato Maru*, an ancient freighter sold by the British to Japan for scrap metal in 1932. The Japanese placed the ship on active maritime service instead. Climbing aboard this ship, as we all watched him, was the good major, wearing a brand new pair of army high top shoes. He had mustered the courage to ask the Japanese for a pair of shoes, *one* pair! Of the three officers in our group, one, Captain Walter C. Hewitt, of Minneapolis, Minnesota, whose unit on Bataan was assigned to my unit, was the only officer with the courage to represent his men's needs at the risk of his personal safety. He paid for his integrity with the numerous beatings he took in the attempt to protect those men.

Ace Faulkner, another captain, was cut from the same cloth as Corey, with an absolute fear of the Japanese so apparent that the Japanese came down on him for no reason other than his fear of them. All three officers were transferred out of our camp in April 1944 to Kanose, Japan, along with the major part of our American and British personnel who had opened the camp in November 1942. The only one we missed was Hewitt.

Bilibid Civil Prison, after our passing through it, became a place of incarceration for many American amputees. Many other inmates however were malingerers who made their last stand against going to Japan or Manchuria by feigning illnesses that kept them off the sailing lists.

Commander Hayes, USN, author of "Bilibid Diary," commanded those in Bilibid for two years. He wrote of the problems concerning American military officers in that camp, and was disgusted by the breakdown of military discipline and the officers' self-seeking ways. He wrote "A person can get used to anything eventually. Man is an adaptable creature, and a most interesting animal when the veneer rubs off. With the outer coat of civilization gone, he lays open his inner structure. There are those among us who have covered their crudities of thought and base concepts of life with a thin filming of schooling and fine clothes. They have nothing but the shallow cloak of civilization to cover themselves and are sad, disgusting creatures indeed. The fine stock—how well they maintain their poise. Their nobility remains evident through ragged clothes and bewhiskered faces. No one can live among these half-starved derelicts and not appreciate the difference in mankind—I have never experienced such a study of man reduced to the lowest common denominator. I will remember it, think of it, speak of it, and write of it all the rest of my life…there are those who are so inverted that they have spent their whole life taking care of themselves. They fought the entire war along these lines, but why shouldn't they. They lived their whole lives doing the same damn thing—only war made them worse. It's the nature of the beast."

Unlike many prison accounts from World War II, Hayes does not emphasize the cruelty of his captors and the courage of the imprisoned. Hayes does try to present an accurate account of how men behaved under the conditions found at Bilibid and other prison camps of the Japanese. While Hayes had no love for the Japanese, in whose hands he died, neither did he for those Americans whose integrity evaporated in the face of hardship.

CHAPTER 14

THE 'HELL SHIP' *NAGATO MARU*

On 7 November 1942, we marched through the deserted streets of Manila in the early morning hours. Taken to Pier Seven, where in pleasant days we would come to see American transports arrive and depart, we saw two ships tied to the pier. One I later learned was the *Umeda Maru,* also headed for Japan. About fourteen hundred men boarded the freighter *Nagato Maru* with approximately the same number boarding the second ship. The ships were ancient by any standards, with wooden gangways leading to the cargo holds below. We descended into the belly of one cargo hold. Some men had to be carried down because of their poor condition. Soon, about one thousand Japanese soldiers, veterans of the fighting, came aboard. They of course remained on the upper decks. On the outer sides of the ships were little wooden huts, the "outhouses," which extended over the sides of the ship. These were for the prisoners' use—if a prisoner could make it to the deck. The sheds were so poorly constructed that they gave the impression they would soon fall off the ship. They had a slit on the floor to discharge the waste. The user had to squat, oftentimes while the ship was rolling in the ocean swells. Waves would often break over the ship and inundate the occupant. To gain entry one had to take a huge step from the ship to the hut. Two very weak prisoners using the facility never made it. They fell through the opening. It goes without saying that the ship never stopped to pick them up.

In the hold of the ship the heat became so intense while we waited to leave that men started passing out. Our ship remained tied to the pier until almost dusk that day. Men who could not make it to the main deck to urinate did so against the metal sides of the ship. The ship's hull was so hot the urine created steam. The stench of unwashed bodies and rotting vegetables lying about from a previous trip, soon sickened most men. Empty five-gallon gasoline cans were lowered by ropes to use for waste. Also lowered by bucket was water. Here again many were never to see the light of day during the entire trip, being unable to ascend to the deck. A number of men on that trip were destined to die from the ordeal.

I found myself on the lowest level, where mules and horses had been kept on a previous trip from Japan. The Japanese left these animals' straw bedding for our use, and the animal smell, coupled with extreme heat became almost unbearable. Regardless, we were happy to finally have a place to sleep, initially. To each bay, approximately twelve feet wide, ten men were assigned. Sleeping became a cooperative undertaking. Each man had to lie on his side until there was a general request for all to turn over. The hold, completely in darkness both day and night, became intolerable. Eventually a very long canvas chute was lowered into our hold, and when the ship finally got underway we had some fresh air "pumped" in. Men however, desperate to breathe, would gather about at the bottom of the chute, gulping in the air. Here again only the strong succeeded. The weak were unable to get near the chute. The sick who attempted to get close to the chute were pushed back by the strong. During the entire trip to Japan, I never saw an officer in that hold take charge and attempt to instill order. They were too busy with personal survival. Plus, I doubt they could have obtained any order among a group of men slowly going berserk.

To assist those too weak to climb to the top deck to use the "toilet" facilities, someone convinced the Japanese to provide buckets and some water. The strong took both over quickly, and the weak went without, as the strong drank all of the water, passing none back to those unfortunates who had to remain where they lay. When the water was gone the utensil became a portable toilet. One bucket the size of mom's floor bucket became the depository for over a hundred men in our bay. It was merely a question of time before it overflowed. Those sleeping nearest the bucket soon had the overflow splashing on them. Each man attempting to use the bucket would be cursed and kicked by those now covered with human waste.

Every morning and afternoon, the bucket would be hoisted to the top for disposal in the outhouses. In the early stages of our trip some men were allowed on top, if they could manage it, twice daily for their issue of pickled fish and rice. After our diet in O'Donnell and Cabanatuan the fish tasted very good. The small amount however, one small fish per man, hardly satisfied anyone. Getting to the deck was the closest to civilized behavior we experienced on the trip. Men could breathe fresh air without recrimination, and many risked the potential fall and visited the "outhouses." This "good treatment" lasted all of three days. The end of it was partially brought about by the behavior of the prisoners of war, without leadership. When some prisoners delayed going down into the hold and allowing other prisoners to come up in their place, the Japanese sentries grew angry and refused anyone permission to go on deck thereafter. Our two "meals" a day were lowered in buckets to us in the hold.

Americans given the job of parceling out food and water were not as fair in their distribution as the Japanese had been. Again the strong prevailed, and by the time the bucket of food was empty, many who were too ill to claim their share sat in the back of the hold and went without. Men would fight with each other to see who would stand nearest the air chute. It was just a question of time until men started to die.

During the trip five men in my compartment died. Each one was carried to the main deck and thrown overboard by fellow prisoners. I had the misfortune to help bury one man at sea. The body received no honors as it was unceremoniously dumped over the side of the ship. I did not see one clergy at the one "burial" I was part of, nor did anyone else mention seeing a clergyman. Yet there were a number of them on board. I like to believe that these chaplains were unaware of the burials, but somehow I cannot convince myself of that.

To my knowledge a total of thirteen prisoners died on our trip to Japan. I have read other accounts of this shipment, and one in

particular written in 1948 states that men died every day. The trip
was twenty-six days in duration. Also claimed in the aforemen-
tioned account was the statement that seven officers had been keeping food and water meant for all, and that all seven officers were
strangled during the night and the next day thrown overboard.
While several other holds contained hundreds of other prisoners,
that trip has been researched over and over again and there is no
evidence of such occurrences.

During the early days of our trip a siren sounded aboard the
ship. I was on deck at that time and heard the Japanese, all of
whom were agitated, yelling "Sensuikan!," meaning submarine.
Americans, who recognized the word and the agitation, soon began yelling, "It's a sub! It's ours!" About that time the single 75mm
gun on the deck began firing at something I could not see. Several
days before the sub was sighted, the Japanese had issued us life
preservers which were so old I doubted they would work. When
the sub alert was sounded, the Japanese chased all Americans off
the deck and gathered all the life preservers from the prisoners.
They then put those preservers onto the boxes containing the ashes
of their dead. The boxes were still sitting on the top deck when the
all clear was sounded. I was among those who climbed to the deck
and saw them. Their honored dead were being returned home at
all costs. It was evident the regard the Japanese placed upon our
lives was indeed small when compared to the reverence they held
for the ashes of their dead. That lesson stayed with me all through
captivity.

By now most of the prisoners were praying that a torpedo would
strike the ship and put us out of our misery. Things slowly went
from bad to worse. During the submarine scare, if there ever was a
submarine, many men tangled with those at the bottom of the air
chute in an attempt to climb up the chute in order to escape from
the hold. Others at the bottom would pull them down and try to
take their place, with others in turn pulling them down. Those
fortunate enough to be in holds above us were already climbing
the chute or making their way up the gangway. Japanese guards on
the main deck ensured that no one reached the top by clubbing
the prisoners with the butts of their rifles. As time passed and no

one heard, saw, or felt an explosion, sanity returned to the prisoner hold.

Several days after the submarine scare, the weather began to turn much colder. The stifling heat of the holds began to be replaced by bitter cold air making its way down the air chute. At this period of our imprisonment we learned how much warmth the human body can project when close to another body. Our first lesson in "body heat" had occurred, and it was to prove to be the only real source of warmth we would know in the Japanese winters ahead of us.

One day I was sent topside to work in a detail. Arriving on deck, I watched the waves come over parts of the ship and add to the ice already covering much of the ship. The old bucket we were on had great difficulty making its way through the heavy seas, creaking and groaning as if it were coming apart. On the deck were cauldrons for cooking rice and a smaller one which contained fish. The fish had been pickled long before our trip had begun. This was the fish given to us twice a day for about a week (I assume they ran out of fish after that.). The fish was about five inches in length and all of it was eaten, head, tail, bones, the whole thing. Fed twice daily, it was barely enough to sustain life. Considering these cauldrons supplied food for 1,400 prisoners and about 1,000 Japanese soldiers returning home, I would say we were lucky to eat. During this visit topside I witnessed three Americans being buried at sea who had died the previous night. Carried to the side of the ship in nothing more than filthy rags, once a uniform of the United States Army, they were dumped overboard as if part of the ship's garbage. No minister or officer said a prayer before their bodies were committed to the sea. Hardly a glance came from their fellow prisoners nearby. In the years to follow I watched newsreels and movies depicting such burials at sea, and could never fail to compare what I had witnessed to those Hollywood versions. There was no comparison between a civilized nation which had respect for human life, and the Japanese who had no respect for life let alone a prisoner of war's life.

After more than two weeks at sea (a trip of five days in normal times) we entered the harbor of Takao, Formosa, now known as

Taiwan. Many prisoners were removed from holds that held coal while the ship was refueled. Black coal dust was all over the ship. We were told by the Japanese that we were the first white men allowed to put into that harbor in thirty years. Formosa was one of Japan's super-military bases before the war. Attacks on the Philippines on Pearl Harbor day came from this island. Remaining overnight in the harbor, we saw anti-aircraft searchlights roaming the sky. Most of us were hoping for an air raid just to see the Japanese get a pasting, but nothing happened. In the harbor were white hospital ships with red crosses on their sides.

Three days later we left for Japan, but a storm caused the ship's captain to pull into a small island harbor. Storms had torn this little island to shreds, and very little vegetation remained. When we left the next morning the seas were still rough, but obviously the Japanese were in a rush to get to Japan. Of course, we too were in a rush to get off that ship!

After more than three weeks at sea we entered the harbor of Moji on the northern tip of Kyushu, near the city of Nagasaki. As we motored into the harbor, bitter winds swept the ship and the huddled masses of prisoners brought topside to disembark felt the cold that would be part of their lives for the next three years, if they survived. We arrived on 25 November 1942, the day before our American Thanksgiving. My twenty-first birthday passed aboard that ship, and I recall telling someone that "Today, I am a man." Someone added, "You became a 'man' long before this trip."

Stepping onto Japanese soil, I remember hearing "Gee, it's Thanksgiving back home." What irony! The only thing we had to be thankful for was that we were still alive, barely. But "still alive" for many prisoners was a questionable blessing, considering their condition. Like cattle, we were unloaded on a windy pier where we were sprayed with a disinfectant from head to toe by jabbering Japanese women. Everyone arriving there that day will always remember the bitter, bitter cold that swept over us. Forced to completely disrobe, we stood naked in front of the women, an added indignity!! Our bare feet actually stuck to the frozen steel part of the pier. The "little women" took rectal examinations from each of us. Nothing I have ever experienced in life was as dehumanizing as that day. Chattering like "a bunch of monkeys," an expression used by most of the prisoners, they completed their work.

Seeing Japanese women for the first time, our curiosity was aroused. But that's all that was aroused. While we understood very little of what they said, their actions were kindly. Japanese women are beautiful in my opinion, as I later learned. But on that day, wrapped up against the cold as they were, it was impossible to tell.

Once ashore, we suddenly witnessed several officers approach and form us into groups of one hundred. Where had these people been during the trip? Counting noses, they arrived at a total of thirteen dead from the trip. Thirteen very cruel deaths that were uncalled for, and with little compassion from their captors. For some reason, according to two American officers who arrived with us, 150 men taken from the ship were placed aside from the main body of prisoners. Obviously very sick and unable to keep up, they were never heard from again. No records of that group have ever been found. Nor did anyone with friends in that group ever see them again.

Taking a ferry boat across the Straits of Shimonoseki, we arrived in the town of Shimonoseki, where we began walking through the streets to the railroad station. On the way, huge crowds of Japanese, seeing Americans for the first time, gathered about us in a threatening manner. Old women and children began running alongside of us, taunting us and striking us with sticks, spitting on us and, in general, doing everything they could to show us their contempt. We were the first enemy troops to arrive in their city and the civil populace was out to express their feelings toward us.

CHAPTER 15

WELCOME TO JAPAN

Arriving at the railroad station after our freezing and humiliating ordeal at the docks, we encountered a pleasant surprise. A long line of railway passenger cars was coupled together awaiting our boarding. Most of the train was reserved for Japanese passengers, but several cars were set aside for transporting prisoners. Sitting on the comfortable seats far exceeded our expectations. It was just too good to be true. Surely this must be some kind of hoax. After our train nightmares in the Philippines, this was beyond our wildest dreams.

Darkness came and we finally got underway. To where, we had no idea, nor did we give this matter, in which we were utterly helpless, as much as a second thought. We were in Japan now, completely at the mercy of our captors to do with us what they wanted. Several hours later, while traveling through the blackness of the night (General Doolittle's air raid on 18 April 1942 was still a fresh memory with the Japanese and blackout conditions existed in Japan), we pulled into a railroad station crowded with Japanese, military as well as civilians. A number of our Japanese army guards got off the train and brought back numerous "bintos." These meal boxes, made out of balsa wood found in model airplane kits of that era, contained rice in the major portion of the box along with pickled seaweed, a pickled cherry, and a pickled miniature bird. The bird bothered us; the remainder excluding the rice was totally unknown to us, but we hadn't eaten in two days at this point so we wolfed it down, bird and all, with great gusto. The pure white rice was a delicacy in itself. It was the first time in my captivity that I had rice not mixed with another grain or water and bugs.

The lunch boxes best resembled an elementary school student's box that contained pens, pencils, rulers, etc. Vendor stands, similar to our hot dog stands, could be seen on the streets.

We traveled through the night and most of the next day, catching whatever sleep we could. Daylight showed us the beauty of Japan, which I have always admired. Late that afternoon, after being fed breakfast and lunch similar to what we had had the night before, we arrived in the city of Nagoya. We were ordered off the train, this most comfortable means of conveyance. Sitting not too far from our train was a group of single electric cars. Some Americans did remain aboard the "luxury" train and were taken to two other camps. My group, originally formed in the Philippines prior to embarkation, were placed in a single car, and we began the second leg of our journey.

After a while the train began to climb and we found ourselves headed for what we later learned were the "Japanese Alps." The countryside looked like the mountainous rural areas found in West Virginia or parts of North Carolina. The guards began dozing off, as they had been on duty since we were first placed in the train at Shimonoseki. Whenever the train stopped to pick up a few passengers, a hissing noise would pierce the air. Hats would be taken off and deep bows to the soldiers on guard would follow.

Several hours later, when completely black outside, the train stopped. No station or lights were visible anywhere. The guards began jabbering at one another and to one who appeared to be a train conductor. Apparently this was an unscheduled stop, as we were about to enter one of the many tunnels on our route. This particular tunnel, however, had had a snow slide on the other side and nothing was allowed to enter.

Inasmuch as it was about 10 P.M., many prisoners were asleep, glad to escape the reality of where they were. With loud "Kuras" (a Japanese shout to get one's attention), each prisoner was forced out of the train into the snow. It had snowed fairly recently, about ten inches on the ground when we detrained, and it was still snowing hard. The Japanese plan was simple. A second car would meet us on the other side of the tunnel. Hardly simple! We would have to climb a strange mountainside in darkness except for the lamps worn by the guards at the head of the line. Soon we became a lost group, with each prisoner instructed to hold onto the clothing of the person in front of him. Many lost their grip and wandered off, not knowing where the line was. They were lucky to hear their fellow Americans calling out to them and find the line again. It began to snow even harder. And the snow was blinding us all.

Somewhere on the mountain my legs, weakened by my illnesses, soon gave out. I lay down alongside the trail not caring whether I lived or died. The cold had become unbearable. Not one American that night had any clothing other than the short-sleeved shirt and trousers cut down at the knees that he had left the Philippines with. I soon found myself freezing to death. All I wanted to do was sleep. Almost asleep, I was roused by a fellow American. This apparently strong individual, later identified as Bill Standish of Chicago, Illinois, literally picked me up off the ground, stood me on my feet, put my arm around his neck, and proceeded to drag me up the hill. Releasing me there, he reasoned I could walk downhill. For that act of kindness that undoubtedly saved my life, I have always been grateful to Bill. Exceptional men like him must never be forgotten. Others were not as fortunate as I. Three members of that climbing group failed to reach the other side. They were left on that mountainside, never to be seen again. Undoubtedly they had frozen to death and were buried by the drifting snow until spring came, when some Japanese may or may not have discovered their remains. At the bottom of the hill's far side sat another electric car, which we reached about daybreak and I wondered why they could not have waited until daylight before making the ascent. I learned the answer when we arrived in our prison camp. Any delay would have caused the prison camp commander to wait for us, and he was the type no one kept waiting.

At this point, an incident happened which made me think it best to learn how to eat using chopsticks. While a fairly simple procedure, it does take practice. Eventually I became adept at using chopsticks and to this day am very comfortable using them when the occasion warrants. On that particular day however I could not pick up any food with my sticks and ended up using my fingers to wolf down the delicious food given to us. While doing so, a Japanese guard walked up behind me and hit me on the side of the head.

Not knowing exactly what I had done to incur his wrath, I went on to drink the green tea, also given us at the station. After learning Japanese customs a bit, I found out that my offenses of that day had been two. One: I used my fingers to eat; and two: I gulped down my food without "masticating" it. During my three years in Japan I repeatedly heard the Japanese admonition against eating fast. "You must masticate your food. Chew each mouthful twenty times." The Japanese seemed obsessed with care of the *hara*, their stomachs. It was not an uncommon sight to see a mostly disrobed Japanese male wrapped tightly in several layers of cloth to protect his stomach from the cold. As to masticating one's food, I had never heard that term before. I had heard an English word which sounded close to it, with a mischievous meaning, so this led to some confusion!

The train continued making its way through the Japanese countryside from Nagoya to Hiraoka. At each stop, hordes of Japanese civilians came to the car windows to get their first glimpse at the Americans whom they had defeated and captured. Despite some of Japan's military setbacks, up to that point the civil population had no idea what their enemies looked like. They were told they were winning the war and soon it would be all over. Some of these civilians entered the car containing myself and the other prisoners, looking for seats. Seeing a Japanese soldier sitting as our guard, they would quickly bow to him and make a hissing noise while doing so. We later learned this was a sign of respect civilians paid to any soldier they encountered. I never saw a Japanese civilian sitting, regardless of his or her age, who ever failed to get up and relinquish a seat to a soldier. The respect that Japanese civilians held for the military was amazing compared to our society, a respect that continued throughout the war and beyond.

Down the platform at one of our train stops, one particularly good vendor's stand intrigued me. Just outside my railway car window stood a vendor selling some type of meat skewered in a barbecue fashion. The aroma of this stand came close to torture. Still, the rice was the most pleasant surprise of all. From my initial capture I had tasted pure rice at only one time. That was in a tin warehouse at Lubao during the march out of Bataan. To be sitting in the most comfortable seat I had occupied since before the war began eleven months before, traveling through Japan like this, was difficult to understand. I later learned those vendor stands were extremely popular throughout Japan, and the aroma came from roasted chicken and pork. Beef was always a scarce commodity in Japan before, during, and after the war. The lack of land for raising cattle caused the Japanese to import much of their beef at a price that average Japanese could not afford.

Trying to rationalize this apparent act of kindness on the part of the enemy, we later arrived at a sage conclusion. This good treatment was for the benefit of the civilians watching us at every opportunity. The Japanese Army was showing how benevolent they were in their treatment of enemy prisoners. However, the Japanese civilian held nothing but contempt for the prisoners, as they exhibited at every opportunity. They had been made aware of the Doolittle raid, and who dared to attack their homeland? Yet, unbeknownst to me at that time, we had already paid for that bombing raid with vicious beatings to every prisoner held at O'Donnell.

But I want to go back to how I learned to use chopsticks. When I was first given my "box," I soon discovered that I had lost my only utensil: a soup spoon. I had lost all of my eating utensils on the march out of Bataan but I had obtained a tablespoon from a dead American awaiting burial in O'Donnell. However, for some reason the handle had been broken halfway down. Nevertheless, it had served me well as that was all I needed to eat with. Knives and forks were meaningless in prison camp, where meals were mainly liquid in form. Wondering how I would manage to eat without my spoon, I soon discovered that the box was complete. Turning the binto upside down, I found Japanese "throwaway" chopsticks. Each respectable Japanese always carried his own chopsticks in a carrier resembling a pencil case. Of excellent quality, they were never thrown away like those at the bottom of our bintos.

Chapter 16

MITSUSHIMA

Hours later our train pulled into a dingy railroad station high above the Tenryu River. While everyone ever held in this camp always knew it as Mitsushima, years after the war when I attempted to locate the camp through the Japanese government I was told they had never heard of such a town. I persisted, and eventually my search uncovered a town, Hiraoka, which turned out to be Mitsushima! In the summer of 1986 I had the opportunity to visit this town accompanied by the daughters of the last prison camp commander, Lieutenant Kubo. While there we went to the town mayor's office, where I was introduced by my Japanese women companions as a survivor of that camp from 1942–45. No, said the mayor, no American or British prisoners were ever held in that camp, "only Chinese." But the two daughters of Lieutenant Kubo insisted, "that cannot be, we lived here as young children and we know there were Americans as well as British in this camp." My presence obviously bothered the mayor and we shortly took our leave. Officially therefore, no American or British prisoners were held in that village during World War II. Another example of how truth becomes a casualty in war.

A check of American records of Japanese prison camps in that area also revealed no such camp. Our records did show a camp in Matsushima however. Upon reading a report on that camp it became obvious to me that Camp Matsushima and Mitsushima village were one and the same. A British prisoner of war who entered that camp in August 1944 had submitted a report after the war using the wrong spelling. The error remained on the books until the late 1970s when I managed to have it corrected. Before that happened I was challenged on my knowledge about the existence of the camp. My three years in that valley left a lasting impression, and I remember all too vividly Camp Mitsushima.

Mitsushima prisoner of war camp was located in central Honshu island and was situated on the eastern banks of the Tenryu River at latitude 35-55-00 north and longitude 1-37-00 east. The night we arrived we witnessed mostly old Japanese men and women scurrying about in their wooden "getas," Japanese wooden slippers which made a clacking noise as they hit the pavement. All through the war Japanese leather shoes were almost nonexistent for the civilian population. Only the military were ever seen wearing leather boots or shoes. Worn inside the "Tabi" were what appeared to be cloth inserts with a split between the large toe and the one next to it. These inserts provided some degree of warmth in the winter. Later we were issued what we called sneakers, which basically is what they were. Sneakers such as these were seen on dead Japanese solders in Bataan. Black in color and closed with two eyelets in the back, we thought then that they were sniper shoes. The split in the toe, we erroneously thought, enabled the sniper to climb better. These shoes contributed greatly to the suffering of the prisoners in Mitsushima.

Marching down the serpentine road from the railroad station to the camp hundreds of feet below us, situated on the rock bed of the river, we examined our future home beneath us illuminated by the prison camp lights blazing brightly. It was Thanksgiving back home, and all of our thoughts turned to those we had left behind and how we had shared that holiday with them in years past. Many felt they would never leave this valley alive, and for forty-eight Americans and British this proved correct. Running down the side of the mountain, often used as a shortcut, was a rail line for boxcars which were let down and retrieved by a cable. The cable broke on occasion and a boxcar would come hurtling down at an unbelievable speed. Men going to work at the railroad station unloading cement and supplies for the camp were forced to climb that incline every morning. In 1986 I discovered that one section of the rail line still existed. That finding brought back many, many memories of many trips up and down the incline.

Once inside the camp compound we again—for the hundredth time—were lined up in formation and searched in the bitter cold. Made to stand at attention, we waited for the appearance of the camp commander to 'welcome' us to the camp. This individual, Captain Nakajima, destined to be executed by hanging after the war, appeared well-fed. Climbing atop a box brought out for him (a scene painfully familiar to us by now) he gave us the usual speech we had heard repeatedly ever since our capture. "Americans and Japanese are eternal enemies.... We will fight you and win if it takes one hundred years...any attempt at escape and you will be shot." I have often wondered where they expected us to escape to? Only the river would provide an avenue of escape, and we had no idea where the river went. Later we did learn that it eventually ran into a much larger body of water, where a Japanese naval base was located.

After the "welcoming" remarks we were assigned to one of three barracks. The other two were reserved for additional incoming prisoners. In all the camp consisted of thirteen structures surrounded by a ten-foot wooden fence with nails protruding from the top boards. Three gates led to this compound but only two were ever really used. The main gate on the southern part of the compound was posted at all times by two or three guards.

The living barracks, approximately 18x75 feet and housing 120 prisoners, were built of one-quarter-inch wood and covered with shingles or tree bark. The interior was divided into three sections with an upper and lower tier for sleeping. Each individual was allowed an area of 30x72 inches for his quarters and storage of clothing. The floor was dirt and sand. As it was not properly drained, water in depths from 2 to 3 inches stood on the floor during the rainy seasons. During the winter, ice formed under the mats in the sleeping area. Prisoners would wash this area down on their day off work and rid the quarters of fleas, but ice would form before it could be properly dried out. These conditions persisted in the three winters I spent there, with no changes made or allowed.

To heat the barracks, a 3x3-foot fire pit was placed in the center of each section and a very small amount of wood and charcoal was allowed to be burned between the hours of 1700 (5 P.M.) and 2000 (8 P.M.). The wood supplied on an average day was ten sticks each about four inches in diameter and two feet long. Inasmuch as there were no flues to carry away the smoke, and as the barracks were inadequately ventilated, smoke became so dense that the prisoners' eyelids swelled to the point where they could hardly see. No dry sticks whether wood or charcoal were furnished even when the thermometer registered as low as nine degrees Fahrenheit. The guards always attempted to justify this action with the claim that some rule or other had been broken by someone.

A small amount of disinfectant given out during the last year of this camp's existence was allowed, but not in sufficient quantities to rid the camp its flies, fleas, and bedbugs. We would have "fly campaigns," when we would spend our rest hours killing flies and vermin to ease this terrible condition. Fleas were uncontrollable and rats were a constant source of worry. Located near the barracks was a small washstand with an overhead covering of wood. The stand, containing twelve spigots, was for washing one's face, clothing and dishes. No hot water was ever supplied.

Water, pumped into the camp from a well along the edge of the Tenryu River, was never fit for human consumption unless boiled. We did however have a small boiler which held about fifteen gallons. All the drainage from the town of Mitsushima entered the river a few feet from the well, which was thirty feet deep. Further upstream was a camp for Korean workers who used the river. Beyond them was a camp of Chinese prisoners of war who also dumped waste into the Tenryu River. Water was not always available and had to be carried in buckets from the river when the lines and pumps froze up.

Next to the washstand were two latrines (marked in English as "water closets," a British term for "toilets") located in a wooden building large enough to accommodate thirty men at a time. They were of the same type as those used throughout Japan. "Straddle trenches" are still found in rural Japan. (During a return trip to that camp in 1986, I had occasion to use the toilet on the train. It still contained a "straddle trench" which dumped the waste onto the railway track.) There were no drainage facilities. Consequently

waste had to be scooped out, and the accumulation was distributed onto the camp garden in 1944 and to the countryside as fer-
tilizer. Latrine openings were not covered, hence flies abounded
and maggots crawled around the building and into the living quarters.

For bathing one bathtub was provided, a boxy affair about 6x3x3
and heated by piping running along one end and fired by a small
fireplace. Cold showers could be had if one wished to risk pneumonia due to his weakened condition. Complete drawing and
"regulation of bathing," dated 29 December 1942, was written by
a Japanese guard whom we had nicknamed "Mush Mouth." He
was our first interpreter. Suffice it to say that a reading of this by
the prisoners generally provoked a great deal of laughter. "No singing is allowed…while taking a bath the observing officers must
call all to attention and one salute. When the saluting order is
given by the observing officer all men must stand at attention…etc."
Read today, the order is hilarious, but when posted on the bath-
room wall then it was dead serious business. One "observing officer" failed to call to attention when a Japanese appeared and was
beaten so severely that he later died.

The camp contained no "mess hall" as the military knew the
words. Instead each barracks was provided with three tables. In
order to eat the men either sat on their bunks or the dirt floor. The
food issued from a bucket, with one to each of the three sections
in each barracks, was a mixture of barley, rice, and millet. Of the
three, rice was the least provided. In fact, as the war progressed
rice became even more scarce, even to the Japanese. In the early
days of the camp we were fortunate to have carrot tops in a so-
called soup. After a while we would occasionally find vegetables
and beans. The most popular vegetable was the daikon, a radish
type vegetable which has only appeared in the U.S. in recent years.
The Japanese did everything with it. They boiled it, grated it, pickled it, and fed on it. In growing the vegetable they would oftentimes
pull it up slowly from the ground, then stop to allow it to continue
to grow. This produced a much larger daikon. I eventually came
to like daikons. Long after the war and to this day I will order
sukimo, or pickled daikon. I might add that the order in a Japanese restaurant usually produced some stares from the Japanese

since this is considered "peasant food."

Meat and fish were seldom provided. During the first two years I don't recall meat ever being in our food. As the war ran down there was some effort to provide a little of both. Unfortunately when "meat" was provided we would get the stomach and bones of cattle butchered in the area. Both the meat and fish would (in our minds) normally be unfit for human consumption, but it would be boiled sufficiently to make it palatable.

Medical conditions in the camp were the worst we had encountered anywhere in our captivity, if that's possible. Our first and only medic for the first year of the camp's existence was a Dutch-Javanese captured when Java fell in early 1942. This individual probably killed more prisoners than the Japanese through his total incompetence as a medic. Fearful of the Japanese, he would order men to work who were totally unfit. As a result they died. About a year after our arrival a British naval doctor captured at Hong Kong in December 1942 arrived, and he brought some semblance of order from chaos. Medicines were practically nonexistent, a condition that remained with us throughout the war. Enlisted men were required to work regardless of their health, as each contractor doing work on any project required a certain number of workers daily. Our project: build a dam to supply Nagoya and its surrounding area with electricity. I might add that the dam—while never operating during the war—is functioning today and is Japan's fourth largest hydroelectric source of power.

The day after our arrival we witnessed over two hundred British prisoners captured at Singapore enter our camp. While most belonged to the British Army's Surrey Regiment, the remainder were Eurasians belonging to Singapore's "Special Training Corp" (STC) of the Royal Air Force (RAF) also captured in Singapore. These men provided service as orderlies and did general work duties in which white RAF members did not engage. These men, all from mixed marriages, were Chinese, Portuguese, and Spanish in their ancestries.

For the most part these were fine men who showed a loyalty to one another that was hard to find in Americans. From this group emerged the best friend I had in Mitshushima, a black lad named

Cecil Fernandez. With his father a Portuguese seaman and his mother an Indian from Ceylon, Cecil was quite dark. His features were definitely Caucasian with a fine aquiline nose and narrow lips. Because of his skin color, he was resented by white prisoners, namely Americans. Our friendship was resented, again by Americans, and I was known as a "nigger lover" by some southerners. Racism was definitely a part of my military era!

My friendship with Cecil began the night that I experienced my first malaria attack in Japan, three weeks after arriving. When the chills began one evening, my fellow Americans either could not or would not help me in any way. Cecil, who slept in the same bay as I did but who hardly knew me, decided I needed to somehow get warm. With this thought in mind he went to the kitchen and placed a good-sized rock in the open fire underneath a cauldron being prepared for next morning's meal. Heating the rock for a long period of time he wrapped it in a burlap covering, brought it back to where I slept, and placed it under my blanket near my feet. While I wondered who the Good Samaritan was, I enjoyed the heat generated by the stone. Several days later I had overcome my malaria attack and, in asking who had helped me, I learned that a "half-breed black" had stepped up to help without even knowing me. I was immediately in his debt, and I vowed to help him whenever I could.

After settling into our daily camp routine I was assigned to the prisoners' kitchen as a fireman, responsible for keeping the fires constantly hot enough for cooking purposes. Shortly after starting this duty I developed a bad case of scurvy and smoke blindness from the green wood we were forced to burn. Scurvy was all over my lips and mouth, both inside and out. One night when the kitchen closed I heard a voice in Japanese offering me a "presento," the Japanese word for a gift of some kind. Unable to see, I reached out my hands and a bowl was put into my hands. The aroma told me it was food but with my poor vision I was unable to see what it was. While wondering why I had been singled out for this act of benevolence on the part of a "Japanese," I eagerly began to eat a dish, which turned out to be very hot Japanese curried rice. I had never eaten any curry dish before and the aroma was terrific. I soon found my mouth on fire, with the pain on the inside of my mouth beginning to mount. Despite my hunger, I spat it out and left the kitchen to the sounds of laughter coming from those who had given me the rice. Unable to see, I found myself making my way to my sleeping quarters by feeling along the walls of the buildings in between. My eyesight got so bad that I was relieved of my duties as a fireman and assigned to duties out of camp. I later learned that a fellow American named Jones working in the kitchen as a wood cutter had contrived with the Japanese in the kitchen to play a trick on a fellow American. This of course endeared him to the Japanese, with whom he curried favor. Jones and I were to meet again numerous times in Japan.

Verble Jones, a "southern gentleman" by his definition from Selma, Alabama, had been chosen by a buddy in charge of the prisoners' mess to work in the kitchen as a wood cutter. Since this type of work required considerable strength, he and two other cutters received extra rations plus what they could steal. Both their diet and exercise led to their being in excellent condition for most of the war, at least in the eyes of their fellow prisoners. Soon after getting himself in good condition, Jones became the camp bully. Nightly he would challenge American, British, Chinese, or Dutch to fight him with his announcement that he was "king of the camp." Jones had many fights. He lost none in three years. The British-Singapore group came to detest him as did the Americans who did not seek anything from him in the way of extra food which he obtained from the kitchen. He engaged in numerous fist-fights, and while the Japanese did not sanction the fights they did not prohibit them either. Since the fights took place in front of a barracks, Japanese guards on duty enjoyed watching the show. The fight would end when Jones' opponent, or victim, would say he had enough. Watching him I felt ashamed to be an American.

Shortly after regaining much of my sight I was elected "rice server" for the third of the barracks where I was quartered. Such an honor—and it was considered an honor—was bestowed only on those the group trusted most. Candidates for the position were nominated and those in that part of the barracks voted. Each breakfast and supper a detail of two men would obtain a bucket of grain

and a bucket of soup, with rations for forty men as prescribed by
the Japanese. In charge of the kitchen was one Kimura, who we
called "The Punk"—a detestable individual if ever there was one.
He eventually was hanged after the war, but I am getting ahead of
my story. The soup was colored with miso paste, a soybean prod-
uct, and carrot tops. Basically, with the addition of a few vegetables,
this was our standard fare for three years in Japan.

During my rice server term of office (we were elected for a six
month period), I would fill each prisoner's rice bowl placed on the
serving table and level off the top. All forty men in the section
would focus their eyes on my action. Under constant scrutiny I
would fill each bowl as evenly as the one before it. We had a system whereby any leftover rice or grain, after filling all forty bowls,
would then be distributed as "leggi," a Malay word meaning anything extra. A list was maintained and each man looked forward to
when he appeared on the top of the "leggi" list. One day when
Jones was off duty from the kitchen, and already fed at the kitchen,
he watched my issuance of the grain. He made the remark that I
was packing Cecil's bowl too tightly and showing favoritism to others. I called him a liar and challenged him to come down from his
perch atop the upper sleeping bay. He did, and we were soon squar-
ing off outside the barracks in a fight. In about two minutes—
which felt like twenty—he gave me a severe beating about the
eyes and nose. A kindhearted Britisher took pity on me and stepped
in, ending the fight. There may be a former British soldier named
Jock Webster running around in the United Kingdom to whom I
am indebted for stopping that fight. I believe I threw two good
punches before my arms felt like weights. I was a fool calling for
the uneven fight, which left me with nothing but bruised pride.

Shortly after my fight with Jones the Dutch-Javanese medic decided I was fit for outside work. So one cold January morning I
found myself attempting to climb the incline I had first seen upon
arriving in Mitshushima. My work assignment: the Igarashi cement contract to supply cement for the hydroelectric dam. Igarashi,
one of the largest employers of prison labor, usually had at least
forty prisoners assigned to him daily. His jobs were many. This
particular day we were to move fifty-kilo cement sacks from the

freight train sitting at the railroad station into a warehouse that bordered the station's platform. I was to work for Igarashi for three years, eventually as the *honcho*, or noncommissioned officer in charge of his assigned prisoners.

That first day outside I found myself in the "loving care" of one Japanese guard we had nicknamed "Snake." A more cruel, sadistic guard never existed. There were others however who equaled the Snake. I never knew his correct name, and as a result I never found out what punishment, if any, befell that deviate. Making no attempt to walk up the road we had come down on that first night, Snake had his forty prisoners take a short-cut up the incline used for boxcars coming down the hill and across the river. The cement incline, with railroad ties to support the tracks, had a grade of about 45 degrees.

Unable to use my legs fully, I was unable to keep up with the main group. Snake helped by striking me over the head and back with his sword, made out of wood. The only way I could possibly climb that incline that day was to grasp one knee with one hand, place my foot on the railroad tie in front of me, then switch hands and do the same with the other leg, placing that one on the next tie. It was slow going and Snake did not like my speed. Shouting "Kura" repeatedly, which means anything the guards want it to mean, he drove me up the incline. Each day that detail received the same treatment from the Snake with his shouts and beatings.

During my three years at Mitsushima I was amazed at the Japanese love for the stick as a weapon. Fashioned from oak and handmade to look as close as possible to the sword carried by officers and noncommissioned officers of the Japanese army, it was the nearest thing to a "badge" these rearline taskmen could ever hope to achieve. These sticks played havoc with every prisoner who came into that camp. The second "badge of honor" was their former army cap with its red star, or the navy cap with its insignia. During the first year of Mitsushima the regular Japanese Army controlled the prison camp with a few civilians who were former military, most of whom had been wounded. They eventually became even more vicious than the regulars, who were primarily very young and had not seen combat. It was merely a question of time before the high number of Japanese casualties required the regulars to move out to the front. They were then replaced by all these former military, all of whom had been wounded. Several had been wounded in the Philippines, China, Malaya, or at sea. Their wounds in nearly all cases made them even more vicious. We were the cause behind the loss of an eye, a leg, or an arm. In only a few cases did they hire guards who had had no service. One in particular was named "Buick" because he wore a Buick emblem from some prewar auto plant on his military-style cap. It was his "badge" since he was not authorized to wear a star on his cap. Buick was the equal of Snake in every respect. A physical reject because of his poor vision which required him to wear the thickest glasses I had ever seen, his viciousness was known to every prisoner. Snake and Buick were called the "gruesome twosome." Where you found one you found the other, and the best word to describe them both was "sadistic." They reveled in seeing someone hurt or bleeding, and their greatest accomplishment was to knock an American or Britisher off his feet. Early in captivity Allied prisoners learned to fall down as soon as the first blow landed. John Wayne and other Hollywood figures would probably have stayed on their feet. Some prisoners attempted this, naturally. They soon learned that this made the Japanese only more furious and determined to knock them down. An immediate fall brought a grunt of pleasure from the Japanese, who left the scene bragging about what he had done.

As time passed and my legs became stronger, I enjoyed working outdoors except in the bitter cold of winter. Then, we never could get warm.

Assigned almost constantly to the cement detail, I became friendly with the Japanese contractor Igarashi. A well-intentioned Japanese who never mistreated a prisoner, he lived on one side of the valley in a small house and had me do all sorts of jobs for him which allowed him to give me extra food. During a heavy rainstorm prisoners would go back into camp, where they often worked harder than they did outside on a work detail. For inside, they were constantly harassed by the camp guards and beaten for little or no reason. During such inclement weather Igarashi would have me report to his house for work assignments.

One time I was to report to the railroad station and pick up a hundred-kilo bag of rice for Igarashi's Japanese civilian employees. My first such assignment taught me a great lesson. We often watched Japanese women carry heavy loads that to us were unbelievable. I even saw a woman carrying a scale used to measure everything heavy, and I wondered how she did it. The answer was simple. Japanese laborers used what we came to know as an A-frame. This frame is strapped to the bearer's back with part of the frame flush against the back and another section protruding at a 45-degree angle, or an inverted A. The bag or any other item to be carried would be placed in the "crotch" of the frame and the carrier would bend over far enough to support the weight with his or her back. On my first attempt at carrying a bag of rice for Igarashi, I ended upon the ground unable to get up with a large crowd of Japanese laughing their heads off at the sight. After they helped me get up several times, each new attempt put me back on the ground. I finally learned that the secret was to bend over as the frame was loaded and to never stand erect until it was unloaded.

Each bag of rice that I carried to Igarashi's home would bring the reward of a pure white rice ball, oftentimes covered with sweet red beans known in Japanese as "mami." Igarashi's daughter, however, was an added inducement to making the long grueling walk with that sack of rice. A most beautiful girl about seventeen years old, I often enjoyed her company as we sat on the steps leading to the house, talking as best we could. She spoke some English learned in school and taught me quite a bit of Japanese. All in all she was a wonderful girl I could have grown very fond of given different circumstances. Terribly frightened of the guards in the camp, she would run away if she saw any of them crossing the bridge directly below us. As she explained it, she would have been punished had they seen her talking to me. Shortly after the war ended she married a local lad, according to her father, whom I managed to stay in contact with for a number of years until his death.

Igarashi was another victim of the war. While disliking all prisoners of war as enemies of Japan, he soon discovered he had no reason to dislike us personally. He and I would sit and talk about democracy and the United States from time to time. In talking to him however, I had to utilize what Japanese I knew plus his daughter's help in translation. Eventually, as a sergeant, I was given responsibility for the forty-man detail and permanently assigned to Igarashi. He had asked for me and the Japanese administration agreed. That assignment kept me in Mitsushima for the remainder of the war. As Igarashi's *honcho*, Japanese for a work supervisor, I found myself responsible for those forty men both in and out of camp.

Igarashi's main duty was to provide cement without any delays in accord with his contract. On the occasions we unloaded cement from the train into the warehouse, we could escape the frigid weather to some degree. Eventually we built the stacks of cement so high they almost reached the one hundred foot ceiling. This warehouse was so huge that later in the war, with tons of cement stored, we actually built a makeshift oven there to bake bread from a mixture of stolen rice pounded into a flour-like substance and mixed with water. As rice was unloaded from freight cars at the station, a prisoner would take a hollow bamboo reed with a sharpened point and insert it into a sack of rice. A makeshift bag, placed inside the shirt or trouser would be the final resting place for the rice pouring out of the bamboo chute. Never stealing too much for fear of being caught, we took some every time we had the chance. Sometimes we brought it to the makeshift oven in the warehouse and other times smuggled it into camp. Searched every night as we returned to camp, the ingenious rice packets were never found.

Never at any time were the Japanese without abandoned stocks of proper clothing for their prisoners. Large supplies of British uniforms awaited us on arrival there. Our warehouse was always filled with clothing items meant for us, yet the army feared allowing civilians to see us well-dressed. Putting chinos over our uniforms led the Japanese to believe that they were clothing us adequately. Shoes were the biggest problem. South African army boots were brought into camp through the courtesy of the Red Cross at the camp's opening, only to remain in the warehouse for the duration of the war. The issuance of these hardy, tough, hobnailed shoes would have saved a number of lives. Again, not having leather shoes for themselves, excluding their army, the Japanese would not allow such shoes to be seen on us by civilians.

To avoid having any prisoner wearing such magnificent boots, the Japanese issued rubber sneakers, or tabis as they became known. These tabis, used by Japanese in almost every civilian occupation during the war, were meant for the small feet of the Japanese. Prisoners with much larger feet couldn't force them inside tabis.

Our Japanese supply sergeant, Tatsuo Tsuchiya, who escaped the death penalty at the end of the war, had lost his right eye in the Philippines. He issued pairs of tabis to prisoners requesting foot cover. If a POW had a foot size ten or larger he was in deep trouble. "Little Glass Eye" as Tsuchiya was known, firmly believed that no one should look a gift horse in the mouth. Whatever size he issued was to fit, no complaining. I made the mistake of saying my tabis were too small. Little Glass Eye proceeded to beat me over the head with his wooden "saber" for my impudence in asking for a larger size. Eventually the size he issued "fitted perfectly." I had learned that complaining not only accomplished nothing but only brought on worse afflictions.

It was not an unusual sight to see a prisoner walking around camp with his feet wrapped in burlap for fear that a beating awaited him if he dared ask for a pair of those boots, which were buried in the camp warehouse, or for a pair of tabis that would come close to fitting. Every morning many prisoners went on work parties which required them to walk through tunnels built to allow box-cars to come and go the entire length of the work area. These tunnels constantly dripped water, and in the winter ice formed on the tracks and ground. Walking through a tunnel one winter day on my way to Oiwa's blacksmith shop down the river, I watched big-footed Americans and Britishers walk through the ice with their feet covered only with parts of a gunny sack from the kitchen. Unable to obtain shoes that fit them they had improvised. Unfortunately the gunny sacks soon became saturated and covered with ice. Several of these men came down with pneumonia and eventually died as a result. To me this was plain murder. Years later I had the pleasure of telling Little Glass Eye just that. Small retribution indeed for this merciless individual.

Despite these hazards in the tunnels, British soldiers would march through them singing songs unknown to us Americans. For the first time I heard Vera Lynn's hit song back in England, "We'll meet again," and "When the lights of London go on again." On one of these morning marches I heard the British soldier's version of "Bless them all," quite different from this soldier's bitter perspective as anyone can imagine.

The cruelest part of the needless illness and dying that resulted from the lack of footgear was that lifesaving supply stored in the camp warehouse: South African army boots. These, if issued to us when we first arrived, would have lasted us the length of the war in that camp. In 1991 during a trip to Japan, I asked Little Glass Eye, "Why did you not issue them?" He gave two reasons. One, we would hurt ourselves slipping on the boulders along the river, and two, "we were saving them, for when you went home." Oh, sure. Tell that to the Marines! The truth was that the Japanese did not want civilians to see us in better shoes than they had, pure and simple. I am sure that the shoes in the warehouse were put to good use during that first winter after we left the valley at the war's end, even if the boot sizes were too big for Japanese feet.

Several months after we arrived in Mitsushima word passed through camp that the International Red Cross was going to pay us a visit. Amidst a hurrying and dashing around the camp, mainly on the part of the Japanese, we suddenly discovered that we had a canteen. It wasn't there one day, but there it was the next. Not too well-stocked as one might expect, but a canteen nevertheless. We felt things were on the upswing. We had no money but had been promised we would be paid for our labor on the dam. Alas, the Swiss representatives paid us a visit, but if they could have come back ten minutes after they left, they would not have found that canteen. It was gone pronto! Things were back to normal with the Japanese. One good thing did come out of that Red Cross visit. A group of musicians were allowed to play for the benefit of the Red Cross. Instruments in the camp courtesy of the Red Cross were given to prisoners who could play. From that point on some effort was made to hold a monthly musical get-together. Only the British attempted to introduce this relief from the utter misery in our everyday lives. The American prisoners showed little if any interest. They were morale boosters however, and I found myself joining a singing quartet of Americans. One British civilian, previously a government official in the Marshall Islands, Pinky Williams, was always putting a show together. Pinky was constant trouble to the Japanese, which is why he was the only civilian held in our camp. His cheerfulness was contagious.

Our existence in Mitsushima began with the issuance of orders from the Japanese as soon as we arrived. All men were to work. Officers who refused to work would be fed less than those who did. Work details would leave camp for their assignments at 7 A.M. and remain at work until 5:30 P.M. before returning to camp. Work weeks would consist of ten consecutive working days. Work details canceled because of extremely inclement weather would be considered a day off. The day off was to be considered our "Sunday," or in Japanese a "yasume" day, a day of "rest." But any days off brought more misery than rest.

Discipline was severe for any insubordination or failure to salute properly. The salute must be in accordance with Japanese army regulations. Our first two weeks in camp the Japanese military conducted forced attendance classes for what we in the U.S. military would call "close order drill." Here soldiers learned the fundamentals of saluting, marching in units, and turning their eyes to salute a Japanese standing on the side. This usually came about as the work detail marched in and out of camp, with the Japanese officer of the day on duty taking the salute from the group. All commands for such "army" training had to be learned and given in Japanese when necessary. When a hand salute was not practical then a proper bow, with the emphasis on proper, had to be given. Westerners hated the very act of bowing. It went against the grain to have to bow. The Japanese soon learned this and insisted on prisoners bowing. During one lesson given by a Japanese guard nicknamed "The Bird," or more properly "Watanabe," to Dr. Alfred Weinstein, the American surgeon who entered our camp in October 1944, I witnessed Watanabe strike Weinstein repeatedly for failing to bow properly. Weinstein must have absorbed at least fifty blows from Watanabe that day. Apparently The Bird did not like Weinstein. He had met the doctor in another camp before Mitsushima. Many Americans and British have memories of the beatings they suffered for failing to bow correctly, including me.

On the so-called day off from work, prisoners were expected to clean their clothing and living quarters as well as the barracks until everything passed inspection of all the guards on duty that day. Personal clothing had to be stacked on shelves above one's sleeping space. Improper stacking brought beatings. Pieces of flat wood had to be inserted in each item of clothing, with each piece piled atop another, and all had to be in a square formation. This was required of all Japanese soldiers, and they expected no less from us.

All instructions to prisoners were in Japanese or translated by a Japanese soldier masquerading as an interpreter who spoke very poor English. Our first interpreter, known as Mush Mouth, was a corporal in the Japanese Army. His English was so bad that very few of us ever knew what he was saying. He wrote better than he spoke, and one had to assume that was the primary reason he was given the job. Eventually he left when the army moved out and was replaced by an American of Japanese descent. Before he left however Mush Mouth beat a number of people, several of whom died as a result. He was tried after the war and executed. In early February 1943, Mush Mouth posted batheing (sic) instructions in the massive tub, and we took our first bath in many months. In my case, my last "bath" was a washcloth bath in a river we crossed walking out of Bataan in April 1942. The sense of warmth, for the first time since we entered that camp, pervaded our bodies. What a wonderful sensation! Even if it meant taking a bath with forty other men! Of course, the rules were violated due to ignorance of what was wanted from us, and men were again beaten. Mush Mouth had some strange rules.

That first winter, November of '42 to April of '43 has to be the worst winter of my life. Men diseased, sick, and hungry, without medications or a trained medic, struggled to stay alive. Forty-four prisoners of war died during that period. While nearly all had entered camp suffering from some disease, their deaths could be directly attributed to the treatment accorded them by the Japanese. Their captors' failure to provide proper clothing, shoes, food, medicine, and housing, aided by the severely harsh punishments accorded every prisoner, led to their demise. Camp records were falsified and entries indicating death due to pneumonia were substituted for plain murder. The details of this inhumanity were brought to light in the Yokohama trials of 1947.

Just getting through the day was a constant challenge to every prisoner at Mitsushima. Because of its location high in the "Japanese Alps" in Nagano Prefecture, about 7000 feet above sea level, winters were especially brutal and lethal. Many men died in the winter months due to a mental state brought on by their low morale. Morale reached rock-bottom during every winter there. Our greatest concern every second was how to stay warm.

While I had not developed the need to shave daily at this point in my life, the Japanese insisted upon a clean-shaven face. Each winter morning in very poor light, every man was expected to line up at one of the five bowls in the washstand and do their morning ritual of attempting to shave using freezing cold water and any blade available. Any kind of scraping action and I was clean-shaven! Winter nights however were the worst. We were issued four Japanese army blankets so thin one could literally see through them. Sleeping on a wooden platform, either on the bottom of a bay or on the top, we had a rice husk mat about a half inch thick. Something similar to this mat could be found in Japanese homes but they were much thicker and provided some back support. They did not rest on a wood platform as in our case. Sleeping on these mats was not conducive to a good night's sleep. I don't recall one single night's sleep that was ever a complete sleep. Between the guards constantly awakening us for one false reason or another and mother nature's frequent calls to urinate, sleep was difficult. On average each prisoner had to make four or five calls to the "banjo" every night. This was due to a bladder irritability caused by a vitamin deficiency.

To reach the "banjo," or toilet, one had to dress completely, or if only partially dressed, endure the wrath of a guard who caught you. If apprehended, the guard (most likely "Buick" or the "Snake") would hit the violator with his fist or a bamboo pole and then stand him at attention for hours. In my case, sleeping on the upper level made dressing completely even more difficult without stumbling on those sleeping. Whenever this happened, it always prompted a curse from those stepped upon. Down from my bunk and past guards looking me over for a violation, I then went into that horrible building called a toilet with its foul odors and maggots crawling all over the place. Many prisoners too ill to squat over the open slit of the toilet often fell and needed help to rise. After each trip to the toilet one had to return by the same route, with the usual sadistic guard watching for violations. All this at two and three in the morning.

Each night some prisoners were required to stand a fire watch. Men selected had to stand guard in the barracks for one-hour stints. The Japanese had a terrible fear of fire, attributed to the many fires that engulfed their wooden towns and cities of that era. When it came to our barracks I always wondered, why their fear? No stoves or fires were burning within the buildings. By 9 P.M. each evening any fire in the fire pits was long since extinguished for lack of charcoal. Those fires never produced any real heat for the barracks anyway. Instead they succeeded in smoking up the entire living area as there were no flues inside the buildings. Smoke rising to where I slept caused me nothing but watery eyes and chronic coughing.

To sleep warm and avoid frostbite in temperatures ten and twenty degrees below freezing, we devised a method of sleeping together to maximize the heat our bodies produced. Two or three prisoners would pool their blankets into bedrolls which we referred to as "French whores" or "Russian whores" depending upon how they were folded. That system really made a difference in keeping warm. Of course these sleeping arrangements displeased some of the guards, who would beat those huddled together for warmth. The positive side of sleeping on top side was there was less chance of being discovered sleeping in such huddles. Those sleeping on the lower level had to determine who the guards on duty were going to be before attempting to huddle together.

Fires were permitted by the Japanese according to the calendar, not the weather. One incident involving Frank Brancaticano, an Italian-American, is a shining example of the Japanese mentality on the topic of fires in the barracks. Frank, who knew very little

English, had the misfortune to misunderstand Little Glass Eye's poor command of the English language. On this very cold first day of Spring, according to the calendar, in 1944, Little Glass Eye came into the barracks where we were enjoying a day off from work. Seeing us huddled around the charcoal pit, he screamed to put it out, stating, "Today is Spring, I prove to you!" He pointed to March 21 on the calendar, which had "First Day of Spring" on it. In poor English, Frank said something to Little Glass Eye, who thought Frank was making fun of him. He asked Frank, "Are you a fool?" Frank thought he had been asked if he were full in an eating sense. Frank responded "No, I'ma not full." Frank received one of the worst beatings I had ever seen a prisoner take when Little Glass Eye ordered him down from the top level and beat him severely in front of all those in the barracks. Days later, when Little Glass Eye had cooled down somewhat, we tried to explain what had really been said, but he accepted none of it.

Every enlisted man, excluding those the Japanese had officially declared as ill, was compelled to work. The camp commander had said on opening night "no work, no food. Japan is in a struggle to survive. You must work hard." Assigned to Japanese contractors Igarashi or Oiwa (blacksmith shop) or Iwatia (general laborers) or Kamijo (machine shops), each prisoner became known to his contractor over the time spent in Mitsushima. In many cases genuine friendships were made. These contractors undoubtedly saved a number of lives by attempting to make the lot of the prisoners life a little better when at their work site. When the war ended each contractor showed up at the camp to give gifts to many of their "employees" (prisoners). Lined up each morning and evening, each detail began to assume the identity of its contractor. Contests often developed between the contractors to see who had the best group of workers. There was never any real animosity between those civilian contractors and the prisoners. Oiwa, the contractor in charge of the blacksmith shop, knew that the work there demanded a great deal of strength from the prisoners.

During a lull in cement work I was assigned to Oiwa as a hammer man. Three prisoners were required to swing twenty-pound sledgehammers in the forge area. A small but extremely strong

Japanese, whose very bad eyesight had kept him out of the service, stood in the pit and held the forging tools while the prisoners, keeping a constant pace, brought their hammers down on the article being forged. We called the Japanese "Muscle Brain," for brainpower was not his strong point. Overhearing the prisoners calling him by that name he asked what it meant. We told him, in Japanese, it meant strong brains. He was never anti-American. Manpower shortages eventually caught up with Muscle Brain and he was called in to the army. To keep his prisoner laborers strong enough to swing such a heavy hammer continuously, Oiwa supplemented our diet with pure white rice. What a delicacy! I hated leaving that detail as it was warm all the time and there was extra food.

CHAPTER 17

LEARNING THE LANGUAGE

L ives lost and beatings absorbed could have been reduced had any officers in the camp, especially that first winter, assumed the leadership role the United States Congress had imposed upon them, and had any of them required that their men take lessons in basic Japanese. Because this did not happen all in camp suffered.

Officers, British and American alike, were more interested in staying alive themselves. One American officer, Walter Hewitt, showed signs of being an officer. The Japanese made sure he was soon shipped out of camp. The other two American officers left did not have any backbone whatsoever. To stay alive was their sole concern and for that they would do anything.

Captain Alfred Weinstein, Medical Corps, summed up the behavior of most prisoners in his book *Barbed Wire Surgeon* when he wrote, "Does man continue to love his brother when steeped in disease, chronic starvation, and death? How low in animal-like behavior can man sink and still revert to manliness?" Weinstein saw prisoners of war and their lives as "a tale of mankind with his veneer of civilization stripped away." No better words were ever written to describe the behavior of most American prisoners of war held by the Japanese. I saw less of this behavior among the British prisoners. I cannot speak for the other nationalities. The heartless actions of my fellow American prisoners are what I remember most fifty years later. To this group as a whole I cannot extend my hand in friendship. Memories of their self-serving behavior will stay with me until I die. In gatherings of former prisoners of war I see men who meet and greet each other as though they had been lifelong friends. This leaves me with an impression of artificial friendliness and shallow insincerity.

While Japanese is a difficult language to learn, counting in Japanese is fairly easy. One can easily learn to count up to one hundred and above using similar words over and over. For example, to count to ten in Japanese you say *ichi, ni, san, shi, go, ruku, sichi, hachi, qu, ju*. For eleven and up, one merely starts over again using the word *ju* (ten) tied to *ichi*, or *ni*, or *san*, and so on. Thus, *ju-ich* is eleven; *ju-ni* is twelve, etc. The same applies to twenty (*ni-ju*), thirty (*san-ju*), forty (*shi-ju*), etc. At one hundred the word *hyaku* is used. The counting can then start all over with *ni-hyaku*, *san-hyaku*, etc. Most prisoners, mainly Americans, felt it was disloyal or unAmerican to learn the enemy's language. It went against their grain. Their rationale was that by learning the language we were selling out to them, or, "who wants to learn the slope-heads' language?" As a result many died and many more were beaten needlessly because of this idiotic attitude.

Being appointed a *honcho*, a position given American and British noncommissioned officers, meant that each such appointee was responsible for the actions and behavior of his group. One cold winter evening, with a raging snowstorm outside, we were permitted to hold our evening formation (*tenko*) indoors. *Tenko* was considered by the Japanese a group formation to honor their emperor. It had to be treated in that fashion by all concerned and carried out with flawless precision. Normally *tenko* was held every morning and evening on our parade ground for the primary purpose of counting the prisoners and to impart any orders from the camp commander. At each formation the Japanese officer-of-the-day (OD) and the prisoner officer of the day, would approach each work detail and expect a smart, military, crisp report from each detail's *honcho*. To compensate for those who would not or could not count in Japanese, as sergeant I provided the individual with his number in Japanese. After that I would report in Japanese to the OD how many men I had in my group, how many were missing, and where they were when this group was in formation. After the completion of the report I would bark out *bango*, or count off in Japanese. The counting off then had to be in rapid, machine-gun-like, staccato barks. Any slow counting or giving the wrong number would result in the entire group being punished, beginning with the *honcho*. The system worked, initially.

When the formation was held inside we avoided inclement weather, but on this particularly snowy night it brought us disaster. This night, Little Glass Eye was the officer of the day. As usual we had given the numbers in Japanese to 120 men in that one barracks, just as we had done on a number of previous inclement weather indoor *tenkos*. This time however, Little Glass Eye decided to come in by the barracks back door. I ran to the back of the barracks, with my heart in my throat. This had never happened before and I knew that the men at the back of the barracks did not know their proper number. I then reported the usual information and yelled *bango!* What happened is what I expected: a disaster. The count went successfully for the first three or four numbers, then hell broke loose. We heard, in Japanese, one, two, three, six, five, etc. The men not knowing their numbers were compelled to guess.

With a total look of disbelief Little Glass Eye shouted, "Nanda?" Loosely translated that amounted to "what the hell is going on around here?" "*Mo iki* one more time!" Glass Eye yelled. Again, a total foul-up. With another yell of *bagaro* or "crazy," Little Glass Eye blew on his ever present whistle to summon help. Feeling he had been made a fool of, Glass Eye ordered us all outside. It was 18 degrees and we were not permitted to take warm clothing with us. We were lined up at Japanese attention position, which is far more rigid than the American army attention. This meant you were not allowed to twitch a muscle. Fingers had to be absolutely stiff alongside the legs. The backbone had to be completely stiff. In this position we awaited what was coming next.

Strands of rope dipped in ice water in a firebox outside the barracks were given to each guard by the OD. Every guard then began striking each prisoner across the face, already frozen by the weather. At each stroke skin would break from the impact. The beatings in this manner were applied to every man in our barracks. In addition, the guards were striking prisoners in a frenzy.

This lasted for almost one hour. To punish us further, every man was forced to stand at attention the entire night. Those who fell down or moved from their rigid attention were kicked into insensibility.

With the coming of dawn we were allowed to enter the barracks and put on warm clothing, and then were marched off to work without our morning meal. All that day wherever they were working, American prisoners received the brunt of Japanese anger by being beaten again by guards not on duty the night before. As a result of that brutal night three American prisoners died from pneumonia in a matter of days. No attempt was made by any of our officers to aid us that night. I am sure their efforts would have been in vain, but from a morale point of view their credibility as officers would have been enhanced. Their failure to appear or even protest the treatment, further widened the schism between officers and enlisted men. After this incident one would think that all prisoners would make an effort to at least learn to count in Japanese. Not so! Americans are a stubborn lot, as are the British. Every roll call (*tenko*) indoors from that point on was a cliffhanger.

Case after case continued to surface where a prisoner—unable to understand even fundamental Japanese—was severely beaten and often died from his injuries. During that first winter of 1942–43, Japanese army personnel in that camp were at their worst. With nothing but victories on the war front to brag about, most of which were propaganda, like all of us they believed what they were told. After all, didn't MacArthur promise us that "relief is on the way"? We believed so. Why wouldn't the Japanese believe their own? In the meantime the average Japanese soldier, positive of the war's eventual outcome, became more vicious with each passing day. The slightest provocation would be grounds for immediate punishment.

From inadequate food, freezing temperatures, and constant and brutal harassment by the Japanese, illnesses increased at an alarming rate. Men began to lose hope of ever seeing the war end. It was fairly common to have someone sleeping next to you, in apparent good health, suddenly decide to die, telling a bunkmate he no longer wanted to live. With that announcement the man would turn over on his side and the next morning be found dead. I learned then that a man could indeed will himself to die. Medically speaking it was called "inanition," the state of being empty or the loss of vitality that results from a loss of blood. Men were dying every other day on average. The cremation detail was constantly walking up and down the hill where the cremation site was located.

Going on that detail, or any detail, was absolute agony. We performed coolie labor by loading buckets with rocks and sand, but found ourselves too weak to fill the cars that ran on the train tracks alongside the river. The cold weather was bone-chilling. Our feet, in only their canvas sneakers, were constantly cold. When given the chance men would put their feet close to a fire that a guard had going for his own warmth. Occasionally, they forgot that the rubber in the sneaker would quickly heat up. When this happened one could see a prisoner or two jumping about from the "hot foot" they had just given themselves. With no means of gaining warmth out on the job, we looked forward anxiously to when the sun would appear over the rim of the mountain and reach its apex. We basked in the glow of that heat, albeit all too briefly. I remember hearing my fellow prisoners saying "no wonder these little b_____ worship the sun, it's the only way they really get warm."

The camp and dam, located along the bed of the Tenryu River, in winter only saw the sun when it was directly overhead. Amazingly the sun was very powerful, and reminded us of the warmth of the Philippines. At this time, how we wished we had stayed there! We most certainly were not blessing the name of the doctor there who had advised us that the cold weather in Japan would benefit us!

In the first week of April 1944 nearly all prisoners, American and British, were removed from Mitsushima and taken to a carbide mine further north. Left behind were thirteen British and thirteen Americans. How the Japanese ever arrived at the makeup of those remaining behind has always been a mystery to me. Looking at both groups one could deduce that the *honchos* of each work detail and the medical and kitchen staffs were selected because of their duties in camp. Nearly all these men knew a small bit of Japanese, and they were to form the cadre of the camp for incoming prisoners. Going out with this group were the three American and some British officers. Outside of Walter Hewitt, the Americans did not miss their "fearless leaders" Major Alan Corey and Captain Wallace Faulkner, both worthless officers. Yet in the case of Corey he remained in the service and eventually retired a full colonel. That only proved to me that mediocrity can indeed rise to success.

Living in that camp, we all witnessed despicable acts perpetrated by prisoners on fellow prisoners. The vast majority would take advantage of anyone, given the opportunity. For instance, prisoner Frank Brancaticano had a severe nicotine habit. He would do anything, sell anything, snitch to the Japanese—anything just to obtain a smoke. In the early days of Mitsushima smokers would obtain from Japanese civilians a form of tobacco that we named "horsehair" because of its willowy, wispy-type strands. This was smoked in a tiny pipe that had a very, very small bulb at the end of it. One would roll this "tobacco" between the thumb and forefinger and pack it into the small bowl. Three or four puffs and it was time to reload. With about six such smokes a prisoner could satisfy his habit. Fortunately I had not smoked up to this point, and so was unaware of the lengths that a smoker would go to just for a smoke.

Frank however never could get enough of the little nicotine contained in this so-called tobacco. Constantly running around camp, he would sell any item he had. Soon the smokers in camp were bumming cigarette butts off the guards and civilians, or picking up off the ground any butt that a Japanese threw away. Many Japanese threw burning cigarettes on the ground just to see the ensuing dash by the prisoners to recover their refuse—another form of humiliating the prisoner, with the prisoner willingly giving them the satisfaction.

A number of individuals would collect cigarette butts during the day while working outside and bring them back to camp to be "sold." Frank was a big "buyer." Having nothing more to sell, Frank then began trading his food for the butts. Eventually, he had "sold" his three meals a day for over a week. Frank's health soon worsened from his self-imposed starvation. It finally became so bad that the two medical doctors in camp declared Frank "bankrupt." Then those who could not collect became furious. To watch my fellow Americans literally kill a prisoner by taking away his food sickened me. Shortly after Frank was sent to Kanose, Japan, with the main group of prisoners in April 1944, he died on 20 June. Here I would attribute Frank's death to his fellow Americans' greed and their complete lack of concern for the man involved. To those who took part in Frank's death and are strutting around today as heroes, I say I hope the next world brings you face to face with him.

The lack of mail during captivity led to great depression. In three years I received a total of three letters, and not until 5 January 1945 were we allowed to write home. That consisted of twenty-five words on a postcard. This card was then allowed on a monthly basis. Most of this mail arrived in the United States after the war. What little mail came in was held by the interpreter, Machida, in the latter part of the camp's existence.

A great deal of animosity existed between Americans and British in Mitsushima, and to me the actions of the Americans caused the situation. Nor did Americans make the least attempt to improve conditions. The British at least tried. What always impressed me about the British was their ability to make the best of a bad situation. They would sing when they had no reason to. They put on shows even though they had very little energy left. They put on a good face even to the Japanese. They just refused to let the Japanese get to them. I admired them then as soldiers, an admiration I carry with me to this day.

Work details of prisoners were scattered all over the valley near the dam. Men worked along the riverbeds lifting rocks and gravel, toiled in blacksmith shops located in key areas, and labored on the cement details. Everyone but officers worked. Most officers insisted that they were exempt from work required of lower ranks. Hence no officers were compelled to work by the Japanese, but their rations were cut accordingly. As a result they sat around the barracks most of the day playing cards or deciphering Japanese newspapers. Towards the end of the war the officers' ranks swelled because of new arrivals, recently captured. These new men became the center of interest because they could give us the latest information on the war.

When the opportunity to work for Igarashi on the cement detail came, I jumped at it. Igarashi always allowed the prisoners to burn fires during the winter months. In the event a Japanese guard came by, Igarashi would claim the fire was for his comfort. Camp rules prohibited any fires being lit to warm prisoners. While I liked the cement detail it was not without its dangers. One prisoner named Skubina from Minnesota fell from a loading platform after slipping on the ice and landed on his head about ten feet below. He fractured his skull and hovered between life and death for two weeks. He then took a turn for the worse, developing weakness and incoordination in his arms, legs, and eye muscles. The medics determined that he had a blood clot in the cerebellum at the base of the skull. Dr. Weinstein, a surgeon, and Dr. Whitfield, the British doctor, appealed repeatedly to Dr. Fugi, the senior Japanese doctor at Omori Camp, where Weinstein had come from, for permission to send Skubina to a military hospital for an operation. (There were no brain instruments available in Mitsushima.) Fugi wrote back "it is impossible. There is no transportation available." Skubina lingered on for months, and when Doctor Fugi visited the camp on a tour of inspection he was shown the patient. "Nothing can be done. You cannot send him to Tokyo." Skubina died thereafter, and an autopsy performed by Weinstein found a liquefied blood clot abscess pressing on Skubina's cerebellum. According to Weinstein this could have been drained if operated on. He should have lived. Dr. Fugi in effect murdered Skubina by refusing to send him to Tokyo.

CHAPTER 18

WORK DETAILS AND CONTRACTS

After a period of American-British failure to produce work satisfactory to the Japanese, the brilliant idea to "contract" their work was originated by an American. A look at the job performance records of the prisoners convinced the Japanese that contract work was a good idea. Poor job performance was in part a deliberate act on the part of the prisoners. Every day, when possible, prisoners would contribute to the war effort by sabotaging any "target of opportunity." Contract work, agreed upon each morning by the detail's *honcho* and the Japanese, consisted of a specified amount of work to be done that day. The incentive was returning to the barracks when the job was finished. An example of such a contract would be the filling, transporting, and dumping of so many small boxcars of sand and stone. The prospect of returning to the barracks meant escaping harsh winter temperatures, but also it usually meant doing work around the campsite. Eventually the prisoners ruined this agreement by finishing so early that the Japanese reneged on the contract setup.

During the latter days of the war the cement detail often found itself without cement. The United States Army Air Corps was destroying railroad tracks, interdicting the shipments of cement. As a result I was assigned to a six-man detail, on a pole-carrying job. Making work to keep the prisoners busy, the Japanese had us carry poles the size of telephone poles from point A to point B. The next day we would carry them back again. On this particular day, I as *honcho* agreed with our Japanese guard, Nishigaki, or "Boy Scout" as we called him, to carry five poles. Nishigaki was no more than eighteen and suffering from tuberculosis. He had no idea of what he had agreed for us to do. Twelve o'clock came and we had just finished carrying the stipulated five poles. Sitting down to have our lunch, brought us by Doc Weinstein, and Doc Whitfield, who enjoyed the opportunity to get out of camp, Nishigaki asked me if we would carry an additional pole after lunch as it was much too early to go back to camp. He knew he would catch hell for bringing us back that early. I discussed the additional work with the men, and they all replied, "no way, a contract is a contract." I heard this comment repeated insistently until I was sick of hearing it. The men simply refused to do any more work, and I had to deliver this message to the Boy Scout. He was almost in tears wondering what to do with this rebellious group.

About this time Nishigaki jumped up from his sitting position, which he was not allowed, and saluted two regular guards touring the work sites. Their purpose: to check on people like Nishigaki. Frightened by being caught sitting down, he began telling the guards Big Glass Eye and Little Glass Eye that his charges had refused to work. Hell hath no fury like Little Glass Eye and Big Glass Eye that day. We six prisoners were stood at attention and beaten numerous times with their wooden swords. Marched back to camp immediately, we were made to stand at attention on the parade ground until the remainder of the work details had returned, and lined up after the evening meal for *tenko* formation. At that time the entire camp was called to attention and out strode Captain Nakajima, the camp commander.

Nakajima began bellowing in our faces one by one. Then he took keen delight in drawing his sword (a real sword, no wooden one) and hitting us over the head with the handle. For me he reserved special attention. After the beatings were administered, all of the errant detail, excluding me, were marched off to the barracks. Nakajima barked orders and I found myself in solitary confinement inside the Japanese administration building. This was known as an *aso*. An *aso* closely resembles a coffin. The one being punished is placed inside the coffin-like box, which is then slid into a wall affair such as might be found in a morgue. At one end of the box is a small peephole for air. With no room inside one can do nothing but lie in one position. When I emerged I was told I had been in there for three days. During that time I was not fed or allowed water. To this day I cannot allow myself to be in a small area or surrounded in any way. This punishment, mind you, while inflicted by the Japanese, was brought about by the pigheadedness of my fellow Americans. To insist upon "a contract is a contract" attitude might go well in a General Motors plant, but certainly not when you are the mercy of a very cruel and sadistic people. This was my judgment then. It continues to be my judgment today.

As I said, work details of prisoners were scattered all over the valley where the hydroelectric dam was located. Some men worked along the riverbed sifting rock, sand, and gravel using a little hand-held spade to dig out the sides of a hill. Others worked in the two blacksmith shops under contract and some were on the cement detail. Everyone worked but officers and the sick and lame. We might change that last word to "lazy," for we had more than our share of malingerers. They would do anything to avoid going out to work, especially in inclement weather. For these deadbeats we used the old army expression "goldbricks." Oftentimes their action compelled legitimately sick patients to take their place on work details. Naturally some of these did not survive. In one such case a private named Williams of Texas, a cardiac patient, was compelled to take a goldbrick's place. Williams returned from carrying wood from the mountain in a state of cardiac collapse, his face purple and his heart barely ticking. He died two hours after returning to camp, another victim of a fellow American's inhumanity.

Both doctors Weinstein and Whitfield conducted a beriberi survey of our camp. Of the two hundred men and officers, a hundred eighty-five had extensive clinical evidence of this disease. Forty of these had weakening of the heart, including Weinstein. Dr. Weinstein died a few years after liberation of a heart attack.

In December 1944 our work on the hydroelectric site was finished. Not that the dam was completed; the work ended because cement was no longer available. Men continued working at small "keep busy" jobs. Each day about 150 men went into the mountains to cut down trees and return them to camp. Trees weighing about one hundred pounds and more were carried by sick men on starvation rations. According to the medics everyone in the camp had developed severe beriberi—swelling of the face, abdomen, and legs, partial paralysis of the extremities, increased blindness, and cardiac failure.

Officers not required to work sat around camp, often wishing they could work out of sheer boredom. Their rations had been cut as a result of their not working, so they remained in camp playing cards as I said, or deciphering the Japanese newspapers that the enlisted men managed to bring back to camp. The Japanese were always curious as to why we wanted their newspapers. Our reason: "for banjo" or toilet paper. Since we were never issued any of that necessary material, our response was readily accepted. One new officer recently captured, a B-24 pilot shot down in March 1945, brought into our camp the words and music of "Tangerine," a song made popular by Jimmy Dorsey and his vocalist Helen O'Connell. He hummed the tune and our musicians picked up the melody.

During the last six to eight months of the war the Japanese began to see "the handwriting on the wall." Materiel of all sorts began to appear at the railroad station. Prisoners began unloading and transporting machinery of all types, with many lathes included for manufacturing ammunition and weapons. Placed in what we called *toros*, these small almost flat cars were lowered down the ramp (incline), across the bridge and up the other side to the tunnels sitting there empty. As the *toros* crossed the bridge small parts of the machinery were tossed by prisoners into the swirling water below. We never had the opportunity to see if those machines ever were put to the test. Which is just as well, as I am sure the Japanese punishment for that sort of sabotage would have been nothing less than death for some unlucky prisoners.

Before this, the Japanese felt (rightly so) that the dam work was not progressing on schedule, and so they relieved the infamous Captain Nakajima, who was sent to the war zone. In his place came a Lieutenant Kubo, a university graduate and lawyer in the Tokyo city government before the war. Seriously wounded in China, Kubo was totally different from Nakajima. He often helped prisoners, and when he did not it was because his hands were tied by his superiors in Tokyo. Scrupulously honest he insured a fair distribution of our Christmas Red Cross parcels in December 1944. Before then any Red Cross parcel went to the Japanese in the camp. He tried repeatedly to improve the lot of the prisoners and reduced the corporal punishment so readily handed out until it went beyond his control, as circumstances later revealed. While Kubo was sent to "improve work production" according the Japanese, his main goal was to reduce the death rate in the camp.

As late as December 1944, shortly after the arrival of Lieutenant Kubo, three men had died of beriberi in a week. From all indications many more would die. News from home was not good. According to our interpretations of Japanese newspapers, fighting to retake the Philippines had bogged down and the Germans were advancing on the Allies at a place called Bastogne. It truly seemed to us on Christmas that the war would never end.

Shortly after Kubo's arrival came Dr. Weinstein. Al Weinstein, a surgeon in Bataan's Field Hospital #1, had been sent to Mitsushima from Camp Omori for punishment. Weinstein had been a thorn in the sides of the Japanese ever since his capture. Warned to behave himself in Mitsushima by Kubo, Weinstein still kept up the fight to improve the lot of the prisoners. He managed to make Kubo see that the problem had been his predecessor's refusal to believe there was a problem. Weinstein held a great deal of respect for Kubo and after the war did everything in his power to aid him, including testifying in Kubo's behalf when charges were preferred against him for "war crimes."

Shortly after the Skubina death, a Japanese Army disciplinary sergeant was sent to Mitsushima to improve the camp's presumed problem. This may have come about as a result of Lieutenant Kubo's improved treatment of his charges after word had reached Tokyo. This previously mentioned disciplinary sergeant named Watanabe had been the scourge of a number of prison camps in Japan. When discipline began to lag in any camp the call went out for Watanabe. Standing almost six feet tall in his stocking feet, extremely tall for a Japanese, he delighted in his reputation for brutality. His nickname The Bird came from his method of operation. He would sit in a cage-like enclosure. From this one could assume he was paranoid about someone slipping up behind him. From his "perch" he could survey the entire parade ground, about a football field in size and appearance, and the walks between the barracks. A loud command from him to anyone passing his cage usually meant a severe beating. He would berate a prisoner called before his cage, first in Japanese, then in very poor English. "Coat no buttoned," bam! "You too slow in coming here," wham! Etc., etc. Without a doubt he was the most vicious Japanese guard I met in my three-and-a-half years as a prisoner of the Japanese. In particular he hated Weinstein, whom he had known in Omori, Weinstein's previous camp. Beaten often by The Bird, Weinstein gave him a wide berth when he could. No one including the camp commander had any control over him. His orders came only from Tokyo. Very recently I read that he was very much alive and very prosperous while living in Tokyo. He had gone underground to avoid prosecution as a war criminal until American authorities signed the odorous peace treaty of 1951. During a press interview in 1995, he not only admitted to his brutality, he offered to allow any former prisoner to hit him in payment for his beatings.

When first subjected to Japanese punching we had learned to roll with the punch—a gesture almost woman-like in its effect—and then fall down immediately. The Japanese had seen enough Western movies to realize they had won the fight when their victim fell. In Watanabe's case one did not have to pretend to be knocked down. With proper coaching Watanabe could have been a terrific middleweight.

About this time a large contingent of the British Navy arrived in our camp. Leading the group into the camp in as military a manner as I had seen in prison life was Captain Oliver Gordon, Royal Navy, former commanding officer of the H.M.S. *Exeter*, sunk in the Java sea battle along with the American cruiser U.S.S. *Houston* and several other American, Australian, British, and Dutch ships in that naval battle in early 1942.

Suddenly it was Christmas 1944. Little did we know that the following Christmas most of us would be home. Still, here we were in the mountains of Japan without any idea of how the war would end. What troubled us more however was the cold. Hunger and homesickness had become a part of our everyday living. In the hospital area, where a fire was permitted all day and night, the many sick patients found staying warm a major task. To offset the cold, patients got hold of some papers, made some glue from rice flour, and attempted to cover the walls. As Dr. Weinstein put it, "they ate more of the glue than they used." They were still cold! As for the barracks, Japanese Army regulations did not allow heat indoors before their official beginning of winter, 4 January of each year. I never ceased to be amazed at the mentality of the Japanese when it came to the weather. The only time we were ever really warm in that camp was when we took our communal bath every five days. Two hundred men passed through the filthy water and no one cared. We were warm!

Just before Christmas 1944 we formed a glee club. I joined because in previous Christmases no one showed any interest in celebrating my favorite holiday. Dr. Weinstein, although Jewish, and Dr. Whitfield put the club together. We spent several nights before Christmas singing Christmas carols. The birth of Christ was celebrated that Christmas Eve with our singing "Holy Night." Despite the conditions around us I felt closer to home than I had ever felt in three previous years. The caroling surely contributed to that. Kubo released Red Cross parcels, one for each man. It surely was a most magnificent night. The excitement of Christmas had returned to us, and we spent Christmas Eve opening our packages and telling one another what we had. Ultimately it led to swapping of goods and the selling of cigarettes, with ten packs in each parcel. It was then that I started my smoking habit, not knowing what else to do with my share. I refused to trade them for food. I guess the memory of Frank's starving to death from trading his food for cigarettes still haunted me.

The next day, Christmas, we pooled some canned meats into a pot in the kitchen, where the cooks came up with something resembling stew. After our stew for breakfast, Dr. Whitfield conducted Christmas services outside in a bitter cold, windswept area. No one seemed too concerned about the weather that day. Christmas was declared a holiday by Kubo and he visited us in our barracks while his guards took photographs (see appendices).

Both doctors decided to deny Red Cross parcels to members of the camp "football teams." About eleven English and eleven Americans qualified for the teams. These were the true "goldbricks." Shiftless, unwilling to work, constant crybabies about everything and the scum of the camp, they were in constant trouble with the Japanese and as a result others suffered for their sickening behavior. That Christmas they were not given their parcels in order to prevent their selling them to others. Time never improved this lot. I am sure that somewhere today they are still around, talking about their "heroic" days fighting the war. Therse prisoners are the ones I call "predators." Basically unfit to live themselves, they oftentimes caused the death of those who truly deserved to live. Yes indeed: "where is justice?" Of course this leads to the subject of religion. How and why could God permit such sufferings and cruelties? Many lost their faith in prison camps. I may add that our camp never had a chaplain of any type. Our first chaplain, a Catholic priest from Australia, arrived the late spring of 1945. He attempted to hold Mass for Catholics in camp, but almost no one attended. Out of embarrassment he gave up the idea. I am afraid that prison camp life under the Japanese created many an agnostic and a few atheists.

CHAPTER 19

THE SKIES BEGIN TO CLOUD UP

Shortly before Christmas 1944, in November to be exact, we witnessed the most beautiful sight we had seen since before the war. Hearing a low but steady hum of aircraft motors, we rushed outdoors and there, in a perfectly sunny day, were long lines of what appeared to be clouds. High in the sky were these plumes of white, so high that the aircraft could not be seen with the naked eye. Our recently downed American pilot soon explained that they were vapor trails caused by the planes' engines at the high altitude they were flying. We had heard that the American Air Force had struck the home islands of Japan, but we who "did not see, did not believe." These raids were to continue until the end of the war, but no flight was as exciting as seeing that first one. We received word from another prison camp, Shinagawa, by way of a friend of Dr. Weinstein transferred to our camp, that a task force of aircraft carriers had hit Tokyo. A thousand Grumman planes followed by three hundred B-29s in the midst of a snowstorm had devastated the city. If there was one word we heard from the Japanese from that first flight on, it was *B-Ni Ju Ku*, or B-29. The very word caused more fear among the Japanese than I had ever seen in three years in that country. At every workplace the word became the center of conversation.

On the first flight over our camp however, we were not allowed too much pleasure in watching them. Shouting "Kuras!" the guards set about beating everyone standing outside and drove us all inside the barracks. They were determined that our enjoyment at seeing American planes would be short-lived.

On that night however, very few prisoners could sleep. We lay awake thinking about what that flight represented. As Americans we were proud in front of the British that they were American planes. "Just think," one individual said, "there are Americans inside those ships, perfectly clean, well-fed, and they slept in a bed last night, not on a wooden floor, and they don't have any lice!" All sorts of questions were asked: Where did they come from? Where were they headed? What airfield did they take off from, etc. We finally went to sleep convinced that now, finally, we as a country were striking back.

We didn't see any more planes for weeks. And we began to wonder exactly what we had seen. Then they reappeared and began flying over our camp sometimes twice a week. Everyone who dared ventured out to watch them fly over. Despite their high altitude, guys would jump up and down wave their arms as if they could be seen or heard. If caught doing so the guards would punish them with beatings. They obviously were angry. Their cities were catching hell! As the weeks went by, the altitude of the planes began to drop to the point where we could actually see them. At first we saw Japanese fighters going aloft to intercept the B-29s, but that ceased after a while when the Japanese decided to hold back their fighters for the expected invasion.

We now grew accustomed to regular flights over our camp by the U.S. Air Force, and we began to grow angry that they were taking so long to finish off the Japanese. I recall one day working on a hilltop and hearing a flight coming over. While lying on my back, I counted about seven hundred aircraft before I grew weary of it. There were so many planes they blocked out the sun for a time. Eventually we could hear them coming over at night as well. Both the sounds and sights of those planes proved the greatest morale booster we had yet felt.

Captain Gordon, the senior Allied officer in our camp, attempted to restrain the enthusiasm displayed by the prisoners, to no avail. He did insist on certain behavior while he was the senior officer. Every inch a British officer of the Royal Navy, he inspired immediate respect among all prisoners. His subordinate officers had served with him as his staff aboard the *Exeter*, and a great deal of organization, previously lacking for almost three years, emerged as a result. His "number one" officer in camp was a Lieutenant Commander Twist.

Twist was destined to rise to the rank of First Sea Lord of the Admiralty. But in our camp he was the one designated by Captain Gordon to organize the men into some semblance of a military group. Military discipline returned somewhat, and the Japanese finally had prisoner officers they admittedly respected in the persons of Gordon and Twist.

Watanabe however was still Watanabe. No one could change him or his methods. Neither Gordon nor Twist feared him or his violent outbursts. Much of the Watanabe "mystique" was created by fear alone. His mere presence in a barracks put everyone in fear that something was going to happen and someone would be his next victim. In retrospect it was fairly obvious why he was selected to re-instill discipline that may have slipped. Yet if one of Captain Gordon's men was beaten by Watanabe, Gordon would present himself to camp commander Kubo and register his protest. I had never seen any officer do that before Gordon's arrival. Without a doubt his protests did reduce the number of beatings.

Still, something had to be done about Watanabe. One of the American "goldbricks" brought the issue to a head. Watanabe had been on a slugfest in the camp and on work details. Several elderly prisoners were beaten almost unconscious by Watanabe because they were slow in rising when he entered their barracks. The American, Daniels, who we called the captain of the camp's "football team" of malingerers, asked our interpreter Machida, "Are we getting our tobacco ration today?" Machida, or "The Goon" as we named him, asked Daniels, "What's your hurry? If you don't get it today, you'll get it next week." Daniels told him, "Keep it. Next week the Yanks and tanks will be here." Machida, always attempting to curry favor with Watanabe, told him of the conversation. As a result, The Bird almost beat Daniels to death. It was a horrible beating as our beatings went, with blood spurting profusely from Daniels' nose and mouth.

Shortly thereafter, the Allied officers in camp held a meeting to examine ways to rid us of The Bird. Murder squads were formed among the officers and plans were drawn up to throw The Bird off a cliff. Always going out on work details with his sword and armed guards, the chance never occurred. In desperation (or as Dr. Whitfield put it, "The Bird is murdering his prisoners by inches.") the idea of poisoning The Bird became a possibility. Digitalis, morphine, iodine, and atropine were considered by Doctors Weinstein and Whitfield. An overdose of digitalis was ruled out as it might cause vomiting, which meant he might throw up the digitalis before it had a chance to work. Morphine and iodine too were ruled out. Both doctors feared that a Japanese doctor might be called in before The Bird died. Contracted pupils and slow respiration from morphine would obviously be seen.

Several days later it was decided to try to kill The Bird with bacteria. As Dr. Weinstein put it, "Swell, if it doesn't kill The Bird, he'll know he's been sick." Some bloody stools were obtained from patients who had amoebic and bacillary dysentery. Dr. Weinstein placed shreds of mucous feces in a solution of saline and glucose as a culture medium. For good measure the doctors added three fat "juicy" flies to the mixture. Not having an incubator, both doctors then carried little jars with the concentration on their person to provide the warmth necessary. After a few days, Dr. Whitfield made a warm saline suspension of the "gravy," as both medics referred to it.

The next and most dangerous step was to somehow get the "gravy" into The Bird's food. An old friend, George Piel, whom I had known from days with the 31st Infantry Regiment, was the cook for the Japanese. Warned that if caught several men could be put to death Piel nevertheless volunteered. For five days Piel flavored The Bird's rice with the "gravy." Nothing happened, so the next batch of "gravy" was made using contributions from half a dozen stools. Piel did his flavoring again, and only on The Bird's food. No thought to killing anyone else was ever mentioned.

Two days after being given the stronger mix, The Bird took sick and asked for Weinstein to see him. Watanabe was throwing up all night. Asked by The Bird to "cure" him, Weinstein's initial thoughts were of the numerous men he had seen die because of Japanese cruelty.

With tongue in cheek, Weinstein said very slowly, "Yes, I'll cure you." The Bird ran a temperature of 105 for ten days while everyone in camp prayed he would die. While Weinstein administered aspirin and sodium bicarbonate grooved to look like sulfadiazine pills, George Piel continued to flavor his diet with the "gravy" mixture. With Weinstein's urging to The Bird to "keep eating your rice," The Bird lost fifteen pounds in his first week of illness. Unfortunately, The Bird was strong as an ox and survived the "treatment." Yet his illness took something out of him and slowed down his beatings. Surely had the plot to kill him ever been discovered, several people would have been put to death.

After my marriage in 1946, my wife and I honeymooned in New Orleans, Louisiana, George Piel's hometown. George's uncle was general manager of the St. Francis Hotel in that city and, through George, we obtained a hotel room at a time when they were still impossible to find. George and I went over the attempted murder of The Bird with keen delight in remembering how it was almost accomplished.

Camp life proceeded along with each day bringing us closer to home. To cheer up the camp inmates, Captain Gordon would meet daily with his staff officers and discuss the news of the day, deciphered from the daily newspapers by British Lieutenant Henderson, who read and spoke Japanese very well. While Japanese newspapers were obviously and primarily propaganda, we uncovered enough evidence of some truths to satisfy us. From the time Henderson came into the camp we were able to follow much of the war both in Europe and the Pacific. Of course the trick was to read between the lines. As an example: one month we would read where Americans had attempted a landing on a Pacific island, only to be repulsed with heavy losses. Two months later we read that B-29s had taken off from that very same island. In this way we followed the movement of the American attempt to take back lost territory.

Just about Christmas 1944, I was offered the opportunity, along with a number of others, to make a radio address to my family. Being extremely careful in what I was saying, I managed to get my message on the air. My mother received hundreds of translations of the message from military planes flying over China, ships on the seas, and civilian ham radio operators, all of whom had picked up Tokyo's broadcast. Many of those messages are among my proudest possessions. Certainly my mother was extremely proud to receive them. Many times they were only partial messages, in other cases they were complete. Eventually the War Department sent my mother an exact copy of my broadcast. (See Appendix of documents.) Having absolutely no idea if the radio address was ever received, I had forgotten about it until I returned home, whereupon my mother produced these many, many messages received from all over the world.

About this time I became a "friend" of Watanabe, The Bird. The Japanese had decided to raise a number of hens and roosters in our camp to keep them from the eyes of Japanese civilians. After some time, the hens were producing eggs, which were consumed in the Japanese kitchen in the camp. About the same time, Japanese guards began growing a garden in the camp. Their propaganda to the local townspeople was that it was for the prisoners. We took care of the garden but never ever ate any of the produce grown there. Years later I was told by a relative of a guard how well-fed we had been. He firmly believed that we were eating the vegetables produced.

As to the eggs: one day we were called out of the barracks on a "Yasume Day," supposedly a rest day, and lined up in formation. Apparently someone had stolen some eggs. The Bird was determined to get to the bottom of the theft. Down the line of prisoners he came with the question, "Who stole the eggs?" When no one admitted to the theft, he punched each one who had denied doing the deed. He finally came in front of me, asking the same question. My reply was more a question, "Could a Japanese soldier have stolen the eggs?" Watanabe's face darkened. I felt I had gone too far and waited for the blow. It came, but was not as severe as the others. Suddenly he broke into a slight smile and addressed me by my number, saying "*Hachi-ban, Nippon haiti dropo ni*," loosely translated: "Japanese soldiers are not thieves." With that he turned away and ended his questioning. For whatever reason, that incident stuck in The Bird's mind and he became very friendly to

me, which I viewed with suspicion. He often adopted such an attitude before working someone over. In that respect he was almost
sadistic. Still, we did get along after that. He asked me to teach
him some English and he would teach me Japanese. We had a
number of conversations in the last few months of the war. His
hostility diminished with each passing month. During our gab sessions he would ask me *"Hachi-ban,* what is democracy?" Inasmuch
as I was not too informed on democracy myself, I found this a
difficult question. In reality he was more interested in what the
United States was all about and how we operated as a country.
When he disappeared after the war to avoid trial, I often suspected
that he had made his way to the United States because of that
interest. I later discovered he did visit the U.S. twice as well as
Australia. Relatives living not far from the campsite had hidden
him for several years. No one deserved to be severely punished
and even put to death more than The Bird. His claim today that
he was only carrying out orders and that was nothing personal in
his beatings is a lot of rubbish. Watanabe thoroughly enjoyed in-
flicting physical punishment. There are no excuses for his many
beatings, several of which led to death. That he escaped punishment is unbelievable. That he was allowed in the United States
and Australia is also unbelievable. Even more unbelievable is his
owning property in Australia, as verified by CBS television. Others
who had committed lesser crimes than he were put to death. While
Captain Gordon in one of his speeches assured us that The Bird
would be punished one day, this never happened, to the dismay of
hundreds of his victims. Still it was Watanabe who, weeks before
the war ended, told me the war would soon be over. An extremely
well-educated, handsome Japanese, he eventually became a very
wealthy businessman in Tokyo. Just how unfair can life be!

A word here on the interpreter Machida, The Goon. Machida
was born in California and lived there until a year before the outbreak of the war. Returning to Japan for reasons unknown to me,
he was caught up in the war, a victim more than anything else.
Coming to our camp in 1944, he at least spoke English well enough
so we could understand him. Yet he spoke so little Japanese, he
could be seen at night reading a Japanese-English dictionary. The

Japanese did not trust him, nor did we. Constantly currying the favor of The Bird and the Japanese administration, he feared them as much as we did. Caught in the middle as he was, he truly was another victim of the war. To be accepted by the Japanese he committed stupid acts like withholding prisoners' mail or tattling on them if he knew something the other Japanese did not. His Japanese was almost a laugh. After several years in camp, some of our people could speak better Japanese. When he was tried after the war as a war criminal, I offered evidence to help him. After a couple of years in Sugamo Prison near Tokyo, he was released. Years later he wrote to thank me for my assistance. He was never a mean individual, more an object of pity. Fearing prisoner repercussions, he fled the camp when news of the war's end came. Compelled to stay in Japan because of his wartime role, Machida eventually died in Osaka, Japan, in 1985. Machida was one of many Japanese-Americans visiting Japan at the outbreak of the war, and many, by no means all, were compelled to join the military. Many, as we found out on Bataan, had volunteered for service due to their dislike of Americans and the American treatment of Asians in the U.S. at that time.

CHAPTER 20

IT'S OVER

S everal weeks after my last conversation with Watanabe concerning democracy, a feeling began to pervade the camp. No
one could define it, but all experienced it. Something different
was in the air, which could be felt by the tempo in camp. Guards
were more conciliatory, beatings almost disappeared, and contractors on the job had a "who cares" attitude. Those last two weeks of
uncertainty saw me as one of five men considered "strong men,"
carrying the heaviest equipment from point A to point B and then
back again the next day. With ropes under the machinery and a
strong pole, five of us could barely lift the equipment off the ground
more than three inches. At about 135 pounds, I hardly considered
myself strong but the Japanese did. With a chant taught to us by
the Japanese, we would try to lift the equipment in unison. If successful, we might move it a few feet before the weight forced us to
put it down.

Eventually our "Sunday" came and we went about the camp
without typical Japanese harassment on a very warm sunny August
day, picking body lice off our blue British army shirts which had
turned dark blue from all the lice. During those sessions the Japanese avoided us as if we had the plague. It was truly, for the first
time ever, a real day off.

The following day, 15 August 1945, we fell out for morning *tenko*
as some of us had done in that camp for almost three years. "One-
Arm," Nishino-san, a victim of an artillery shell in China, was officer of the day. I have always believed that he volunteered for that

job that particular day. When he announced that "There will be
no work today. Today you rest," translated by The Goon, Machida,
we went into a semi-state of shock. This had never happened before. Walking back to the barracks that morning, everyone was so
animated that we could hear a steady buzz from all the talking
most of the day. Few really slept that night. Guards were noticeable by their absence. For the first time in almost a year the air raid
siren atop a mountain peak nearby failed to sound off. No aircraft
flying at all. Up to this point we could count on B-29s flying over
almost daily on their way to Nagoya or other major targets. In many
ways we were fortunate to have been placed in this camp as opposed to prison camps in or near major cities. Many, many prisoners of war were killed by friendly fire when their camps were near
targets of the B-29s. The next day we again lined up for *tenko*.
Again, One-Arm appeared and said, "No work today. Rest!" At that
moment we truly knew the war was finally over. There simply could
be no other reason for two days off in a row.

Dismissed, we all gathered around Captain Gordon's quarters
in one of the barracks to learn what was going on. An American
prisoner named Willie Campbell wormed his way through a slight
opening in the fence surrounding us and brought back from the
Oiwa blacksmith shop that day's newspaper. Gordon's staff officer
Henderson went to work translating the contents. Two "uncivi-
lized" bombs had been dropped by the Americans, and the Emperor had accepted the Allied powers' demand for surrender. Still
not sure what this all meant to prisoners of war, and following
Gordon's advice, we lined up the following morning for *tenko*.
Again we were dismissed, only this time with absolutely no comment from the Japanese.

Waiting for a clear understanding of what was happening on
the "outside," we turned to those Americans most recently captured. Captain Van Warmer, a B-24 pilot from Michigan captured
a mere nine months before, and an optimist, explained that the
war was due to end any day considering the number of American
troops moving into position for an invasion of Japan. Submarine
Lieutenant George Brown, New York, captured when his sub was
sunk seven months previously, shared Van Warmer's assessment.

Van Warmer was a pleasant addition to the prison group. A lover of popular music, he would hum the latest hit songs from back home, and in no time, my buddy Cecil Fernandez would be strumming the tune on his guitar. Cecil had been a professional guitarist before the war. Subsequently he resumed his career and performed all over the world.

One of our two camp doctors, Whitfield, knowing that one of his fellow British prisoners was dying and in need of immediate medical attention unavailable in Mitsushima, convinced Nishigaki The Boy Scout, in charge of the camp hospital, to take him and the dying prisoner to Tokyo for treatment. Whitfield never returned. He did however send a note back to Weinstein, who read to us that note that night. It read, "I got on board a hospital ship. He's O.K. The harbor is swarming with Allied ships of all classes. I saw the Admiral. He says formal surrender ceremonies will take place on the battleship U.S.S. *Missouri* on September 2. After that, the Yanks will come for you. I had my first chocolate ice-cream soda. Oh boy!"

While Dr. Whitfield was gone on his errand of mercy, I had the unfortunate experience of coming down with a case of yellow jaundice (hepatitis). Coming at a time when the entire camp was excited beyond description, it hit me doubly hard. Feeling I was going to die and be deprived of my "victory" over the Japanese, I was visited by Al Weinstein, on a "house call," something rare in that camp. While the good doctor had very little to give me in the way of medication, he did give me a verbal "kick in the pants." Hearing him tell me, "we are on the homestretch, get tough," I soon found myself on my feet. To this day I treasure Al Weinstein's book *Barbed Wire Surgeon* published in 1947. In signing a copy of the book for me, he paid me a compliment that was exactly how I felt about him. "To my buddy Dick, a guy with plenty of guts, who made life more livable for me in Mitsushima." Years later when I met him on a trip through Atlanta, Georgia, we had a lengthy chat and I said as much to him then. He was one of the few heroes in prison camp.

Shortly thereafter, our camp guards, including The Bird, disappeared. All but Nishigaki, Machida, and Nishino. Later I learned that an order was issued to all prison camps allowing any guard who felt he might be the victim of prisoners' revenge to leave his post. Our Japanese camp commander Kubo insisted however that The Bird had deserted and that he would be held responsible for that act by the Japanese Army. Unfortunately, Kubo did not know The Bird. Watanabe had disappeared one morning. But just the previous night he and I had a long talk outside my barracks, again concerned with the subject of democracy. In a way I felt Watanabe was trying to explain his actions to me to clear his conscience.

Nevertheless, all the guards were now gone. Sleep without interruption was possible at last. Nishino, a very special Japanese, would visit us in the barracks each evening and tell us how fortunate we were to have been prisoners of war in a "safe area." He never did understand that we would gladly exchange the life of a Japanese prisoner to become a front line soldier once more. Still, each night when on duty he could be seen praying, and he openly admitted he prayed for the end of the war and our safety. Every living prisoner of Mitsushima can readily recall Nishino, with his one remaining arm lifted to his forehead, openly praying. Quite a man was Nishino-san. All the prisoners were fond of him. All left testimonials behind when they departed camp attesting to his good treatment of the prisoners. What food we had was given to him along with new clothing held in the warehouse for three years. When we left that camp, Nishino-san had tears streaming down his face. He was the most human Japanese guard I encountered during my entire captivity. He and I corresponded a number of times after the war. In sworn affidavits he readily admitted to what he witnessed happen to prisoners beaten and mistreated.

After the guards left Machida The Goon remained behind. He literally had nowhere to go. When he was charged with being a war criminal after the war, I along with Weinstein helped him as best we could by testifying in his behalf. My support was offered in a letter to the authorities in Sugamo Prison where the former Californian Machida was being held. Released shortly thereafter, he lived out his life with distant relatives in Osaka. In many ways he was more a prisoner than we were, and definitely a man without a country.

How does one describe the happiest day of one's life? Beginning with the 15th day of August 1945, happiness became an every-day feeling. The euphoria we felt upon awakening each morning defies description, a feeling that lasted for months! It was truly a "high," unequaled at any time in all my life. To suddenly rejoin the human race with the rights, respect, and dignity we had been deprived of for three-and-a-half years is indescribable. Ask any former prisoner of the Japanese. I know that a description on my part is impossible. How does one describe being born? Old memories deliberately suppressed for years were suddenly allowed back in my mind. Thoughts of family, friends, and one's country flooded our waking moments. It was a feeling akin to intoxication. Paramount in our thoughts was our pride in our country. We had placed our faith in our country and it did not let us down. Over and over I visualized going home after a six-year absence.

During the last days of Mitsushima—speaking for the majority—I can say that our hatred of the Japanese began to diminish. We were going home. We had no room, no time, to think of what they had done to us. Undoubtedly every man in that camp could have taken revenge on their guards, and no court in the land would have ever held them responsible. To their everlasting credit, most fellow prisoners held themselves in check as Captain Gordon had asked them to do. He firmly believed that our captors would receive their just punishment. Had he known the outcome of some of the trials held in Yokohama in 1946–47, he might have had a different outlook, especially where The Bird was concerned.

Still, there were the "ugly Americans." I witnessed two members of the "football team," our "goldbricks" who had whined their way through the years, strike out at an aged Japanese civilian bookkeeper we had rarely seen. He had done nothing to merit being struck by these two derelicts. Later that same week, two more of the same "team" decided they would leave camp, despite orders to the contrary by Gordon, and seek "wine and women." They never found the women. Most shirkers remained indoors during that period, but they did manage to get some denatured alcohol from a Japanese truck. One almost went blind from the alcohol's effects. We were to see more of such "ugly Americans" later.

One day while we were waiting for something to happen, since very little had changed since the war ended, a large commotion in the camp interrupted my sick sleep. Something exciting was taking place outside my barracks and I went out to see what it was. Everyone was pointing to the sky, where we could see six tiny specks flying way above us. Inasmuch as there had been no Japanese aircraft in the air for months, we assumed they were ours. Waving and shouting at them produced no apparent reaction. They flew away after cruising back and forth over the area apparently looking for us. Japanese newspapers of the day had told us that American fliers were dropping food to prison camps and we placed large signs indicating POW on the roofs of our barracks. Being located in a valley as we were, any airmen would have difficulty seeing us unless they knew exactly where we were. They did not. Joy turned to gloom quickly as the aircraft disappeared over the mountains to the accompaniment of our cursing and moaning.

Exactly one hour later we heard their engines again, flying much lower this time. Suddenly the flight leader made a dive at our camp. At about three hundred feet above us it let go a fifty-five-gallon drum with an orange parachute attached to it. The drum dropped squarely in the middle of our parade grounds where we had stood for so many times in three years. The accuracy of that drop has always amazed me. There could not have been more than fifty feet of a clearing, yet, that pilot dropped his "load" right on target. As soon as he pulled out of his dive, with very little room to maneuver, the second, third, fourth, and fifth planes repeated his actions. Not as accurate as the flight leader, their drums hit all around the camp, with one drum going right into Japanese headquarters. Attached to the drum that had hit squarely on the right target was a red streamer with a note attached which read: "Hello folks. The crew of the U.S.S. *Randolph* send their best. Hope you enjoy the chow, keep your chin up. We'll be back." This was our very first word from free Americans in over three-and-a-half years. What a glorious feeling to read that note. It was passed among every prisoner in that camp and then reread by all. Everyone in camp was asked to sign one of the white parachutes expressing thanks, with his name, rank and organization, for the sole purpose of presenting that chute to the crew of the *Randolph* as quickly as we could. Years later, I attempted to find the *Randolph* to see if the chute with our signatures was ever returned. I never found the ship, and I later learned it had been salvaged.

In the containers dropped to us was an assortment of goodies. Most things we had not seen for years. Gallon cans of fruits, hams, corned beef, meats, milk, cigarettes, and candy. One drum dropped in the riverbed, was filled with Baby Ruth candy bars. Brought to the kitchen, the cooks made a sweet hot soup from the candy bars. Every pot in the kitchen had something cooking from these drums. The following day a second flight of planes, in this case torpedo planes from the U.S.S. *Lexington*, bombed the camp with all sorts of food. A few containers crashed through the roofs of homes, with some injuries to those living in them. From that point on we did nothing but enjoy the variety of foods dropped to us. The stomachs of many, however, could not handle the rich food, myself included. My hepatitis had caused my appetite to all but disappear for several days. After the food drops, we lounged around literally enjoying our newfound sense of well-being, and then boredom set in. We wanted to go home. We had always feared that if the Americans invaded Japan, we would be put to death. We had been told so many times, and evidence after the war uncovered just such instructions. For us, the atom bomb gave us back our lives. While we had heard several months previously that President Franklin Roosevelt had died, we wondered who this President Harry Truman was. None of us knew him, but every one of us owed our lives to him and his courage in dropping the two bombs.

Our Japanese contractors, for whom a number of us had worked closely for three years came to the camp after the guards left. Each one brought some tokens of his firm as gifts for several members of their working parties. Igarashi brought me what we knew to be a "happy coat," a thin silk jacket in several colors with his name in Japanese characters on the back. I treasured that coat, which was stolen from me in an army hospital in Fort Lewis, Washington. So much for my one and only Japanese souvenir of Mitsushima.

The fourth of September 1945 finally dawned and, with it, our orders came to leave that valley. We pooled together all the yen we had and presented this gift to Boy Scout and One-Arm, who had done so much to protect us prisoners. We also gave them the American army blankets that the Japanese had stored in warehouses for three years, along with the South African shoes.

With everyone in a glorious mood at leaving, we Americans made our way up the winding road to the railroad station, and not in any military fashion. Looking down, I witnessed an event that I recall with great pride for the British soldier. Assembled in the parade area were the British troops with their heads bowed. A Sergeant Major Maile, of the Surreys I believe, was leading his group in paying their respects to those who had died in the camp, while we Americans were practically running out of the place in our anxiety to leave. As I watched the British, they formed into a military unit and marched out as if on parade in England. A most impressive sight.

CHAPTER 21

GOING HOME

The word finally came from Captain Gordon to pack up and be prepared to move out on a moment's notice. While we were unaware of it, security of the prisoners was a major concern of our senior officers. They feared Japanese fanatics would attempt to prevent the prisoners' release.

The railroad station platform was a bedlam of excitement, with everyone talking about what they were looking forward to most. The Japanese citizens of Mitsushima turned out as if it were a major holiday, and in many respects the event had a holiday atmosphere. We boarded the train without any Japanese shouting commands at us. What an unusual feeling that was! As the train pulled out of the station, several Japanese were crying. Whether the tears were for us or the defeat of their country, I shall never know. I would prefer to think they were for the prisoners whom many of them had come to know fairly well. All of us aboard that train, however, had our own feelings about leaving a place that many of us had resigned ourselves to as our place to die. Mixed emotions were common. Strange as it may seem, we were leaving familiar surroundings. While tremendously happy to be leaving, there was a strong sense of "family" about the place, something akin to leaving "home." I have never understood those feelings.

Two years after the war ended, I learned that the Mitsushima Prison Camp (Tokyo Camp 2-D) was the worst camp in Japan for brutalities and atrocities. More convicted Class A Japanese war criminals were stationed in that camp than any other camp in Japan. A total of six death sentences were meted out to Japanese guards of Mitsushima, with numerous others sentenced to life imprisonment and other terms of imprisonment. It is a sad commentary on our military criminal justice system of that day that all those imprisoned were then dismissed no later than December 1957, twelve years after the war. Many, many Japanese escaped trial by going underground until the odorous treaty of 1951 was signed by the United States and Japan. This came about when we as a nation needed a strong ally in the Far East to counter the Soviet Union's threat in Korea. The leniency shown to the Japanese is in vast contrast to President Truman's stated purpose of a few years before, when this country promised "to punish those who had inflicted pain and torture upon our POW." It is even more difficult to understand when one considers how Nazi war criminals were hunted for years and still are being hunted at this writing. This dual standard concerning war criminals of Japan and Germany is inexplicable.

As our train rolled through the mountains of Nagano Prefecture (county), passing through small towns which looked like exact duplicates of Mitsushima, we left the mountains thrilled to know we would not have to spend another winter in them. We began to pass through flatland country and see the devastation wrought by our bombers. While the train made no planned stops, we were slowed down by the destruction as we passed through railroad stations. They were completely demolished! Nothing was left standing for miles around the towns and cities.

About four hours after leaving Mitsushima (Hiraoka), we finally made a stop at a railroad station near a major body of water. The town was Hamamatsu, a seaport south of Yokohama. Looking out my window on the train, I saw a group of Caucasians of some type. They appeared very large in stature. Wearing dark blue denims and lighter blue shirts, with weird looking helmets on their heads, they appeared to be from another country. Sticking my head through the open window, I asked one of these men if he were getting aboard the train. I assumed we were picking up additional prisoners for liberation. The one I asked replied "No, Mack, you're getting off." As he turned away from me, I could see a Thompson submachine gun strapped to his back. He either stole it or it was issued to him by our country, I thought. The latter proved correct, and we were finally back in the hands of our countrymen. Just knowing that sent chills up and down my spine.

Getting off the train, we were assembled on a beach by a United States naval landing party which had come ashore there in landing ships designed for the invasion of Japan. Hundreds and hundreds of prisoners of war were gathered on the beach that warm sunny afternoon. Basking in both the glow of the day plus the glow of liberation, we milled about, anxious to start our way home. Walking among the prisoners were a number of war correspondents interviewing and filming those who met their specifications. A reporter from the *New York Times* asked for a number of prisoners of war from New York. My interview with this reporter about my release was published in the *Times* about a week later and my family had the opportunity to read of the event.

Waiting our turn—and everyone waited, regardless of nationality—we watched those who had arrived before us taking off in landing ships which headed for a number of large ships anchored in Tokyo Bay. Soon the waiting prisoners became several thousand in number: American, British, Australian, Chinese, Dutch, and other nationalities. We were all waiting for instructions to board, so we sat and watched the excitement of the Navy operation in rescuing prisoners. A naval commodore with a bullhorn kept some semblance of order.

Finally my group began to go aboard the landing craft. I saw a "complete" American flag positioned on the aft of the landing ship, blowing in the breeze. This was our first glimpse at an American flag since we had moved out of Fort William McKinley on 10 December 1941 on our way to Bataan. No explanation on my part could ever do justice to my feeling of pride on seeing that flag for the first time in years. We had always believed that our country would come back to get us. The flag was proof positive that believing as we did, we were not forgotten. I was never more proud to be an American than on that day. That flag represented everything that we had lived and died for. No one who has not been deprived of seeing his country's flag can ever understand that feeling. Freedom is taken for granted by too many Americans, but, as an un-named Marine wrote on a wall in Beirut, "for those who fought for it, freedom has a flavor the protected will never know."

There, as before, the "ugly American" phenomenon once again reared its ugly head. An ancient Japanese civilian policeman with his little toy sword strapped to his side, whom we had never come into contact with before that day, stood waving farewell to each departing craft. Suddenly a "hero" from my camp threw a can of soup he had been carrying with him since leaving Mitsushima and struck the old man squarely in the forehead. His brow imme-diately opened from the force of the blow and blood spurted from his wound. The act was deliberate, but there was absolutely no reason for it. Turning on the thrower of the can, I discovered it was my old friend Jones, who in his words was "paying them back." I promised Jones then that I would see him again when we got home. That Jones was a coward had always been evident and this latest incident was further evidence of his cowardliness.

There were many "Joneses" in prison camp. Bullies, cowards, non-soldiers, and goldbricks, they were that way before they ever entered the army. Constantly crying about what they did not have or what they had lost by being soldiers, they sickened me. Even in peacetime these were the same characters who complained about the food in the army, and upon close examination you invariably found out they had never eaten as well when they were civilians. Unfortunately, the "Joneses" of the prison camps survived while decent men died, often as a result of the actions of such predators. Many of these same individuals now sit about in convention ho-tels attempting to convince others and themselves how well they had fought the good fight necessary to survive. Worst of all, they are believed by the gullible as "evidence" of what a prisoner's life was all about. They were camp predators then, and they predators today. Their cloak of civilization may have been put back on, but inside they remain exactly what they were. It's in their blood and bones.

The actions of many of these predators in camp paid off hand-somely for them. Many have written books, or had someone write one for them, and you can find them peddling their memoirs at the conventions of former prisoners of war. Truly, these men are "professional prisoners of war," ready to tell whatever it is that one wants to hear. Their stories, if examined closely, could never withstand analysis. As the years go by the stories become more obscene in their exaggeration.

A number claim that the Japanese on Bataan tortured them because the Japanese believed they had knowledge of an underground tunnel between Bataan and Corregidor. First, the Japanese would never ask an enlisted man for such information. There would be no reason for any enlisted man to possess such knowledge. Second, if all the men alleging such torture for this lack of knowledge were lined up, they would run the length of two football fields. Years after the war, these very same individuals can still be found distorting the true extents of the war. But, on with my story.

Going aboard the landing craft on that day, we headed out into the bay, one of almost one hundred such landing craft, all awaiting the signal to approach the hospital ship *Rescue* anchored several miles offshore. With our craft bobbing up and down in the water my old nemesis, seasickness, returned in full force. With very little in my stomach due to my illness, I found myself retching repeatedly to the point that, after a while, I retched nothing but blood. Finally we were signaled to approach the hospital ship, but getting from the landing craft onto the steps leading to the main deck became quite a chore. Finally aboard, we knew definitely we were "home."

On board, the joy of being back in American hands began to register. Those carrying old overcoats and equipment given to them in their camps were told to throw it all overboard or have it burned aboard ship. Very little was allowed on board. British troops who had known the hardships of war before their capture attempted to take certain items back "to old Blighty," only to be disappointed when the ship's crew took away everything they had and burned it. We were immediately undressed to the bone and sent into steaming hot showers, deloused by corpsmen, and then issued totally new Marine Corps fatigue uniforms, insignia and all, down to socks and underwear. We began to look military and American for the first time in a long while.

Assigned to a folding cot temporarily set up on the deck of the ship due to the patient overload aboard, I spent my first night trying to sleep. Nurses in crisp white uniforms that rustled as they passed by helped keep me awake. Their aroma of perfume was maddening. Long since impotent from the poor diet we existed on, the presence of an American woman was still exciting. This was my first contact with a woman in almost four years, and being normally shy of women I found it impossible to talk to one. So I spent the night looking up at the stars with a thousand thoughts running through my mind and just basking in the thought of being free.

At daybreak, prisoners began to assemble on deck near my cot, preparing to go to breakfast. Completely without an appetite, I had to content myself with merely watching them go down to the galley. Dr. Weinstein walked past after emerging from the galley, and urged me to go for some food. I declined. I asked him what he had for breakfast. He replied, "Eggs…thirty-two of them. Yes, thirty-two eggs went down and thirty-two eggs came up!" Even the good doctor forgot that our stomachs could not yet handle most American food. I prefer to think he knew but disregarded his own advice. Staying aboard the *Rescue*, Doc Weinstein received first-class care by the ship's staff. He remained with the ship as it went along the coast of Tokyo Bay, picking up prisoners of war on its way to Yokohama.

That was the last I saw of Dr. Weinstein until April 1947. For me the first day aboard the hospital ship was also my only day aboard her. The ship was overcrowded with prisoner patients, so I was transferred along with others to the destroyer U.S.S. *Lardner* at anchor nearby. Again the ride across the pitching sea started my retching over the side. Once aboard the destroyer my stomach settled down. Knowing the reputation of destroyers however, I refused to go below deck. After a spell the ship got underway and, surprisingly, was cutting smoothly through the water. I then decided to try going down to the galley, as some prisoners were emerging from the bulkhead carrying trays of pancakes, sausages, and eggs. Food we once would have died for! Going below however, was a mistake. I finally reached the galley, several decks below.

But as I started through the chow line the familiar feeling of nausea swept over me again.

Trapped in line by men in back and in front of me, I got my food and started up the gangway to fresh air. Each step brought me closer to vomiting. Barely reaching the main deck, I knew I was going to "lose my cookies" and headed for the railing. Having nowhere to put down the tray, I retched into the tray and threw the contents overboard. Unfortunately, I chose the wrong side of the ship to do that, as the wind swept everything back, dousing three sailors who were sunbathing with the mess. Much cursing ensued, and one sailor told me that being a POW had saved me from being thrown overboard. Fortunately the ship docked at Yokohama shortly thereafter.

We were marched to a liberty ship tied to the pier. I felt I was finally safe from my seasickness, and after several days of normalcy and eating regularly we were sent to Atsugi Air Base, a former Japanese Air Force base, where General MacArthur had landed several days previously when he entered Japan. Waiting in one of the field's large hangars, we received our first Red Cross coffee and doughnuts from some very pretty American women working for the organization.

Planes were flying in so fast, as one touched down, another one took off immediately. This pace was kept all day. Put aboard a B-24 bomber, for my first airplane ride ever, I found myself flying off to Okinawa, a flight of about five hours. The plane was overloaded. Years later I heard that one of these planes had lost four prisoners who fell from a bomb bay as a result of bad weather. Still, thousands of prisoners were safely flown out in this fashion.

CHAPTER 22

MANILA—THE SECOND TIME

Landing at Okinawa on our way to Manila, we were taken to a camp city. A sea of huge pyramidal green canvas tents dotted the landscape. There were hundreds of them. No sooner had we arrived than a torrential rain came down. For three days and nights it was nonstop rain. Mud everywhere. In the sleeping tents, the mess tents, the hospital tents, and post-exchange tents. Wherever we stopped on the way home, we had free access to exchange items at absolutely no cost. Signs were erected at exchange tents advertising that items inside were free for POWs. Our excitement at being safe was dampened by the warning that a number of Japanese soldiers had refused to surrender and were still hiding out in caves and tunnels on the islands. The camp had already experienced "hit and run" tactics from these renegades.

Issued an army poncho as our rain gear, an item we had never seen before, along with a steel helmet, we were given the opportunity to watch our first American movie, in pouring rain. While I fail to remember the title of the film, I have always remembered the song "Drinking Rum and Coca-Cola" by the Andrews Sisters from that movie. I never thought I could sit in a driving rain and watch a movie, but that was a "first" in a long time, and I did! In a way, watching a film that way reminded me of the time I was a very young boy, and a settlement house, the Hudson Guild in New York City, would show movies on a sand baseball field. We would sit on the ground waiting for the movie to start. Invariably someone would start throwing sand in the air, which landed in one's hair. I thought of those summer nights in New York City while sitting in that pouring rain.

Despite the rain that first movie night, not a single prisoner of war left the area. Those assigned to show the movie thought we were crazy to sit there, but since we insisted on seeing it they allowed the film to continue. We were watching film stars we had never seen before and we took the jokes and music in hungrily, as if seeing our very first movie.

Once again, five days later, my turn came to move on another leg of our journey home. Jammed again into a plane, another B-24, we took off for the Philippines. Several airfields on Okinawa were used to return prisoners of war home. Ten years later, while stationed on Okinawa, I had the opportunity to return to the field we had used then for our departure. Overgrown with weeds and no longer in use, the sight of that field brought back every memory of my 1945 stop on Okinawa.

At no point in our return trip home were we ever told where we were going. Only after we arrived did we know where we were. It seems the army of that day did not feel it had to convey any information to its men. They just picked up and moved out on orders. What impressed me during my stay on Okinawa was the fairness exhibited by the Americans in shipping out prisoners to the Philippines. All prisoners regardless of nationality were flown out in the order they had arrived. British, Canadian, and Dutch troops returned to their country by way of Okinawa and the Philippines. With over 140,000 Allied prisoners of war held in Japan alone, such figures put a huge demand on American military to manage their safe return.

After another short flight of about four hours we found ourselves circling Manila. We had now completed a full 360 degree circle since leaving the islands. The pilot, aware that many of us were returning to a city we once knew, graciously flew slowly in circles so we could see the sights of the city. The scene was staggering in its destruction. Manila was in ruins. We were totally unable to recognize streets familiar to us. We soon landed and were immediately trucked about twelve miles outside the city.

After disembarking from our trucks, we found ourselves once

again in a city of tents. In this case however there were thousands of tents with thousands inhabiting them. We were at the 29th Replacement Depot, famous to every returning prisoner of war held by Japan. Men of every nationality were held here pending their return home.

After arriving at the 29th we were assigned to tents, and upon entering them we found two rows of ribbons to be worn on our newly issued suntan uniforms. Not having an idea as to what the ribbons represented, we had to rely on a cadre of the 29th to inform us. We then learned about the "point system." They told us we had enough points to go home, but we insisted we were going home, points or no points! To a serviceman stationed overseas, the accumulation of points gathered either soldiering so many months overseas or by having medals awarded, etc., provided that ticket home which all desired. But a prisoner of war had more than enough "points" to return home. For our category military points were unneeded. Each returning American prisoner was issued a patch of gold stripes, with each stripe representing six months overseas. At no time during World War II did any other service-men wear seven such stripes, as worn by prisoners of the Japanese, all of whom had been overseas the first day of the war. Wherever one of these prisoners traveled, he could be recognized as a prisoner of Japan by the seven overseas "bars" he wore on the arm of his shirt or uniform blouse.

Our stay at the 29th Replacement Depot was fascinating as new sights and new sounds dazzled us daily. Unlimited food constantly outside our sleeping areas, with American cooks standing by for one's request twenty-four hours a day, seemed too good to be true. Working alongside Americans assigned as cadres for the camp were Japanese prisoners of war. They appeared somewhat odd to us, and then we realized why. They were mere boys. Nothing like the Japanese soldier who had fought us in Bataan or guarded us in Japan. Apparently very fearful of returning Allied prisoners, these Japanese kept their distance despite our several attempts to converse with them in Japanese. Whenever we did this a look of great surprise came upon their faces, but they never responded to us. Whenever we walked about the camp the eyes of these young Japanese prisoners followed us. They obviously knew that we had been prisoners of their country and were leery of getting too close to us.

For the next two weeks we were subjected to a battery of tests and probing by Army doctors. It was easy to recognize a prisoner in the 29th. If you saw someone walking about camp who resembled a skeleton with some flesh hanging on him, it was a "horyo." The vast majority of returning prisoners were nothing more than skin and bones. A strong resemblance to what we looked like can be seen in photographs of inmates of Nazi concentration camps, or in photos of American prisoners held by Japan which were later released. Many of our men were mere skeletons. I myself was considered a heavyweight. I weighed all of about 130 pounds, down from my prewar weight of 185.

At night, after spending most of the day in the hands of the medical people, we would head down to the Red Cross building and listen to the latest American music, check for mail, and stare at the American women in camp. Seeing these women came as a shock to me. I had never seen so many American women in one place. We learned they were wearing the uniforms of the Women's Army Corps, WACs, with ranks of private, corporal, and so on. We were seeing a totally different facet of army life. Yet most prisoners still avoided them based on the old thinking that the American women held rank, and enlisted men could never mingle with them for that reason. Here they initiated the mixing! It was more like Lil Abner and Daisy Mae, with Daisy Mae of cartoon fame doing the chasing!

Finally, several nights after my arrival, I received a letter from my mother. While fairly brief (it contained about seventy-five words), to me it appeared to be a book. After being permitted no more than twenty-five words on a postcard in Mitsushima, this was great. My first real letter from home since before the war, I spent hours reading and rereading it over and over again until I had it memorized. Truly, letters from home and loved ones are a soldier's treasures.

From that letter I learned that my brother Roy was in the Navy, somewhere in the Philippines no less. Another brother, a Marine aerial photographer, was also somewhere on an island near the

Philippines. I made every effort through the Red Cross to locate them. "Sorry," said the Red Cross people, "unless you have their serial number, etc...."

While waiting to go home I had the opportunity to visit Cecil Fernandez, my old buddy from Mitsushima. Cecil was in the British compound waiting to be sent back to Singapore. Expressing a desire to go to the United States, he asked me to help him get there. Not knowing myself what awaited me, I had to vaguely promise to help one day. Going to America was Cecil's constant dream in prison camp. I never found out if Cecil succeeded in his quest. We maintained contact for a number of years but eventually lost that touch. I regret that. Cecil was the one person who I felt had befriended me above all others. I owed him a debt and failed to repay him, mostly because I was in no position to do so.

Finally I received word we were leaving for the United States. Loaded one morning into a Canadian Army truck, strange in appearance to me (the nose of the truck disappeared into its cab), we unloaded at Pier Seven in Manila's harbor, the very same pier I had arrived at, in what seemed like a lifetime before, in 1940. It was also the very same pier whence I had boarded the *Nagato Maru* for our hell-ship trip to Japan in 1942. Sitting on the other side of the pier was the *Empress of Australia*, a British ship taking Cecil back to Malaysia. Cecil was getting off his truck about the same time I was, and we bade each other a final farewell standing on the pier between the two ships. We made a few brief remarks about staying in touch with each other, but like so many wartime friendships it was merely talk.

Later I learned from my mother that my brother Roy, upon learning I was back in the Philippines, had obtained a leave of absence and made his way to the 29th. Somehow he contacted my other brother Freddie, who flew in from his island in the Pacific, and together they came down to Pier Seven just as our ship, the Army transport *Gosper*, was pulling out of the harbor. We missed a reunion that would have been the greatest surprise of my life. Freddie it seemed could not get a leave so he went away anyway just to surprise both brothers. By appearing at the dock, at least he and Roy had a reunion which, I understand, was a real "winner."

Freddie was later given a hearing before his CO and reduced from sergeant to private. Always the perfect Private, Freddie never wanted or sought rank, but was merely happy flying about the Pacific taking photographs of Japanese positions from an open cockpit. He became known in the family as "Flashbulb Freddie," ace photographer, destined to die relatively young after the war and a very unhappy marriage.

Boarding the transport U.S.A.T. *Gosper*, we learned that no former prisoner of war was to do anything that resembled work. We were to be treated "first-class" on our way home. Those on board the *Gosper* were of every rank from corporals to master sergeant, all of whom had volunteered to do the necessary chores aboard a transport of those days. Their reward: an immediate ship home! Thousands of servicemen with sufficient points to return home were being held up pending available ships. None of those volunteering had the slightest hesitancy about doing work aboard ship. They wanted home at any cost! We then set sail from Manila harbor, and all that had happened to me since I first viewed Manila harbor in 1940 flooded my mind. Here I was, almost six years after first seeing Manila, on my way home. When I first arrived I had wondered how I could spend two years in the Philippines before returning home. Little did I dream what life held in store for me. I was lucky however. Here I was, on my way home. Thousands of others would never return. As the Memorial Plaque on Corregidor puts it (which moved me greatly in the 1990s when I visited there):

> Sleep my sons, your duty done,
> For Freedom's light has come.
> Sleep in your hallowed bed of sod
> Or in the silent depths of the sea.
> Until at dawn you hear the clear
> *Low reveille of God.*

Still wary of sleeping below deck, I slept in my usual place, under a lifeboat. This new transport however, was a much more modern and rapid ship than the old *Grant*. In addition, it had a ship's orchestra which played on deck every day. The very first song each day was "Sentimental Journey," made popular by Doris Day. Indeed it was a sentimental journey for all of us aboard the *Gosper*. The orchestra played songs most of us had never heard before. The ship's newspaper filled us in on world affairs we knew nothing about. Hitler had killed himself in May 1945; the Russians had joined the war against Japan just days before the war ended; certain Germans were scheduled to be tried as war criminals, a new phrase to returning prisoners. On and on it went. We were catching up on four years of news in a short period of time and happily absorbing it all.

At night, movies were shown to those interested. Many former prisoners were content to just lie in their bunks, or under the stars as in my case, and dream of home. Having already seen our first movie since liberation, most of us were content to wait until we reached the United States. Food was unlimited. It was the only transport I was ever aboard that fed "midnight buffets," found only on cruise ships.

CHAPTER 23

RETURN TO THE U.S.A.

As we neared the West Coast of the United States, we could feel the excitement growing. We were about the see the Golden Gate Bridge of San Francisco again. While in prison camp we had made up ditties concerning the date we would be going home. One in particular stood out in my mind, "the Golden Gate in forty-eight." That was a scary one! I preferred "home alive in forty-five." Two days before San Francisco came our first disappointment. The ship's captain went on the intercom to state that our ship held the roughly five hundred Canadian former prisoners captured in the war. Washington decided to be a "good neighbor" and drop off the Canadians first. The Americans' disappointment over not having the chance to see the "golden gate" was unbelievable. We felt cheated. Told we would be docking at Victoria, Vancouver, B.C., howls of protest went up, with screams of "Who the hell's ship is this anyway?!" Or words to that effect. Today I am still pleased we took the detour.

We arrived at that harbor about midnight. It was blacked out with not a light visible anywhere. We thought this odd since the war was over. This was taking security too far. Suddenly our transport was illuminated by one tremendous ship's searchlight coming from nearby. Then another ship's light hit us. Then a third, a fourth—until every ship in the harbor, and there had to be hundreds of them, had focused their searchlights on our ship. We were lit up like a Christmas tree at Rockefeller Center in New York City. From every ship in the harbor and from the shore itself came the sound of whistles and horns. Literally, hundreds of them were blasting their welcome to us. It had been a planned surprise for the Canadians and what a surprise it was! There wasn't a dry eye — Canadian or American — aboard that ship that night. The din continued for at least thirty minutes as the ship slid alongside its pier.

After docking, each Canadian soldier walked down the gangplank after his name, rank, and organization were announced to the crowd of three thousand plus assembled on the pier. Each one so introduced received a terrific burst of applause as he stepped on Canadian soil again. Canadians were proud of their former prisoners of war and they showed their pride that night. Americans were moved by this very touching display of patriotism and love for their Canadian counterparts. Many Americans remarked, "This is great, but wait until we get home." Our homecoming was scheduled for the following morning after the ship crossed the sound to Seattle. During another hard-to-sleep night we waited for the morning to see our first sight of the United States.

Crossing the sound in almost complete fog we arrived in Seattle at 7 A.M. As the fog dissipated we drew near the pier. No sounds could be heard and nothing could be seen on the pier. As the fog lifted from the pier there was our "welcoming committee," one lone drunk sleeping it off on the pier. Shock hit us! How could our country greet us in this fashion after what we had witnessed the night before? In fairness to the army, Washington had made the last minute switch from San Francisco to Seattle, thus leaving a number of families of returning prisoners waiting on the pier in San Francisco. At the very last minute someone official remembered their being in San Francisco while their sons and husbands were now landing in Seattle. So the families were hastily put on buses in San Francisco and made a hurried overnight ride to Seattle, arriving at our pier about two hours after we docked.

Upon our docking some other official realized that this was a "hell of a homecoming" and rushed an army band to the pier. The band set up their instruments hastily and we were soon serenaded with music. This was the nearest that any of us arriving on the *Gosper* came to a welcome home ceremony. Apparently the majority of Americans were busy welcoming home the veterans from

Europe. So once again, we of the Pacific theater received the short end. Still, we were home! The music sounded great, if somewhat ragged. We were not allowed ashore until the relatives from San Francisco arrived, so we could do nothing but look from the ship's rails at the band and the drunk. I remember that drunk remaining asleep through the whole period I was aboard the ship. In later years I wondered if he was dead.

Finally, after the arrival of the West Coast relatives, we were allowed to disembark. A Red Cross bus and truck had arrived just as we were leaving the ship. As we came down the gangplank we were handed a doughnut and a cup of coffee. What more could a returning soldier ask for?

Throwing our duffel bags aboard trucks as instructed, we soon boarded buses and sped through the city of Seattle. While we waved, shouted, whistled, and screamed out the windows, the natives of Seattle looked at us as if we were crazy. Some waved back and smiled. The vast majority however did not even bother to look. We were sure by this time that the Canadian prisoners dropped off at Vancouver had the last laugh when it came to being welcomed home.

At Fort Lewis, Washington, the home of Madigan General Hospital, we found ourselves truly at home. The hospital staff could not do enough for us. As soon as we were assigned beds we were told to recover our duffel bags placed aboard the trucks at the pier. Another surprise awaited us. When we retrieved our bags from the storerooms where they had been placed, we found every one cut open. Anything of value had been stolen. Welcome home! Taken from my bag was the happy coat Igarashi had given me on my leaving Mitsushima. Others lost similar items. No one was spared the theft of their possessions, as little as they were. To those who have, more shall be added. To those with little, even that little shall be taken away.

Examinations and testing of all types were scheduled for us daily at Madigan General. Almost from the first day we arrived there all of our former "cell mates" were scattered to the four winds. One might pass a buddy in one of the many hallways or corridors of the hospital with scarcely enough time to ask, "What ward are you going to?" Even in the hospital's mess halls, gigantic in size, it was difficult to see a face one recognized. After spending three years with about seventy other American prisoners, that number was swallowed up among the thousands of prisoners in the hospital. Food was great! We managed to eat all we could and many times paid for it with upset stomachs.

Nearly every prisoner of war held by the Japanese had intestinal parasites. Often it took months of hospitalization treatment to resolve this problem. Often only partially. That the army medics allowed prisoners with such delicate stomachs to eat everything and anything has always surprised me. In my own case, I would pay a price for eating in a restaurant if I ate the wrong foods. Terrible cramps would strike me in the abdomen almost immediately to the point where I was doubled up from the pain.

While at Madigan however, we feasted. The kitchen police (K.P.'s), a duty assignment no soldier ever wanted, went to enemy prisoners of war, in this case Germans working at the hospital. Captured in Europe, they were sent to Fort Lewis. Bigger and fatter than any prisoners of war I had ever seen, they seemed to enjoy working in the kitchens of Madigan. Dressed in old blue army fatigues not seen since before the war, with a large "POW" in white painted on their backs, they were objects of our curiosity. I could never understand how this country went out of its way to handle these European enemy prisoners of war with great concern when Japanese-American citizens on our West Coast—as we later learned—were treated as the enemy. Outside the main gates of Fort Lewis we would find American girlfriends of the German prisoners. Later in my career I was assigned to Fort Hamilton, Brooklyn, New York, where Italian prisoners were held during the war. They too fared well, especially among the Italian-Americans of Brooklyn. Countless women would be found pressed up against the steel pole fences separating them from the Italian prisoners, usually in some love gesture. Such treatment—so different from that accorded American prisoners in all theaters of war—was a constant source of irritation among American former prisoners of war.

The American public, swept up in the excitement of their sons, fathers, and husbands returning from Europe, soon forgot that some Americans were returning from prison camps in the Pacific. Many prisoners, equally anxious to put their military lives behind them, signed waivers in the hospitals to get out without receiving adequate medical care, only to regret this later. The medics, overloaded with patients, asked simplistic questions such as "How do you feel?" No prisoner wanting to go home would ever say anything negative in answer to that.

At Madigan General, lists were posted of those who would not be released, and of who would be sent home via hospital trains if their homes were on the East Coast. Among those names posted for leaving was mine. Not knowing what was wrong with me that would require hospitalization while crossing the United States on a train—while others flew home—I entrained for the East Coast with a large number of total strangers from other prison camps.

On board that hospital train we found that Uncle Sam had committed another snafu. A young corporal from the Bronx, New York, whose leg was seriously wounded in Italy, was being sent home to New York by way of California. We all wondered what he was doing on the West Coast. After landing in New York from a hospital ship he was looked at by doctors on the pier. His family, who had been notified of his homecoming, was being held beyond a restraining rope nearby. Tagged, he was then placed in an ambulance, taken to a railroad station, placed on a hospital train—the same one we were on at this time—and sent to Madigan General Hospital in Seattle. Despite his protests he still went to Washington. When he arrived on the West Coast some medical authority recognized the mistake and left him on our train to return to New York. He kept us company all the way back across the country. Laughlin, as I recall his name, never lost his sense of humor and contributed greatly to a very pleasant railroad trip without beefing about the situation. He was glad to be alive and home, even three thousand miles away from his real home. All across the nation, as we stopped in small towns, little old ladies would board the train and offer us candies, cakes, and the like. We received instructions that whenever we arrived at such a stop we were to remain in our bunks, in our hospital robes. All of us were capable of mobility, but the orders were "remain in your bunks." I guess it made the little old ladies happy to see the "wounded and sick" in the shape they expected. I am sure it was nothing more than a public relations gimmick on the part of the army.

Arriving in New York's Penn Station, I approached the meeting with my family with a great deal of trepidation. Since I had written a number of times and informed my mother of when I would be arriving in New York I fully expected to see her there. Yet I was suddenly overcome with the crazy desire to have the train turn around and take me back to Japan. I have never fully understood that compulsion on my part to run away from what I had wished, dreamed, and hoped for almost six years. And to actually want to return to Japan no less! It was a totally mystifying version of the approach-evasion syndrome.

As the passenger car I was in came to a stop I saw my mother. She was going up and down the outside of the car pressing her face up against the smoke-laden windows. Her face was blackened by the soot of the engine, and despite the years in-between I recognized her immediately. Standing alongside her, however, were two strangers. One was a little girl about eleven years old, the other a skinny eighteen-year-old lad, my brother Danny. He was twelve when I left for the army and I knew it had to be him even though he had grown so much. He entered the car asking other former prisoners, "Do you know Gordon?" I actually turned my face away from him so he wouldn't see me, and then another soldier pointed me out to him. Again a feeling of panic overcame me. I wanted to have the train pull out and take me back. That feeling soon passed, however. I was then removed from the train onto a stretcher, and except for my mother grabbing my hand and walking beside me, we were not allowed any time together at the station. She was told abruptly by some "stateside commando" that I was being taken to Halloran General Hospital on Staten Island and she could visit me there.

Hours later, after being assigned to a hospital ward and issued new hospital clothing, I was allowed to visit with my mother, brother, and my young sister Lorraine, the little girl I saw standing next to my mother at the station. I must confess to spending a most uneasy time during our first reunion. I felt out of place. My family was not too comfortable in my presence either. I felt they were examining every inch of me looking for something, but not know-ing exactly what.

After my family's hospital visit I found myself in a huge ward with at least forty former prisoners of war. On one side were Americans captured by the Germans and on the opposite side were those captured by the Japanese. We rarely mixed as we had absolutely nothing in common other than temporarily losing our freedom. At the end of our ward was a dining area specifically for prisoners. Pool tables, card tables and telephone booths were also located there. After meeting my wife-to-be, Jean, I called her every night from those booths.

During my first weekend pass from the hospital I stayed at my mother's home, sleeping in late each morning. On Saturday of that weekend I was awakened by a sailor in uniform—my brother Leroy. To me he was totally unrecognizable, but I knew he was my brother. He kept telling me so. That weekend my mother planned a Thanksgiving dinner over our protests since Thanksgiving was only two weeks away. "No," she said, "this is our first turkey we have been able to have and I promised myself we would celebrate Thanksgiving as soon as you came home." So we had that dinner just as she planned, which was just as well as she did not live to see Thanksgiving Day.

That weekend was even more memorable because that's when I met and fell in love with the woman who shared my life for forty-seven years. My brother Roy made the introduction on my twenty-fourth birthday. I can't thank Roy for much, but I surely thank him for that introduction. A typical sailor of that era with a girl in every port, he eventually toured New England with me and visited his "every port."

Back in the hospital after my first weekend home, I was sitting on my hospital bed when I saw my brother Roy coming into the ward from the opposite side. From his face I knew something was wrong and he confirmed this when he bluntly stated, "Mom's dead." His coldness at that time always bothered me. He might have been telling me that Prime Minister Tojo had died. Such callousness. In retrospect however I realized that he had seen enough of death and dying that he became hardened to it. In addition, he never was close to Mother, preferring to spend his leaves from the navy in the company of friends. What I have always resented him for was his lack of respect for his mother. In those days one did not admit to having an alcoholic mother. He not only admitted to it, he talked about her alcoholism openly. I was now home again, with new problems. The more things had changed, the more they had, indeed, remained the same.

I had to report back to the hospital during the week with weekend passes home until late March 1946. I was examined and reexamined almost daily. Diagnosis: severe malnutrition, severe intestinal parasites, hepatitis (yellow jaundice as I knew it then), and several malaria attacks. My permission to "go home" on weekends, when it came, proved not too beneficial for me. "Home" for me was the YMCA on 34th Street, New York City, still there at this writing and known as the Sloane House. After several weeks I knew I could not remain there. I had better quarters in the hospital. Each weekend when I ate at the local "grease shack," I experienced terrible stomach cramps so severe that they doubled me up. During a couple of these episodes I attracted the attention of New York's finest, the police. They always urged me to go back to the hospital as I wasn't well enough to be out.

I have already recounted how I met Jean. I had fallen in love with her immediately. Jean was Italian-American, and having grown up in the streets of New York City almost every friend I had was an Italian-American. I have never met a warmer or more hospitable ethnic group, and so I felt right at home. Jean's mother, famous for her cooking, took me under her wing, insisting that I spend weekends at her house. She fed me various foods known to be good for one's stomach. I am convinced that Mrs. Frances Pellechi, known as Fanny, did more to cure my ailments than all the doctors I had in the hospital.

On 12 January 1946, Jean's birthday, we announced our engagement while I was on continuous leave from the military. My first leave was for all my accumulated leaves for six years. I had never taken leave up to this point. Following that leave, I was given 104 days as former prisoner of war leave. I returned to the army at Fort McPherson, Georgia, where I reenlisted for the regular army and was given ninety days additional leave for reenlisting. In brief, almost my entire first year after coming home from Japan was spent on leave. Checks arrived at the house for me, and I never really knew what they were for. My back pay had accumulated to over four thousand dollars, a lot of money for that time. I should add that I did not keep it too long. It had come the hard way and was going to go the easy way.

Shortly after returning to the army I was stationed at Fort Hamilton, New York, and a new life began for me. Less than a year from my last day as a prisoner of war in Japan, I was settled down to my army career with a wife. For our honeymoon, as I already mentioned, we selected New Orleans, Louisiana, home of a fellow prisoner of war from Mitsushima, George Piel. George and I talked on a number of occasions concerning our prison experience. Each time we did, we ended up as we began, with wonderment. How did it happen? How were we so unprepared? Who was responsible for the debacle known as Bataan? The answers were few, but the thoughts were many.

Suffice it to say, I and my fellow prisoners of war of the Japanese had gone through a virtual nightmare. Those fortunate enough to return have been haunted by their experience. Hardly a single day ever passes in our lives without the subject of Bataan and our subsequent imprisonment somehow coming up. It will only end with our deaths.

Within two years of leaving my prison camp existence, I was recalled to active duty as a second lieutenant assigned to Germany. Truly my life had turned full circle. From the position of an "animal" in the eyes of the Japanese, I was now a commissioned officer of the United States Army, the proudest achievement of my life. My mother, God rest her soul, would be happy, equally proud. I had begun my military career with the dream of being a West Point cadet. Failing that, I still reached the commissioned ranks, the goal of all military academy graduates. Life has been good to me and I have no complaints. To paraphrase General MacArthur: "We did our duty as God gave us the light to see that duty. I would—if given the chance—relive my life exactly as I lived it." As the song goes, "I did it my way...Regrets? I have a few, too few to mention."

EPILOGUE

Today, a certain number of the survivors of Bataan and Corregidor have become what some call "professional prisoners of war." These individuals have spent the last fifty years pretending to have a camaraderie with each other that goes all the way back to their days as Japanese "horyos." Such camaraderie existed only among a few. This is not to denigrate the large number of fine men who served their country under exceedingly difficult circumstances. Our feelings are directed to the minority of the men of Bataan and Corregidor. Yet, this cannot be overlooked if one analyzes what happened in those days.

These former "horyos" meet periodically to convince each other that they have been lifelong friends all along. These "friendships" certainly did not exist during captivity. Time has not only changed their physical appearances, it has also diminished their memories of each other. Some do remember, but they opt to forgive each other for acts far in excess of Japanese cruelties, all the while claiming that everyone "hates" the Japanese. It is not rare to hear one lie about his experience and have the other swear it to be the truth. From these sessions always come the latest demands these "professionals" place on their government to give them due award because of their "hero" status.

Underneath all of these outward signs of mutual friendship are gnawing questions. Were you the medic who refused me quinine while I was on the verge of dying from malaria, but offered to sell it to me? Were you the one who wanted to sell me that diseased piece of sugar cane candy for twenty pesos (ten dollars) after you had purchased it for twenty centavos (ten cents)? Is it possible that you were the one who deliberately stepped on my face as you attempted to climb over me in your anxiety to reach the deck of our prison ship during a submarine attack? Are you the one who cursed me for being in your way to that deck? Or are you the one who stole milk from the sick and dying patients at O'Donnell so that you could use it in your ersatz coffee at an officers' party? Are you the one who deprived me of a drink of water at O'Donnell by "crashing" the water line under the excuse that you were obtaining water for the sick? Were you the one who filled that container with enough water for twenty men, causing others to go without when the Japanese turned off the water at their prescribed time? And so on.

"Does man continue to love his brother when steeped in disease, chronic starvation, and death? How low in animal behavior can man sink and still revert to his humanity?" Dr. Alfred E. Weinstein asks in his book *Barbed Wire Surgeon*. Written immediately after the war while the events were still fresh in his memory, Weinstein was not referring to a minority of prisoners but to the majority. Sharing the very same experiences as Weinstein, I know full well the meaning of Weinstein's remarks, having shared numerous conversations with him both during and after the war.

Several other books echo Weinstein's feelings on his fellow prisoners' behavior. Unfortunately, if my experiences as a "horyo" are any basis, the answer to Dr. Weinstein's questions is that most men will sink to any level that is necessary to sustain their life. That level in prison camp was often intensified by our leadership, or rather *lack* of leadership, which was more the case. While there is no question that prisoners of the Japanese were treated much more severely than those held by the Germans, the absence of leadership so prevalent in Japanese camps compared to the leadership displayed in Nazi camps brought about the death of many Americans. (About 37 percent of the Japanese prisoners perished compared to less than 4 percent of those held by the Germans.)

That discipline was almost nonexistent among American prisoners of the Japanese was an established fact. One American naval corpsman assaulted an American officer in Bilibid because that

officer had reported him for sleeping on watch. Because the corpsman was a favorite of the prison's naval chaplain, the so-called
disciplinary board exonerated him, thus encouraging a greater
breakdown of military discipline. "Officers and men become animal derelicts with only the crude law of the jungle as the order of
the day—the primal urge to survive. The veneer of civilization
thinly spread to begin with was wiped off like chalk from a slate.
Still, here and there through the pandemonium and graveyard of
decent human behavior, an occasional self-disciplined courageous
personality would emerge. But their number was so small that they
cast only the feeble light of a tiny candle throughout the black and
crumbled world."

The author of those words, Commander Hayes, writing in his
diary, correctly predicted the future. "Of course, when the war is
over, there will be old soft-soap and whitewash act. The politicians
will come out of the woodwork. It will be hands across the sea and
all is forgiven." Such a statement was obviously prophetic. Commander Hayes was a regular naval officer with a code of conduct
that should have been emulated by other officers. Unfortunately,
few could lay claim to being a Commander Hayes.

This then is my story. One that I have been anxious to tell for
over fifty years. Time has not diminished the memory of my fellow
prisoners or of the Japanese. In many ways I hold my fellow American prisoners more accountable for their loss of manhood and self-
respect than I do the Japanese for their brutality. Those Americans
who even today sit around hotel lobbies telling their lies also commit a "crime" when they thus, in effect, blaspheme our dead. It is
not my intent to accuse all former prisoners. Many were, and are,
decent men. The predators I refer to are known to themselves. All
they need to do is examine their conscience. If the shoe fits, wear it.

APPENDIX I: MAPS AND DOCUMENTS

Still Picture Branch (NWDNS), National Archives, College Park, Maryland.

American newspapers announce the fall of Bataan

The American effort to rouse the public

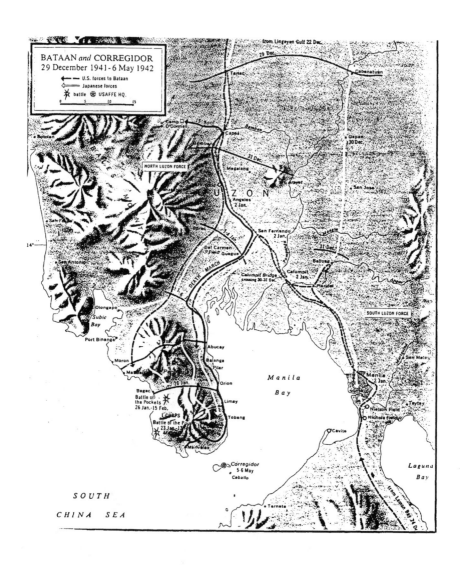

Maps of Bataan Peninsula and Corregidor

They·shall·not·grow·old·as·we
that·are·left·grow·old.
Age·shall·not·weary·them·nor
the·years·condemn.

At·the·going·down·of·the·sun
and·in·the·morning,
We·will·remember·them.

*From the hands of the
UNKNOWN SOLDIER
in Edinburg Scotland*

GRADUATES OF THE UNITED STATES MILITARY ACADEMY
WHO DIED WHILE PRISONERS OF WAR
IN THE HANDS OF THE JAPANESE 1941-1945

Code

D—Died in Japanese prison camp or on prison ship of disease, malnutrition, etc., (other than wounds).

K—Summarily killed or executed while prisoner of war or in process of capture.

Ks—Killed in Allied air or submarine attack on Japanese prisoner of war ship or died later from wounds suffered in such attack.

Code	Name	Rank	Organization	Number	Class
D	Paul D. Bunker	Col	CAC	4154	1903
K	Vicente Lim	BG	PA	5282	1914
K	Videl V. Segundo	Col	FA	5804	1917
K	Eustaquio Baclig	Lt Col	PS	6195	1918
K	Robert H. Vesey	Lt Col	Inf	6232	
D	Edwin V. Kerr	Lt Col	FA	6327	1919
Ks	Leo C. Paquet	Lt Col	Inf	6339	
Ks	H. R. Perry, Jr.	Lt Col	Inf	6374	
Ks	Edwaxd H. Bowes	Lt Col	Inf	6385	
Ks	Kenneth S. Olson	Lt Col	FD	6454	
Ks	Russell J. Nelson	Lt Col	Inf	6457	
D	Howard D. Johnston	Lt Col	Inf	6515	
Ks	George D. Vanture	Col	FA	6603	1920
K	Pastor Martelino	Col	PS	6605	
K	John T. Ward	Lt Col	Cav	6806	
Ks	Albert Svibra	Lt Col	JAG	6860	1922
D	Ronald G. McDonald	Lt Col	Inf	6952	
K	U. J. L. Peoples, Jr.	Lt Col	OD	7058	1923
K	H. E. C. Breitung	Lt Col	CAC	7158	
K	DaJose A. Garcia	Maj	PS	7167	
Ks	Cyril Q. Marron	Lt Col	JAG	7173	
Ks	David S. Babcock	Lt Col	FA	7183	
Ks	Hal C. Granberry	Lt Col	Inf	7202	
Ks	J. R. Lindsay, Jr.	Lt Col	FA	7218	

Code	Name	Rank	Organization	Number	Class
Ks	Floyd A. Mitchell	Lt Col	CAC	7260	1924
D	Lester J. Tacy	Lt Col	FA	7357	
Ks	Albert D. Miller	Lt Col	CAC	7395	
D	L. S. Kirkpatrick	Lt Col	CAC	7435	
D	J. E. Macklin, II	Lt Col	Inf	7512	
Ks	Reed Graves	Lt Col	CAC	7544	
K	Ralph T. Garver	Lt Col	AGD 7646		1925
Ks	John H. Bennett	Lt Col	Inf	7796	
Ks	Harry J. Harper	Lt Col	FA	7801	
D	Edward C. Mack	Lt Col	Inf	7805	
D	John L. Lewis	Lt Col	FA	7814	
Ks	Clarence H. Smith	Lt Col	Inf	7822	
D	Thaddeus E. Smyth	Lt Col	Inf	7824	
D	Claire M. Conzelman	Lt Col	CAC	7943	1926
Ks	John P. Woodbridge	Lt Col	FA	7979	
D	Thomas R. Horton	Lt Col	Inf	8016	
D	Maurice F. Daly	Col	AC	8056	1927
Ks	Stanley B. Bonner	Maj	FA	8086	
K	Harold J. Coyle	Maj	FA	8117	
D	Theodore Kalakuka	Lt Col	QMC	8130	
D	Joseph Ganahl, Jr.	Lt Col	FA	8143	
Ks	Montgomery McKee	Lt Col	Inf	8206	
K	Martin Moses	Lt Col	Inf	8213	
D	James S. Neary	Maj	OD	8310	1928
Ks	Leslie G. Ross	Maj	CAC	8314	
Ks	Fred O. Tally	Lt Col	AC	8371	
D	Leigh A. Fuller, Jr.	Maj	Inf	8393	
D	H. E. Montgomery	Lt Col	Inf	8425	
D	Eugene T. Lewis	Lt Col	Inf	8450	
D	Allen Thayer	Lt Col	Inf	8451	
K	James M. Ivy	Lt Col	Inf	8464	
D	Frank E. Fries	Maj	Engrs	8512	1929
D	William J. Latimer	Maj	OD	8585	
Ks	Dale J. Kinnee	Maj	Inf	8677	
D	T. B. Smothers, Jr.	Maj	QMC	8728	
D	Cornelius Z. Byrd	Lt Col	Inf	8755	
K	Arthur K. Noble	Lt Col	Inf	8775	
Ks	Robert B. Lothrop	Maj	Engrs	8797	1930
Ks	L. A. Boswoxth	Maj	CAC	8803	
K	James N. Vaughn	Maj	SC	8839	
Ks	Robert F. Haggerty	Maj	CAC	8850	
Ks	Harry B. Packard	Maj	FA	8956	
D	M. H. Hurt, Jr.	Maj	Inf	8953	
D	Joe E. East	Maj	Inf	8959	
Ks	Winston R. Maxwell	Maj	Inf	8992	
Ks	Frederick G. Saint	Lt Col	Engrs	9031	1931
D	James C. Blanning	Maj	Cav	9135	

Code	Name	Rank	Organization	Number	Class
Ks	Harry J. Fleeger	Maj	Cav	9136	
Ks	John N. Raker	Capt	AC	9156	
Ks	Howard M. Pahl	Maj	Inf	9234	
D	C. I. Humber, Jr.	Lt Col	Inf	9278	
Ks	James T. McClellan	Maj	Inf	9306	
D	Robert D. Glassburn	Maj	CAC	9400	1932
D	Erven C. Somerville	Maj	CAC	9404	
K	Dwight D. Edison	Lt Col	CAC	9456	
D	William H. Maguire	Lt Col	Inf	9488	
D	William R. Thomas	Maj	FA	9560	
D	William H. Ball	Maj	CAC	9613	1933
Ks	Harry Julian	Maj	CAC	9628	
Ks	Thomas K. McNair	Maj	CAC	9656	
D	Harry W. Schenck	Capt	CAC	9662	
Ks	George H. Crawford	Maj	CAC	9714	
D	S. McF. McReynolds	Capt	CAC	9718	
Ks	Peter P. Bernd	Capt	Inf	9747	
K	Charles F. Harrison	Maj	CWS	9802	
Ks	Roy D. Gregory	Lt Col	Inf	9889	
Ks	M. P. Warren, Jr.	Maj	Inf	9912	
D	Byron E. Brugge	Col	AC	9962	1934
Ks	Thompson B. Maury	Maj	FA	9964	
D	H. M. Batson, Jr.	Maj	FA	9988	
D	Lawrence K. Meade	Capt	FA	10065	
D	Edmund W. Wilkes	Capt	Inf	10092	
Ks	Richard A. Smith	Capt	Cav	10095	
Ks	Stanley Holmes	Maj	Inf	10104	
Ks	W. S. VanNostrand	Lt Col	Cav	10105	
Ks	Paul M. Jones	Maj	Cav	10367	1935
Ks	John Neiger	Maj	Inf	10400	
Ks	Carl Baehr, Jr.	Maj	FA	10628	1936
Ks	Harry R. Melton, Jr.	Col	AC	10631	
Ks	L. F. Prichard	Maj	Inf	10640	
Ks	William J. Priestley	Maj	Inf	10649	
Ks	Karol A. Bauer	Maj	Inf	10652	1936
Ks	John C. Goldtrap	Maj	Inf	10697	
Ks	Campbell H. Snyder	M aj	Engrs	10737	1937
Ks	W. E. W. Farrell	Capt	Inf	10768	
Ks	William P. Baldwin	Maj	Inf	10828	
D	Godfrey R. Ames	Capt	CAC	10841	
Ks	P. G. Lauman, Jr.	Maj	FA	10844	
Ks	William J. Dunmyer	Maj	Inf	10845	
D	Homer H. Uglow	Maj	Inf	10878	
Ks	Charles J. Browne	Maj	Inf	10896	
Ks	Richard F. Hill	Maj	Inf	10917	
D	Horace Greeley	Maj	Inf	10921	
Ks	William H. Traeger	Maj	Inf	10942	
D	William L. Robinson	Lt Col	Inf	10944	

Code	Name	Rank	Organization	Number	Class
Ks	H. R. Wynkoop	Maj	Inf	10962	
Ks	Charles S. Hoyt, Jr.	Maj	Inf	10982	
Ks	William A. Gay	Maj	Engrs	11051	1938
Ks	George Kappes	Capt	CAC	11106	
Ks	Frederick A. Miller	Capt	CAC	11108	
K	J. R. Barker, II	Capt	Cav	11137	
D	Edgar S. Rosenstock	Capt	CAC	11141	
Ks	Frederick J. Gerlich	Capt	CAC	11142	
D	L. C. Baldwin	Capt	CAC	11153	
K	Ralph B. Praeger	Maj	Cav	11167	
Ks	James R. Holmes	Capt	CAC	11177	
D	S. L. Barbour, Jr.	Maj	FA	11200	
D	Earle M. Shiley	Capt	CAC	11216	
Ks	Louis N. Dosh	Capt	Inf	11272	
D	Robert A. Barker	Capt	Inf	11280	
D	Coral M. Talbot	Capt	Inf	11295	
D	Edgar H. Dale	Capt	Inf	11296	
Ks	C. B. Whitehurst, Jr.	Maj	Inf	11333	
D	John H. Davis, Jr.	Capt	CAC	11371	1939
Ks	Charles E. White	Capt	CAC	11376	
Ks	Philip H. Lehr	Capt	CAC	11438	
D	Kenneth C. Griffiths	Capt	FA	11445	
Ks	George T. Breitling	Capt	Inf	11550	
D	Sarnuel A. Madison	Capt	CAC	11554	
Ks	Donald R. Snoke	Capt	CAC	11573	
D	Rudyard K. Grimes	Capt	Inf	11633	
Ks	H. H. Eichlin, Jr.	Capt	Inf	11722	
D	Wiley L. Dixon, Jr.	Capt	Inf	11728	
Ks	John F. Presnell, Jr.	Capt	Engrs	11793	1940
Ks	R. G. Cooper, Jr.	Capt	CAC	11797	
D	J. V. Iacobucci	Capt	SC	11813	
D	Robert L. Wheat	Capt	CAC	11821	
K	Vicente E. Gepte	Capt	PS	11832	
Ks	John J. Murphy, Jr.	Capt	FA	11894	
Ks	Walter I. Wald	Capt	FA	12057	
D	Augustus J. Cullen	Capt	CAC	12069	
Ks	Robert P. Pierpont	1Lt	Engrs	12307	1941
Ks	Hector J. Polla	1Lt	Inf	12576	

Statement Drafted by Lt. Kermit R. Lay
Signed by Prisoners in Cabanatuan Camp No. 1*

Page 1

CABANATUAN PRISONERS OF WAR CONCENTRATION CAMP NO. 1
CABANATUAN, P.I.

August 18, 1942

      We the undersigned, on the 18th day of August, 1942, A.D., under the command of Lieutenant Kermit R. Lay, United States Army, do solemnly swear, being in out right minds and without malice toward any member or members of the Second Platoon, Fifth Company, Building ( ), that in the event of any man or group of men who escapes from Cabanatuan Prisoners of War Concentration Camp No. 1 causing the death or punishment of any remaining member or members, will be apprehended at the expense and effort of the remaining members and most definitely and properly punished by either Army or civilian court or as the Group sees fit.

[Signatures of men in the building follow]

[Attestation by G.B. Gross, Major, Infantry Adjutant, Group II, American Prisoner Headquarters]

---

*Copies of the original statments with signatures for prisoners in buildings 17 and 19 are in the possession of the author.

Deaths at Cabanatuan Camp No. 1
Deaths by Month and Year

Year / Month	1942	1943	1944
January	—	73	—
February	—	10	1
March	—	9	1
April	—	2	—
May	—	1	—
June	503	4	—
July	786	2	—
August	287	2	1
September	262	1	—
October	262	2	—
November	296	1	—
December	149	1	—
Total	2545	108	3

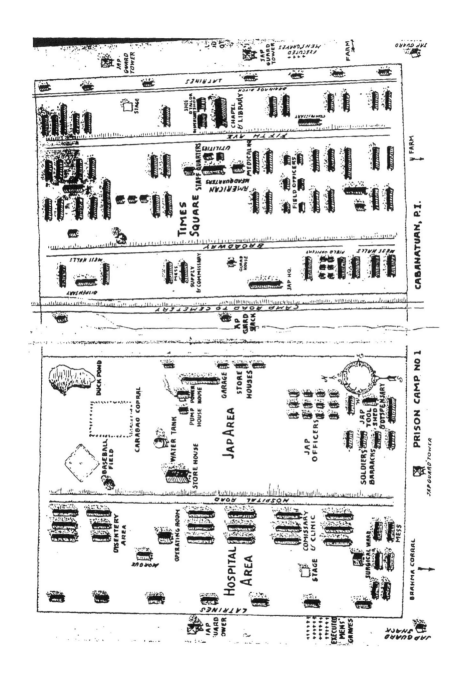

Sketch of Cabanatuan Prison Camp from Of Rice and Men

1942 Aerial Propaganda Leaflet dropped over Bataan to suggest
pipedreams for the native troops to break down the American
flag and revolt.

1942 Aerial propaganda leaflet dropped over Bataan and
Corregidor to discourage the defenders by the suggestion that
General MacArthur had abandoned them and gone home.

American Prisoners of War
Captured in the Philippines 1942
Who Entered Mitsushima Camp 2-d Japan
26 November 1942

Name	Rank	Asn	Pow#	Status
Atkin, James Taylor 17th Ordnance Company	Pvt.	15045534 dob 12/11/21	70	Kanose, Japan, 04/16/44
Atnip, Beverly Franklin 59th Coast Artillery Regt	Pvt.	18052228 dob 1/11/22	71	Kanose, Japan, 04/16/44
Atwell, John Rowlins 194th Tank Bn.	Cpl.	37042049 dob 4/13/05	18	Kanose, Japan 04/16/44
Bandish, William Edward 27th Bomber Group	Cpl.	697102 5	19	Kanose, Japan, 04/16/44
Bass, James Ozie (Sam) 3rd. Pursuit Sqdn.	T/Sgt.	6971025 dob 1/25/10	9	Kanose, Japan, 04/16/44
Berry, Cullen Wilkerson 27th Bomb Group	Pvt.	6250483 dob 07/03/16	72	Kanose, Japan, 04/16/44
Briner, James R. Air Warning Company	Pvt.	13022538	73	Remained until 09/04/45
Bolin, Bedford Forrest 803rd Engineers Bn.	Pvt.	34049133 dob 07/27/14	74	Kanose, Japan 04/16/44
Brancaticano, Frank 31st Infantry	Pvt.	6993549	75	Kanose, Japan, 04/16/44 Died June 20,1944
Braun, Mathew Baxter 192nd Tank Bn.	Cpl.	32045386 dob 11/30/16	76	Kanose, Japan 4/16/44
Brokaw, Glen Dale, Sgt. 194th Tank Bn.		20900657 dob 04/04/21	48	Kanose, Japan, 04/16/44
Burke, Alfred John 93rd Bomb Sdqn.	T/Sgt.	6718582	80	Died 12/04/42 – diarrhea (Dysentery)
Campbell, Kenneth, C. 21 St. Pursuit Squadron, Rec.	Cpl.	13001451	20	Remained 9/4/45 Appendicitis, 02/28/43
Chaves, Mike Narvis 200th AA	Sgt.	20842496 dob 6/22/22	49	Kanose, Japan 04/16/44
Chavis, Raymond 200th AA	Pvt.	20843361	49	Died Feb. 16, 1943 Pneumonia
Corey, Allan Murray 51 St. Inf. Bn, Pa	Maj.	0317610	1	Shipped 1943
Cupp, Burlen Clayton 192nd Tank Bn.	PFC	35001552	23	Kanose, Japan, 04/16/44

Name	Rank	Asn	Pow#	Status
Dement, David, Allen	PFC	14014561	24	Kanose, Japan 04/16/44
Derr Roger Glenn	PFC	35050891	25	Died Feb. 6, 1943
803rd. Engineers				Diarrhea/dysentery
Duncan, Joseph Johnson	Sgt.	20843956	51	Kanose, Japan, 04/16/44
200th AA		dob 08/17/23		
Dunn, Eugene Cecil	Cpl.	6972999	21	Kanose- Japan 04/16/44
16th Bomb Squadron		dob 12/10/20		
Engle, Elmer Earl	Pvt.	35121426		Died June 29,1943
192nd Tank Bn.				Dysentery
Ennis, Earl Edward	Pvt.	19052117	36	Kanose, Japan 04/16/44
803rd Engineers				
Faulkner, Ace E.	Capt.	0308907	3	Shipped in 1943
14th Engineers (Pa)				
Fields, Beranard Anthony	Cpl.	7040173	31	Kanose, Japan 04/16/44
17th Ordnance		dob 5/14/21		
Francis, Sherwood B.	Sgt.	19052825	52	Died Feb. 11, 1943
60th Coast Artillery				Dysentery
Gavord, Charles B.	PFC	20842474	26	Kanose, Japan 04/16/44
515th Coast Artillery		dob 10/26/21		
Goff, Marshall Wayne	1st Sgt.	6253514	4	Kanose, Japan 04/16/44
409 Signal Corp Aviation		dob 4/17/12		
Gordon, Albert Richard	Sgt.	12007159	53	
31st. Infantry & Hdq. Company, Phil Division				Remained 9/4/45
Grabowski, Leo James	PFC	6878147	29	(Skull Injury 8/3/43)
808th Military Police				Remained 9/4/45
Grassick, Paul Alexander	S/Sgt.	35001515	30	Kanose, Japan 4/16/44
192nd Tank Bn.		dob 5/6/19		
Groves, James Thomas	PFC		31	Unknown Whereabouts
17th Ordnance				
Hayes, Winfred Ordell	PFC	6931832	32	Confined W/lumbago
Hdq. Co. 31st. Inf.				Dysentery, Died 4/11/43
Hendrickson, Clarence H.	Pfc.	37028042	33	(Beri-beri)
803rd Engineers,				Died Feb. 27,1943
Holstein, Arthur, Jay	Sgt.	20500721	54	Kanose, Japan 4/16/44
194th Tank Bn.		dob 1/2/16		
Hewitt, Walter John	Capt.	0338977	2	Kanose, Japan 4/16/44
12th Signal Company, PS				
Hunter, Kenneth, Gilbert	Sgt.	8038791	10	Died Feb. 4,1943
60th Coast Artillery,				Dysentery

Name	Rank	Asn	Pow#	Status
Hyde, Revis Charles	PFC	6396050	59	Kanose, Japan 4/16/44
803rd. Engineers		dob 9/14/18		
Ivy, John B.	Sgt.	6265784	11	Kanose, Japan 4/16/44
48th Material Squadron, Ac		dob 1/4/17		
Jackson, Asa A.	Sgt.	6248651	12	Died April 16,1943
Ordnance				Beri-beri
Johnson, Leo Leslie	S/Sgt.	6970422	41	Kanose, Japan 4/1/644
Hdq. 5th Bomb Command		dob 1/6/17		
Marble, Verner Berner	S/Sgt.		13	Kanose, Japan 4/16/44
Ordnance Det. Hdq.		dob 1/29/21		
Martindale, Donald Allen	Pvt.	19050911	27	Kanose, Japan 4/16/44
7th Material Squadron.		dob 12/4/19		
Mcgill, Ray Hayden	Pvt.	38022993	79	Kanose, Japan 4/16/44
17th Ordnance Co.		dob 7/1/20		
Mitchell, Arthur Jesse	T/Sgt.	6864512	42	Kanose, Japan 4/16/44
3rd. Bn. 31st. Infantry		Sent to Shinagawa for		
		Hernia, 6/10/45		
				Returned 7/24/45
Peil, George Joseph	Cpl.	14042451	56	Remained until 914/45
31st. Infantry				
Pratt, Dorris Robert	S/Sgt.	6960136	43	Kanose, Japan 4/16/44
5th Interceptor Command		dob 3/29/18		
Richards, William Roy	PFC	1804985	43	Kanose, Japan 4/16/44
Richardson, William B.	PFC	38012566	82	Died Jan. 7, 1943
200th AA,				Diarrhea (Dysentery)
Roberts, Albert Henry	PFC	6334878	62	Died March 1, 1943
19th Bomb Group				Diarrhea (Dysentery)
Rogers, Joel Lee	Sgt.	38011946	14	Kanose, Japan 4/16/44
200th AA		dob 8/22/18		
Jones, Eugene	Cpl.	6292899	50	Kanose, Japan 4/16/44
Hdq. 3rd. Bn. 31st. Inf.		dob 3/2/20		
Jones, Verble Lee	Pvt.	14014390	38	Remained 9/4/45
Quartermaster		dob 3/21/14		
Kirch, Raymond S.	Pvt.	14014390	39	Remained 9/4/45
27th Bomb Group				
Klassen, Ray Joseph	T/Sgt.	6565295	5	Kanose, Japan 4/16/44
Hdq. Battery		dob 6/24/17		
Kolilis, Fred Louis	PFC	20956487	40	Kanose, Japan 4/16/44
194th Tank Bn.		dob 3/6/20		

Name	Rank	Asn	Pow#	Status
Krouse. Gusta Ray 194th Tank Bn.	T/Sgt.	2072032	6	Died Jan. 28,1943 Dysentery
Lilly, Donald Clifford 31st. Inf.	PFC	15061732 dob 7/22/21	60	Kanose, Japan 4/16/44
Lobe, John Alex 3rd. Pursuit Squadron	Cpl.	19051950	22	Remained 9/4/45
Lujan, Errett Louis 515th Coast Artillery	Cpl.	20843147 dob 5/14/22	55	Kanose, Japan 4/16/44
Mann, William Hearne 803rd Engineers	Pvt.	33043704	78	Remained 9/4/45
Sutterfield, James Edward 49th Material Squadron	Pvt.	14002078	46	Kanose, Japan 4/16/44
Teas, Robert Gordon 19th Bomb Group.	PFC	6915655	66	Died March 5, 1943 Listed as Diarrhea

Died from beatings given him over two days.I witnessed it and testified.

Name	Rank	Asn	Pow#	Status
Tison, Thomas Powell 27th Bomb Group	Sgt.	6973420	15	Remained 9/4/45
Vallerga, Simone Nicola 809th MP. Co.	PFC	19052525 dob 1/14/13	67	Kanose, Japan, 4/16/44
Wasson, Wayne Nile 200th Coast Artillery AA	PFC	3801212123	68	Remained 9/4/45
Wilson, Frank Elbert 515th Coast Artillery	S/Sgt.	39012385 dob 9/24/06	47	Kanose, Japan
Williams, Russell Aubry 48th Material Squadron	Cpl.	6270737 dob 12/25/12	69	Kanose, Japan 4/1/644
Wilson, Jack Dudley 27th Bomb Group	Sgt.	6286742 dob 11/4/14	17	Kanose, Japan 4/1/644
Holland, Pete Boyce 48th Material Squadron	PFC	14014943	34	Remained 9/4/45
Rouse, Samuel James Chemical Warfare Service	T/Sgt.	6842414 dob 3/12/12	44	Kanose, Japan 4/16/44
Roy, John Cabbell Far East Air Force	M/Sgt.	6896934 dob 12/12/1899	63	Kanose, Japan 4/16/44
Silver, Alvin Air Warning Co, Phil Dept.	PFC	12026748 dob 3/12/14	7	Kanose, Japan 4/16/44
Simpson, Guerald M. Signal Corps, Air Warning Co, Phil Dept.	Cpl.	6384738	57	Died March 26, 1943 Diarrhea (Dysentery)
Smith, Alfred Glen 3rd, Bn. Hdq. 31st. Inf.	PFC	20938926	6	Died 5/4/45 Diarrhea (Dysentery)

Name	Rank	Asn	Pow#	Status
Smith, J.N. 200th AA	1st Sgt.	20843476	81	Died May 4, 1942 Diarrhea (Dysentery)
Snodgrass, Clifton Otto 903rd Engineers	1st Sgt.	6624975 dob 9/3/14	8	Kanose, Japan 4/16/44
Spencer, Paul Richard F Company, 31st. Inf.	Sgt.	18050440 dob 5/23/22	65	Kanose, Japan 4/16/44
Stanford, Kenneth D. 26th Pursuit Squadron	T/Sgt.	6265574 dob 1/29/18	45	Kanose, Japan 4/16/44
Steele, Arivl Leon 3rd Pursuit Squadron	Cpl.	6861252		Remained 9/4/45

Major Corey and Captain Faulkner left Mitsushima for Zentsuji camp on July 28,1943.

Following Americans left Mitsushima on April 16,1944 and arrived in Kanose on April 16, 1944 at about 9pm.

Hewitt	Chavez, M.	Bass	Hyde	Bandish
Dement	Berry	Fields	Rogers	Rouse
Wilson, F.	Silver	Holstein	Johnson	Spencer
Aiken	Grassick	Braun	Lilly	Dunn
Goff	Jones, E.	Ivy	Wilson	Stanford
Gavord	Bolin	Jones, V.	Mitchell	Vallerga
Brokaw	Snodgrass	Lujon	Richardas	Cupp
Atnip	Ennis	McGill	Atwell	Sutterfield
Klassen	Duncan	Marble	Pratt	Williams, E.
Martindale	Brancaticano	Kollis	Roy	

#102 Kingen, Harold, PFC, 190952225, Medical Corps, Station Hospital, Ft. Milss, PI, arrived in Kanose, Japan 6/12/44

#207 Robinson, Donald W., Captain, Md, 038099, 1st Bn. 57th Inf., arrived Kanose, Japan Jan. 28,1945

After departure of main body of Americans for Kanose there remained thirteen American Prisoners of War selected by the Japanese to become the cadre for the new group of American and British prisoners to come into Mitsushima. In addition to the thirteen Americans, thirteen British prisoners were also selected to remain, creating a "Ku Horio" or "Old Prisoners" to become the cadre.

The American prisoners selected to remain were:

Bitner, James

Campbell, Kenneth

Gordon, Albert Richard

Grabowski, Leo James

Piel, George

Jones, Verble Lee

Kirch, Raymond

Lobe, John

Mann, William

Tison, Thomas

Wasson, Wayne

Holland, Pete Boyce

Steele, Arvil

Eighteen died of various diseases always listed as less than the actual cause. One (Teas) was killed, One (Brancaticano) died immediately after leaving Mitsushima, for a total loss of 19 of the original 82. The vast majority of the deaths occurred in the first five months in the camp.

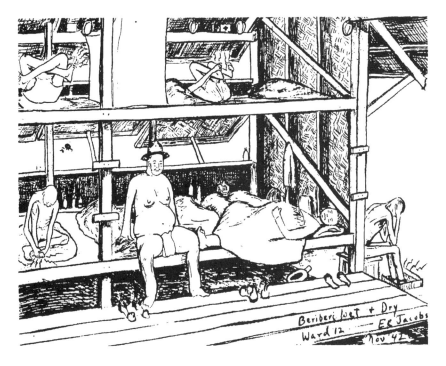

Beriberi Wet and Dry, Ward 12, courtesy of Dr. Jacobs

Description of the Mitsushima Camp from a U.S. Intelligence Report dated 1 July, 1945.

Coordinates: 36°53' N, 138°16' E [Actually: 35°16' N, 137°51' E]

Strength: U.S.: 65 Allied: 209

Description: Located Tenryu R., Nagano Pref., with newly constructed one-story wooden bks, shingled roof, wooden fence, five billets of 173 sq. meters each or 865 sq. meters total. Camp is reported to be in a wooded gorge of the above river. POW said to be working on a hydro-electric plant in the river bed. (C-Oct 44, J-Mar 45).

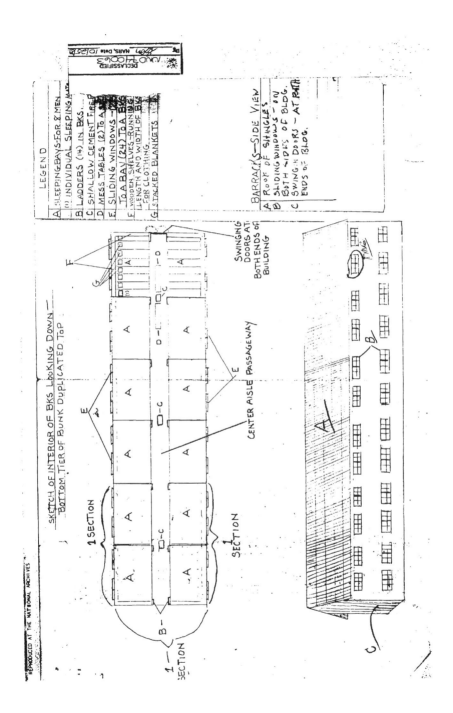

GENERAL HEADQUARTERS
SUPREME COMMANDER FOR THE ALLIED POWERS
LEGAL SECTION

APO 500
21 Feb 47

File No. 014.13

Public Relations Informational Summary No. 56

SUBJECT: Result of Trial of Sukeo NAKAJIMA and six others. (By Sgt.Wm.D. Cox)

The four man EIGHTH Army Military Commission having heard the prosecutions case against these seven accused today returned a verdict of guilty on all seven accused. The accused were sentenced as follows:

Sukeo NAKAJIMA — Death by hanging (Camp Commander)
Sadaharu HIRAMATSU — Death by hanging (Big Glass Eye)
Kunio YOSHIZAWA — Death by hanging ("Mushmouth" — Interpreter)
Tamotsu KIMURA — Death by hanging ("Punk" — No. 1 Cook)
Harumi KAWATE — Death by hanging ("Rivet Tooth")
Takeo KIRISHITA — Life Imprisonment at Hard Labor ("Buick")
Rikio SHIORI — Life imprisonment at hard labor ("Shorty" — Medical Orderly)

Following one of the longest trials on record at the Yokohama District Wars Crimes Trial Court House, Yokohama, Japan, the Sukeo NAKAJIMA commission reconvened 21 February 1947 for its final session. Following a weeks deliberation, in closed session, the four man EIGHTH Army Commission, headed by Colonel Clair F. Schumacher, of St. Peter, Minnesota, punishments for these seven accused war criminals were meted out subject to rulings by the Commanding General, United States EIGHTH Army.

With over three months in trial, scores of witnesses were produced by both the prosocution and defense panels. Four former Prisoner of War survivors of the Mitsushima Camp, Nagano, Japan, testified in behalf of prosecution. Their opposition introduced a number of Japanese witnesses, both civilian and former camp personnel. The principle charge against these seven accused was, included in two specifications involving the death of scores of American and Allied Prisoners of War. These Japanese engaged in daily acts of brutality against all the internees, charged prosecution, and through their brutal treatment, the withholding of foods, medicines and other supplies, they brought death to these prisoners.

From among the innumerable affidavits introduced by prosecution, are the following exerpts: "We were addressed by the commandant and threatened with death and dire penalties for any attempt to escape or for other breaches of regulations" ... "On this day, November 29, 1942, all personnel, including the seriously ill, were ordered outside, naked, for measurement and weighing"... "There was a sharp frost and thick ice on the ground"... "One dead officer was kicked by the Japanese because he did not rise to attend the weighing"... "Those who could not adapt themselves to the diet of half-cooked barley, died of diarrhea and starvation" ... "He (NAKAJIMA) weeded out the sick according to his own ideas, ignoring the doctor, and sent most out to work. Many returned to sick quarters shortly afterwards to die" ... "All men in the hospital were made to go outside in freezing weather and stand at attention all night, three men died"... "All camp personnel looted Red Cross supplies" ... "Teas was beaten to death."

The prosecution representatives for Legal Section, General Headquarters, Supreme Commander for the Allied Powers, were Mr. Max Schiffman, New York Attorney, of 2155 East 24th Street, Brooklyn, New York, and Mr. Alexander Pendleton, of 89 Valley Circle, Mill Valley, California. In his closing argument, Mr. Schiffman stated before the commission that prosecution had proven its case beyond a reasonable doubt, and requested the penalty of death for each defendant.

APPENDIX II: PHOTOGRAPHS

Author as a young soldier in the 31st Infantry, Manila

Author as a prisoner of war, March 1943, Mitsushima, Japan

Author's brothers, Le Roy, US Navy and Fred, US Marine Corps, WW II

Author visiting Pacific War Memorial, Corregidor, P.I. 1995

Cabanatuan Memorial to those who died there

Plaque given to U.S.S. *Bataan* (LHD5) by Battling Bastards of Bataan

Author (on left) and brother Fred, ages 3 and 4 respectively New York City

Barracks of 31st Infantry Regiment 2nd & 3rd Battalion, Estado Mayor (prewar)

Company F, 31st Infantry Regiment, December 1940, greatly understrength

Bataan Death March

Mt. Samat, scene of heavy fighting April 1942

Cross monument built by American prisoners June 1942, Camp O'Donnell

Present monument atop Mt. Samat

Former prisoners visit the last remaining boxcar used in transporting prisoners

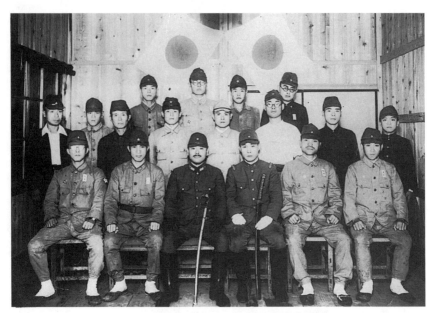

Camp guards, Mitsushima (Hiraoka), Japan

Group shot of Allied prisoners in Mitushima, Japan, October 1944

Monument to victims of Bataan Death March, Capas, P.I.

Author revisiting Mitsushima 1991

Author meets with "Little Glass Eye," 1991

Author pays visit to "Big Glass Eye" widow, 1991

Five survivors of 31st Infantry Regiment meet in Minneapolis, Minnesota, 1993

INDEX

Note: *Page references in italics refer to illustrations, maps, or photographs.*